W9-BEV-581

easy

Microsoft®
Word 2010

Sherry Kinkoph Gunter

que®

800 East 96th Street
Indianapolis, Indiana 46240

CONTENTS

EASY MICROSOFT® WORD 2010

ISBN-13: 978-0-7897-4329-9
ISBN-10: 0-7897-4329-9

UK ISBN-13: 978-0-7897-4374-9
UK ISBN-10: 0-7897-4374-4

Library of Congress Cataloging-in-Publication Data

Gunter, Sherry Kinkoph.
  Easy Microsoft Word 2010 / Sherry Kinkoph Gunter.
    p. cm.
  Includes bibliographical references and index.
  ISBN-13: 978-0-7897-4329-9
  ISBN-10: 0-7897-4329-9
  1. Microsoft Word. 2. Word processing. I. Title.
  Z52.5.M52G86 2010
  005.52--dc22

                           2010013054

Printed in the United States on America

First Printing June 2010

TRADEMARKS

WARNING AND DISCLAIMER

BULK SALES

Que Publishing offers excellent discounts on this book when ordered in quantity for bulk purchases or special sales. For more information, please contact

U.S. Corporate and Government Sales
1-800-382-3419
corpsales@pearsontechgroup.com

For sales outside of the U.S., please contact

International Sales
international@pearsoned.com

Associate Publisher
Greg Wiegand

Acquisitions Editor
Michelle Newcomb

Development Editor
The Wordsmithery LLC

Managing Editor
Kristy Hart

Project Editor
Andy Beaster

Copy Editor
Julie Anderson

Indexer
Cheryl Lenser

Proofreader
Dan Knott

Technical Editor
Vince Averello

Publishing Coordinator
Cindy Teeters

Designer
Ann Jones

Compositor
Nonie Ratcliff

ABOUT THE AUTHOR

Sherry Kinkoph Gunter has written and edited oodles of books over the past 18 years covering a wide variety of computer topics, including Microsoft Office programs, digital photography, and Web applications. Her recent titles include *Sams Teach Yourself Facebook in 10 Minutes, Craigslist 4 Everyone, Teach Yourself VISUALLY Microsoft Office 2007, Microsoft Office 2008 for Mac Bible,* and *Master VISUALLY Dreamweaver and Flash CS3.* Sherry began writing computer books back in '92 for Macmillan Computer Publishing, and her flexible writing style has allowed her to be an author for an assortment of imprints and to write in a variety of formats. Sherry's ongoing quest is to aid users of all levels in mastering ever-changing computer technologies, helping users make sense of it all, and showing them how to get the most out of their machines and online experiences. Sherry currently resides in a swamp in the wilds of east central Indiana with a lovable ogre and a menagerie of interesting creatures.

DEDICATION

I'd like to dedicate this book to my new sister, Candace Gunter Noland—her enduring grace and endearing wit are an inspiration.

ACKNOWLEDGMENTS

Special thanks go out to Michelle Newcomb for allowing me the opportunity to tackle this exciting project; to project editor Andy Beaster, for his dedication and patience in shepherding this project; to copy editor Julie Anderson, for ensuring that all the i's were dotted and t's were crossed; to technical editor Vince Averello and development editor Charlotte Kughen, for skillfully checking each step and offering valuable input along the way; and finally to the production team at Pearson for their talents in creating such a helpful, much-needed, and incredibly good-looking book.

WE WANT TO HEAR FROM YOU!

As the reader of this book, *you* are our most important critic and commentator. We value your opinion and want to know what we're doing right, what we could do better, what areas you'd like to see us publish in, and any other words of wisdom you're willing to pass our way.

As an associate publisher for Que Publishing, I welcome your comments. You can email or write me directly to let me know what you did or didn't like about this book—as well as what we can do to make our books better.

Please note that I cannot help you with technical problems related to the topic of this book. We do have a User Services group, however, where I will forward specific technical questions related to the book.

When you write, please be sure to include this book's title and author as well as your name, email address, and phone number. I will carefully review your comments and share them with the author and editors who worked on the book.

Email: feedback@quepublishing.com
Mail: Greg Wiegand
          Associate Publisher
          Que Publishing
          800 East 96th Street
          Indianapolis, IN 46240 USA

READER SERVICES

Visit our website and register this book at www.informit.com/title/9780789743299 for convenient access to any updates, downloads, or errata that might be available for this book.

INTRODUCTION

Microsoft Word 2010 is the latest release of the world's number one word processing program. Like many users, you might have mixed feelings about this new and improved software. On one hand, it's exciting to see what sort of changes Microsoft has made to the program, but on the other hand, it might mean more time and effort on your part to learn it all over again. Don't worry. Whether you're a new user or a seasoned pro, you can get up and running fast with the newest version of Word with the help of this book.

So what sort of changes are we talking about? Most of the changes are subtle. The good news is the user interface hasn't changed considerably between Word 2007 and Word 2010. As a matter of fact, they've added the Ribbon to all of the Office suite of programs now, including Outlook and Publisher. If you upgraded to Word 2007 awhile back, you're already familiar with the overhaul that produced the Ribbon at the top of the program window instead of menus and toolbars. If you're new to the Ribbon, don't panic—it's not nearly as intimidating as it sounds.

In addition to the Ribbon, Word 2010 has revamped the Office button into a File tab filled with document-related operations. In Word 2007, the Office menu gave you access to standard document tasks like saving and printing. The new File tab, when selected, opens a full page menu screen, called the Backstage view, from which you can control various aspects of your documents, such as saving, printing, and controlling who has permission to open, copy, and edit your documents.

Along with subtle improvements to the Office suite of programs, Word users can also find a new screen capture tool for taking instant pictures of what's on the computer screen. You'll also find enhancements to the picture tools, language tools, themes, a paste preview option, and additional document coauthoring features, just to name a few.

When it comes to learning how to use Word, this book focuses on helping you get your work done instead of trying to show you every nuance of the software. Rather than teaching you a hundred ways to do the same thing, *Easy Word 2010* focuses on teaching you the most direct way to accomplish a task, and you'll learn easy shortcuts along the way. Relying on lots of visuals and easy-to-follow steps, you'll quickly see how to perform a task without having to rely on reading a lot of text. *Easy Word 2010* is both a tutorial and a reference book; you can read it from start to finish to learn everything you can about Word, or just pick and choose the topics you need to know about at the moment. The point is this—without a doubt, Word is a powerful program, but at the end of the day you just need to use it to get your work done. Why not have a little fun along the way?

Chapter 1

GETTING STARTED WITH WORD

Before you jump in and start clicking buttons and scrolling willy-nilly around the screen, take a few moments to orient yourself to the Word program window. Much like learning your way around a new town or city, learning your way around Word takes a little navigating. You need to figure out where to find the commands you need and which direction will get you where you want to be.

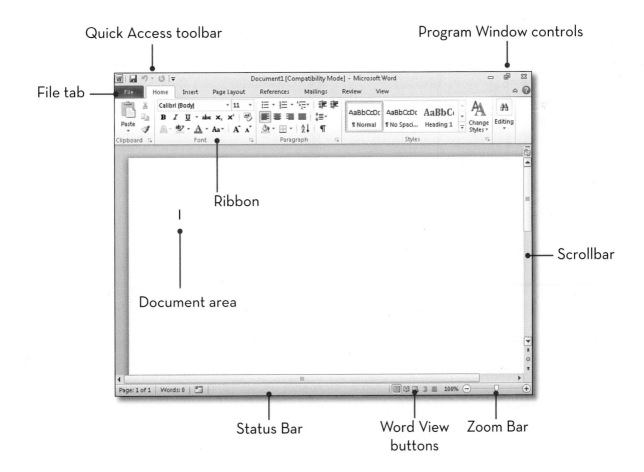

Quick Access toolbar

Program Window controls

File tab

Ribbon

Document area

Scrollbar

Status Bar

Word View buttons

Zoom Bar

STARTING WORD

If you're ready to start using Word, the first thing you have to do is open its program window. Any time Word is open, you'll see a document button for the program on the Windows taskbar at the bottom of your computer screen. If you're using Windows 7, you can hover the mouse over the Word icon to view multiple documents. If you're using Windows Vista or earlier and have more than one document open at a time, you'll see buttons for each document. You can easily switch between open documents by clicking their respective buttons or thumbnails on the taskbar.

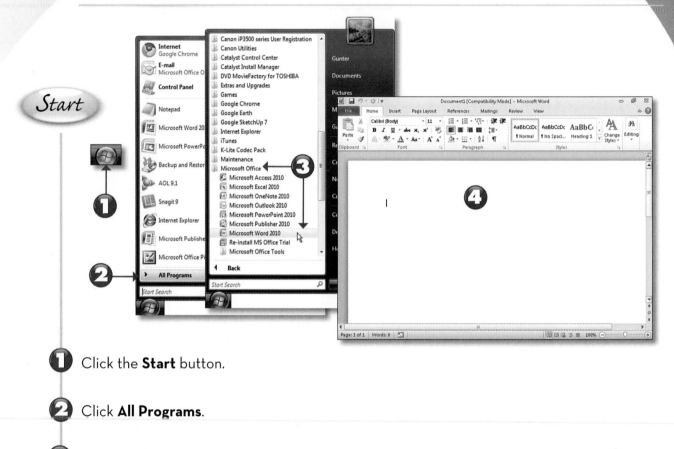

① Click the **Start** button.

② Click **All Programs**.

③ Click **Microsoft Office**, then click **Microsoft Word 2010**.

④ The Word program window opens.

End

TIP

Other Start Methods   If you click the Start button and see a listing for Word 2010, you can click it instead of going through the All Programs submenu to open Word. Depending on how you installed Word, you might also see a shortcut icon on the desktop you can double-click or an icon on the taskbar you can click to open the program. ■

TIP

Taskbar Button   When you open Word, a Word document button also appears on the Windows taskbar. If you have more than one application open at a time, you can click the Word document button anytime you want to return to the Word window. ■

EXITING WORD

After you finish using Word, you can close the program window. If you have unsaved work in the document, Word might ask you to save your document before exiting. As soon as you exit, the Word document button disappears from the Windows taskbar, too.

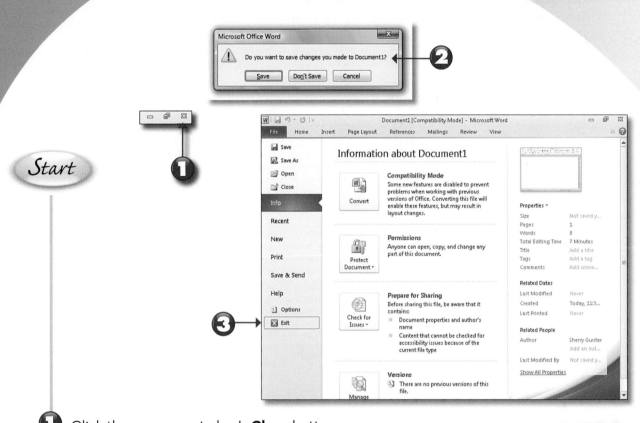

1 Click the program window's **Close** button.

2 If you haven't saved your work yet, Word prompts you to do so. Click **Save** to save your document, click **Don't Save** to exit without saving your changes, or click **Cancel** to keep Word open.

3 You can also exit Word by clicking the **File** tab and clicking the **Exit** option in the Backstage view menu.

TIP

Exit the Document but Not the Program Window To close a document but leave Word open, click the **File** tab and then click the **Close** option. ◼

NAVIGATING THE PROGRAM WINDOW

The Word program window features several key elements you need to know about. First and foremost, you need to know where to find all the commands you'll use to build and format your documents. The File tab, Quick Access toolbar, and Ribbon contain all the commands you'll use the most. The middle of the window is where you'll create and edit your document, and you'll use the scrollbars to move your view of the document. The Status bar at the bottom keeps you apprised of page numbers, word count, and zoom settings.

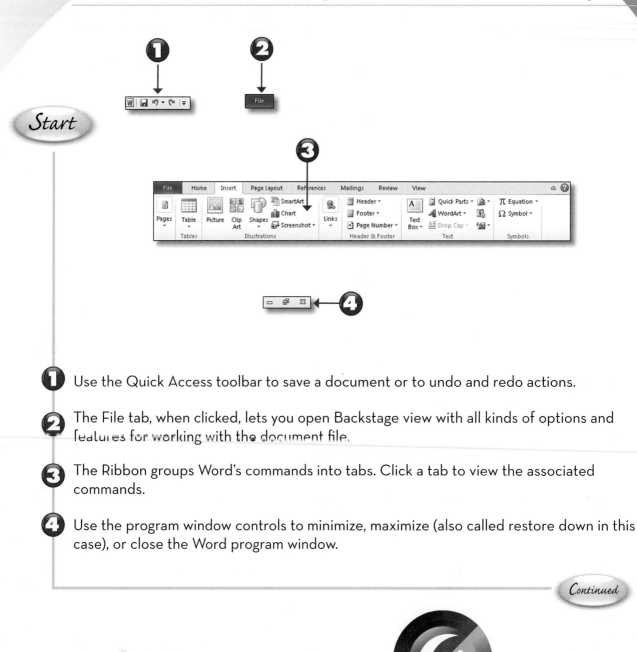

Start

1 Use the Quick Access toolbar to save a document or to undo and redo actions.

2 The File tab, when clicked, lets you open Backstage view with all kinds of options and features for working with the document file.

3 The Ribbon groups Word's commands into tabs. Click a tab to view the associated commands.

4 Use the program window controls to minimize, maximize (also called restore down in this case), or close the Word program window.

Continued

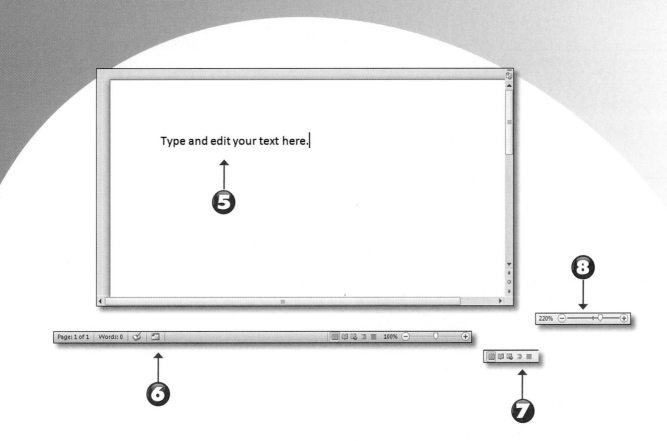

Type and edit your text here.

220%

Page: 1 of 1 | Words: 0 | 100%

5 The document work area is where you type and edit text and other document elements, with scrollbars on the right and bottom for moving around the screen. Click the scroll arrow buttons to move your view of the document page or drag the bar.

6 The Status bar displays status items, such as the current page you're viewing and word count.

7 The five View buttons let you choose a layout view for the document.

8 Use the Zoom bar to change the magnification level for viewing your document.

End

TIP

Turn on Rulers You can click the **View Ruler** button located at the top of the vertical scrollbar to turn on the horizontal and vertical rulers to help you with spacing actions. ■

TIP

How Do I Find Help? You can click the **Help** button located in the far right corner of the program window to open Word's help files. Learn more about finding help in the task "Finding Help with Word 2010" later in this chapter. ■

MINIMIZING AND MAXIMIZING THE PROGRAM WINDOW

You can control the program window by minimizing or maximizing the window. When a window is minimized, it appears as a button on the Windows taskbar. When a window is maximized, it fills the whole computer screen.

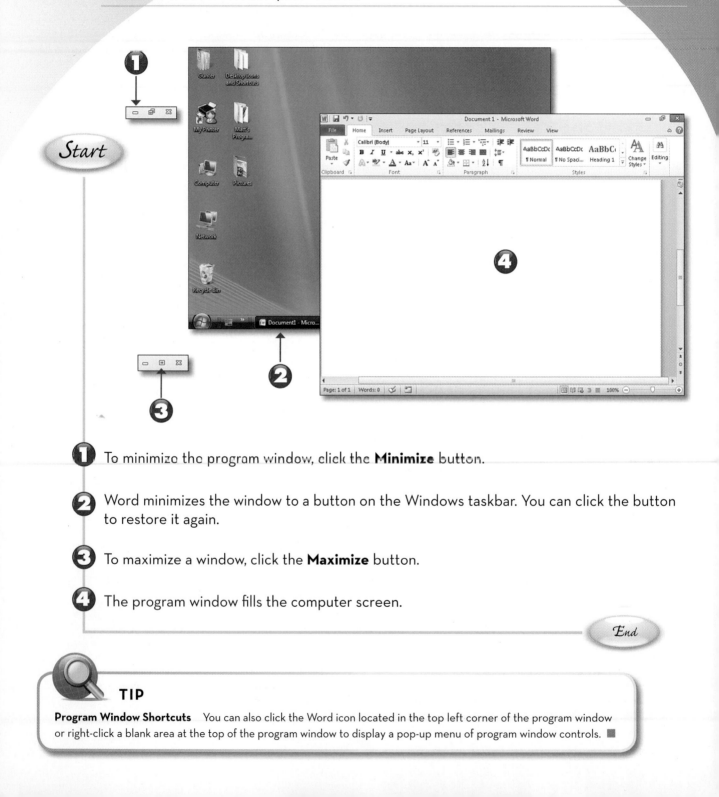

1. To minimize the program window, click the **Minimize** button.

2. Word minimizes the window to a button on the Windows taskbar. You can click the button to restore it again.

3. To maximize a window, click the **Maximize** button.

4. The program window fills the computer screen.

End

TIP

Program Window Shortcuts You can also click the Word icon located in the top left corner of the program window or right-click a blank area at the top of the program window to display a pop-up menu of program window controls. ■

WORKING WITH THE FILE TAB

The File tab, when activated, is actually a combination dialog box and menu system that acts as a repository for various document-related tasks, such as saving files, opening new and existing files, printing files, controlling permissions and sharing, and accessing program customization options. Microsoft calls this special full-screen menu the Backstage view, because it offers you options for controlling things that happen to a document rather than in a document.

1. Click the **File** tab.

2. Word displays the Backstage view menu with document tasks organized into groups that are listed in the left pane.

3. Click a command to view associated options or open another dialog box. In this example, the New options are displayed, and you can open a new document based on a template.

4. Click the **Home** tab or any other tab on the Ribbon to return to Word without selecting anything in Backstage view, or just press the **Esc** key.

End

CUSTOMIZING THE QUICK ACCESS TOOLBAR

The Quick Access toolbar is located at the very top left corner of the program window. It contains just a few shortcut keys commonly used by every Word user: Save, Undo, and Redo. You can edit the toolbar to include other commands you use the most. When you display the customize menu, you can check or uncheck the commands you want to display on the toolbar. To find more commands, you can open Word's Options dialog box to further customize the toolbar.

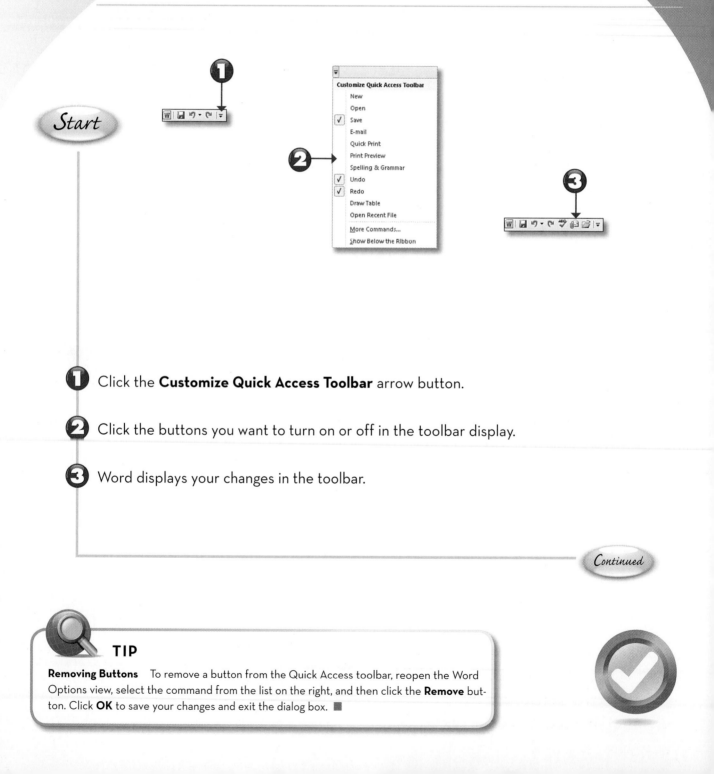

① Click the **Customize Quick Access Toolbar** arrow button.

② Click the buttons you want to turn on or off in the toolbar display.

③ Word displays your changes in the toolbar.

Continued

TIP

Removing Buttons   To remove a button from the Quick Access toolbar, reopen the Word Options view, select the command from the list on the right, and then click the **Remove** button. Click **OK** to save your changes and exit the dialog box. ■

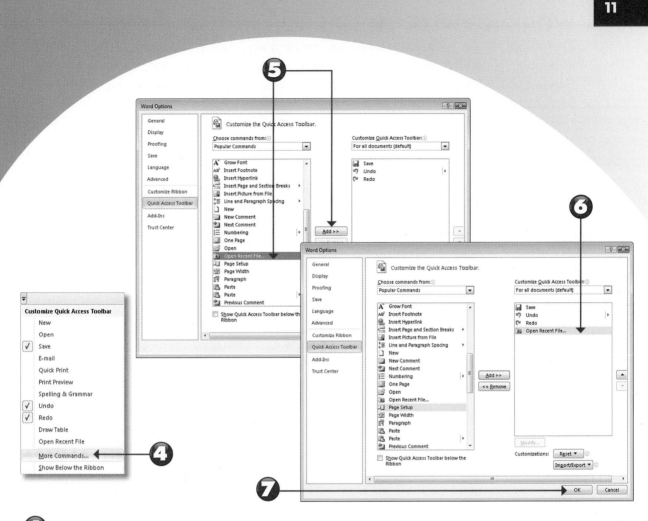

4 Click the **Customize Quick Access Toolbar** arrow button and then click **More Commands**.

5 In the Word Options dialog box, click the command you want to add and then click the **Add** button.

6 The command is added to the list of toolbar buttons.

7 When you finish adding all the commands you want, click **OK**.

End

TIP

Move the Toolbar If you prefer, you can orient the Quick Access toolbar to appear beneath the Ribbon. Click the **Customize Quick Access Toolbar** arrow button and then click **Show Below the Ribbon**. ■

TIP

Finding More Commands You can click the **Choose Commands From** drop-down list in the Word Options dialog box to view other command groups. ■

WORKING WITH THE RIBBON

The Ribbon displays the commands you need to accomplish various Word tasks and presents them as intuitive tools you can activate with ease at the top of the Word window. Related commands are displayed in groups represented by tabs along the top of the Ribbon. To view a group, click its tab.

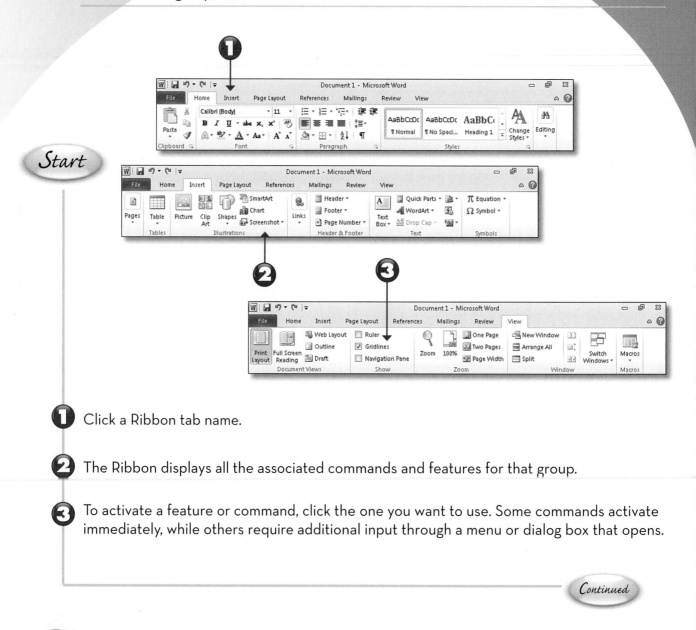

Start

1. Click a Ribbon tab name.

2. The Ribbon displays all the associated commands and features for that group.

3. To activate a feature or command, click the one you want to use. Some commands activate immediately, while others require additional input through a menu or dialog box that opens.

Continued

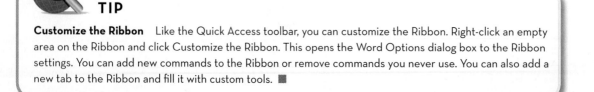

TIP

Customize the Ribbon Like the Quick Access toolbar, you can customize the Ribbon. Right-click an empty area on the Ribbon and click Customize the Ribbon. This opens the Word Options dialog box to the Ribbon settings. You can add new commands to the Ribbon or remove commands you never use. You can also add a new tab to the Ribbon and fill it with custom tools. ■

④ Anytime you see this icon near a group of commands, you can click it to open a dialog box with additional controls you can set.

⑤ When you finish fine-tuning the settings in the dialog box, you can click **OK** to apply the changes.

⑥ Click the **Minimize the Ribbon** button to reduce the Ribbon to show only the tab names.

⑦ Click the button again to view the full Ribbon.

End

TIP

Quick Minimize You can also minimize the Ribbon by double-clicking on a tab name. Click a tab name again to bring back the full Ribbon display. ■

FINDING MORE CUSTOMIZING OPTIONS

Word 2010 offers you all kinds of ways you can customize how the program works and what features appear on screen. You can find settings for proofing, saving, language, and display, as well as advanced options and settings for customizing the Quick Access toolbar and the Ribbon. All of the options are controlled through the Word Options dialog box.

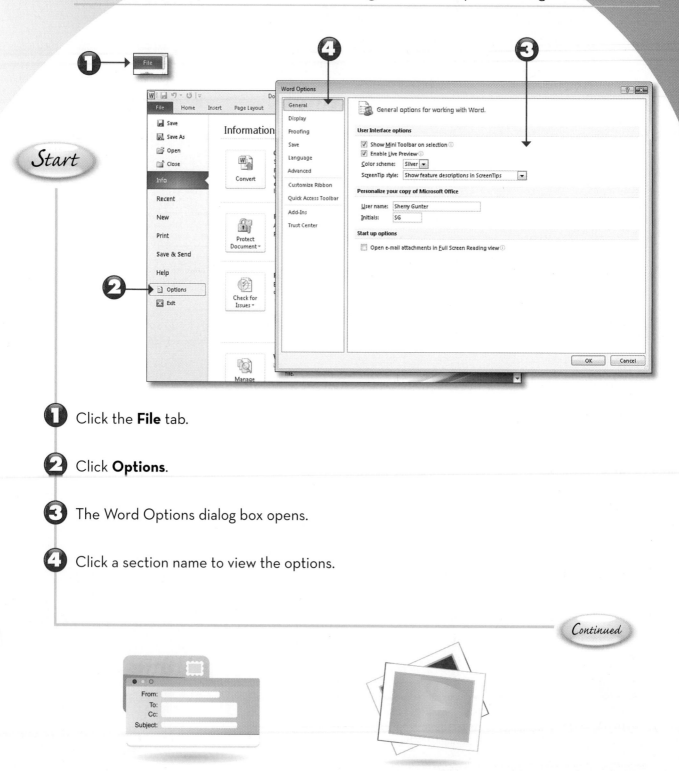

Start

1 Click the **File** tab.

2 Click **Options**.

3 The Word Options dialog box opens.

4 Click a section name to view the options.

Continued

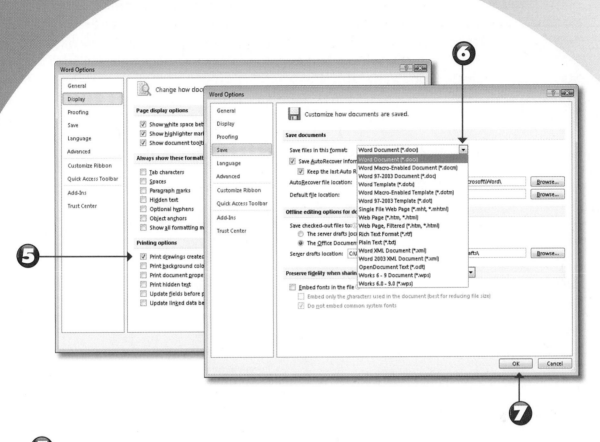

5 Many of the options can be turned on or off with a check box.

6 Other options include selections from a drop-down menu.

7 After making any changes, click **OK** to apply the new settings.

End

TIP

Help with Options To find out what a group of options in the Word Options dialog box does, simply click the tab name and a description appears at the top of the dialog box. Also, look for option names that have a circle icon with an i inside next to them—this is Word's helpful information icon. Hover your mouse pointer over the icon to reveal a ScreenTip that tells what the feature does. ■

WORKING WITH VIEW MODES

You can use Word's view modes to change the way in which you look at a document. Print Layout view, which is the default view, shows you what your document looks like when printed. You can use Outline view to see your document in an outline format, or view your document as it looks in a Web browser window using Web Layout view. Full Screen Reading view optimizes your document for easy reading onscreen. Lastly, Draft view displays a draft version of the document, without text or graphics. You can access view modes on the Status bar or in the Ribbon's View tab.

Start

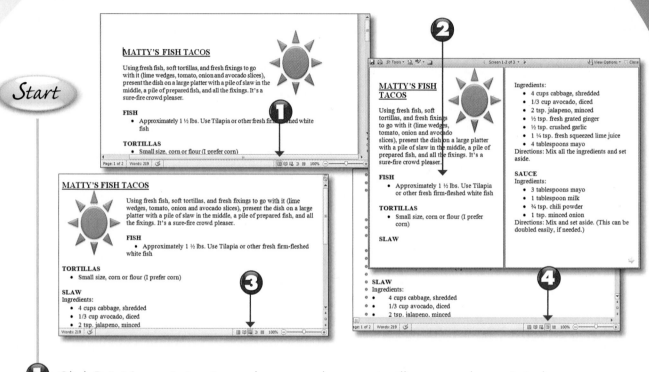

1 Click **Print Layout** view to see how your document will appear when printed.

2 Click **Full Screen Reading** to see your document much like a book.

3 Click **Web Layout** to see your document as a Web page.

4 Click **Outline** to see your document in outline format.

Continued

MATTY'S FISH TACOS

Using fresh fish, soft tortillas, and fresh fixings to go with it (lime wedges, tomato, onion and avocado slices), present the dish on a large platter with a pile of slaw in the middle, a pile of prepared fish, and all the fixings. It's a sure-fire crowd pleaser.

FISH
- Approximately 1 ½ lbs. Use Tilapia or other fresh firm-fleshed white fish

TORTILLAS
- Small size, corn or flour (I prefer corn)

SLAW
Ingredients:
- 4 cups cabbage, shredded
- 1/3 cup avocado, diced
- 2 tsp. jalapeno, minced

Previous Page (Ctrl+ Page Up)

Page: 1 of 2 | Words: 219 | 100%

5 Click **Draft** to see your document without graphics or other added elements.

6 Another way to switch views is by clicking the **View** tab on the Ribbon.

7 Click the document view you want to apply.

End

TIP

Outlining Tools When you switch to Outline view, Word displays an Outlining tab in the Ribbon with tools for changing heading levels, viewing different levels of the outline, and moving different outline headings around in the document. When you click another view mode, the Outlining tab is hidden again. ∎

MAGNIFYING YOUR VIEW WITH ZOOM TOOLS

You can magnify your view of a document using the Zoom tools. You can zoom in to see the document up close or zoom out for a bird's eye view. The Zoom tool is based on percentages, with 100% being the normal document view just as it appears when printed. If your font size is small, you can zoom in to better view your text; or if you want to see how the document's margins appear, you can zoom out to see the entire page. The Status bar features a Zoom bar you can use to zoom in or out, or you can use the Zoom tools featured on the View tab on the Ribbon. The Zoom percentage always appears on the Status bar to let you know the current magnification setting.

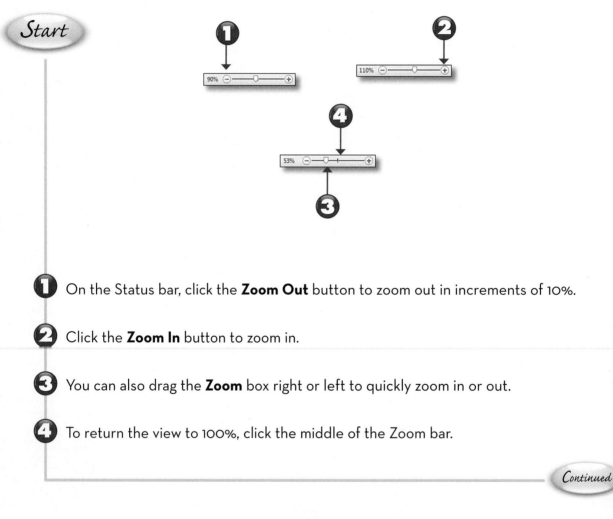

Start

① On the Status bar, click the **Zoom Out** button to zoom out in increments of 10%.

② Click the **Zoom In** button to zoom in.

③ You can also drag the **Zoom** box right or left to quickly zoom in or out.

④ To return the view to 100%, click the middle of the Zoom bar.

Continued

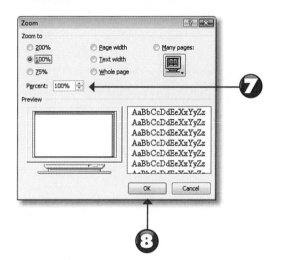

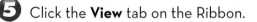

5 Click the **View** tab on the Ribbon.

6 Click the **Zoom** button.

7 From the Zoom dialog box, click a new zoom option or use the spinner arrows to set a unique zoom percentage.

8 Click **OK** to apply the new setting.

End

TIP

100% Please To return a document view to normal, click the **100%** button on the View tab. ■

TIP

Page Views Among the Zoom options on the Ribbon's View tab are buttons for viewing a document's pages by choosing a singular page, two pages, or full page width. For even more page views, open the Zoom dialog box. ■

FINDING HELP WITH WORD 2010

Anytime you run into difficulty using Word, you can find assistance through the program's help files. With an online connection, you can access the Microsoft Office Online center directly and look up topics you want to learn more about. You can view a table of contents for all the available topics and click the one you want to read more about. The Word Help window works much like a browser window, letting you navigate from topic to topic.

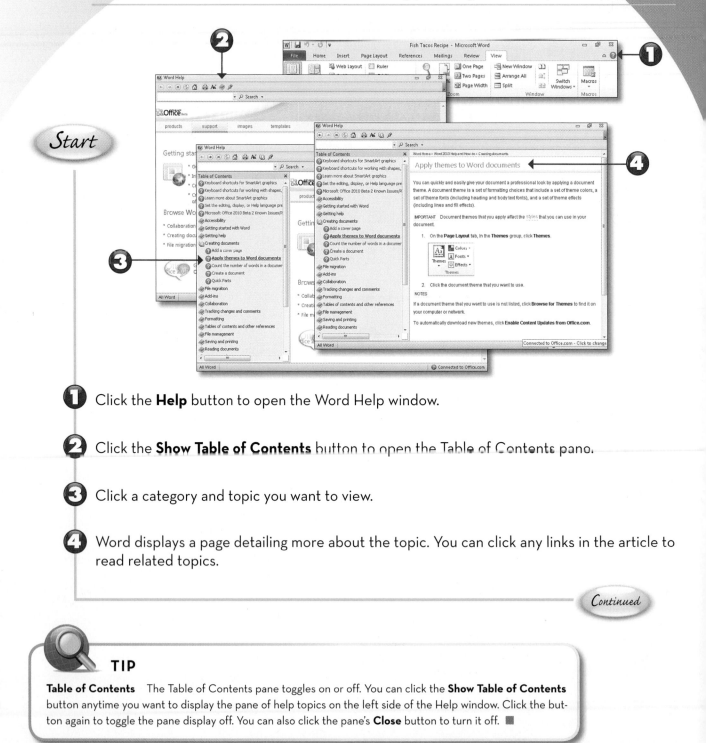

1 Click the **Help** button to open the Word Help window.

2 Click the **Show Table of Contents** button to open the Table of Contents pane.

3 Click a category and topic you want to view.

4 Word displays a page detailing more about the topic. You can click any links in the article to read related topics.

Continued

TIP

Table of Contents The Table of Contents pane toggles on or off. You can click the **Show Table of Contents** button anytime you want to display the pane of help topics on the left side of the Help window. Click the button again to toggle the pane display off. You can also click the pane's **Close** button to turn it off. ■

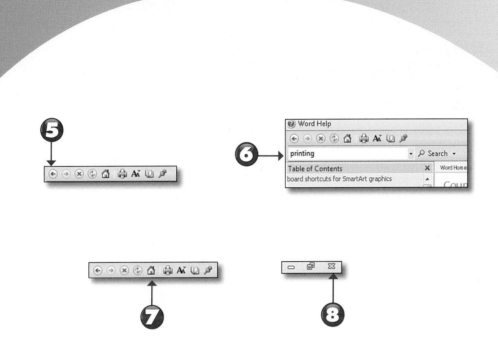

5 You can use the Help window's tool buttons to navigate the Help pages just as if they were Web pages.

6 You can type in a keyword and click **Search** or press **Enter** to look up a specific topic.

7 To return to the main Help screen again, click the **Home** button.

8 Click the window's **Close** button to exit the Help window.

End

TIP

Larger Print You can adjust the size of the font found in the Help window by clicking the **Change Font Size** button and selecting another setting. ◼

Chapter 2

WORKING WITH WORD DOCUMENTS

Files you create in Word are called *documents*. You can create, edit, and save your documents, reuse them again as new documents, turn them into templates to build more documents, and print them out. You can also tap into Word's security settings to assign permissions to control who edits your documents or use passwords to control who can view your documents. The tasks in this section focus entirely on working with document files. You'll learn how to save Word documents in different file formats, how to view multiple documents, and how to move or copy data between documents. All of the commands and features you use to work with documents are found in the Backstage view through the File tab.

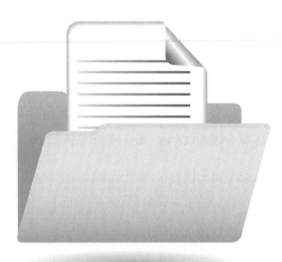

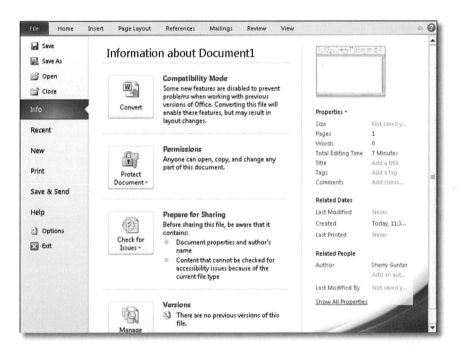

The Backstage view lets you control your Word documents
in various ways all in one convenient spot.

STARTING A NEW DOCUMENT

Whenever you open the Word program window, there's a brand new document waiting for you to begin working with. After you start adding content to the document, you can save it as a file and revisit it again. You can also start new documents at any time. To start a new document, use the File tab to open the Backstage view. The Backstage view is your one-stop spot for all things related to documents. To start a new blank document, choose the Blank Document template. To learn more about using templates, see the task "Applying a Template" later in this chapter.

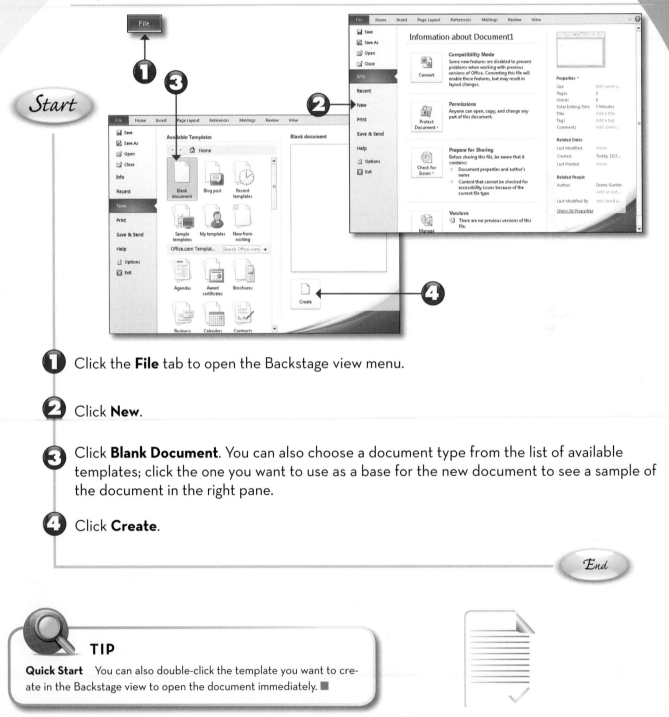

1 Click the **File** tab to open the Backstage view menu.

2 Click **New**.

3 Click **Blank Document**. You can also choose a document type from the list of available templates; click the one you want to use as a base for the new document to see a sample of the document in the right pane.

4 Click **Create**.

End

TIP

Quick Start You can also double-click the template you want to create in the Backstage view to open the document immediately. ■

CLOSING A DOCUMENT

You can close documents you no longer want to edit to free up some processing power on your computer. Closing a document does not close the program window, just the file you were working on. If you haven't saved your work before exiting, Word prompts you to do so before exiting the file.

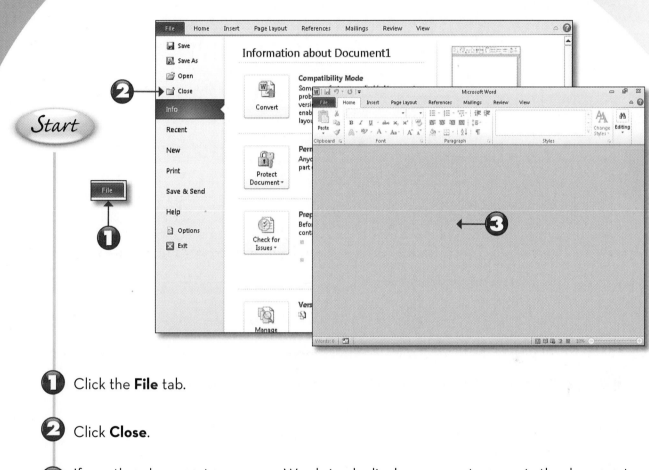

Start

File

1 Click the **File** tab.

2 Click **Close**.

3 If no other documents are open, Word simply displays an empty space in the document area.

End

SAVING A DOCUMENT

After you start adding content to a document, you can save the file to reuse it again later. Word document files are saved in the .docx file format unless you specify otherwise. For most users, the file format designation works behind the scenes and you never see the .docx file extension as part of the filename unless you have the feature turned on. You can save your Word documents as other file formats, if needed. For example, you can save a document as a PDF file or a Web page to share with someone who doesn't have Word.

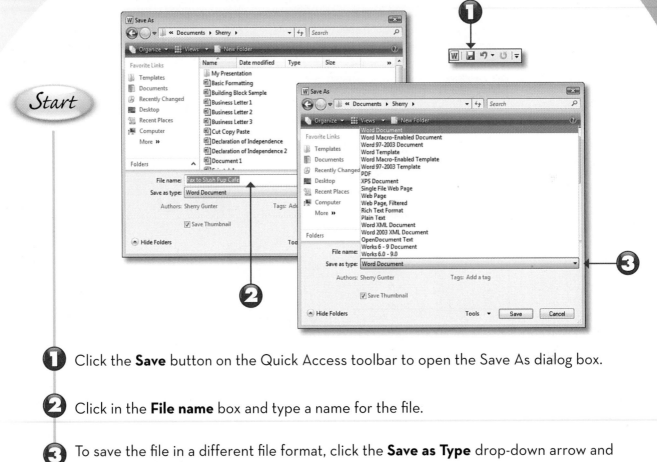

1 Click the **Save** button on the Quick Access toolbar to open the Save As dialog box.

2 Click in the **File name** box and type a name for the file.

3 To save the file in a different file format, click the **Save as Type** drop-down arrow and choose another format.

Continued

TIP

File Naming Rules   When it comes to naming your documents, avoid using the following illegal characters: **/ \ : < > |
* ?** or **"** in your filenames. You can use a period as part of your filename, such as **memo1.sherry.docx**. ■

TIP

Quick Save   If you've already saved a file, you don't have to name it again. You can just save it to its existing name by clicking the **Save** button in the Quick Access toolbar. ■

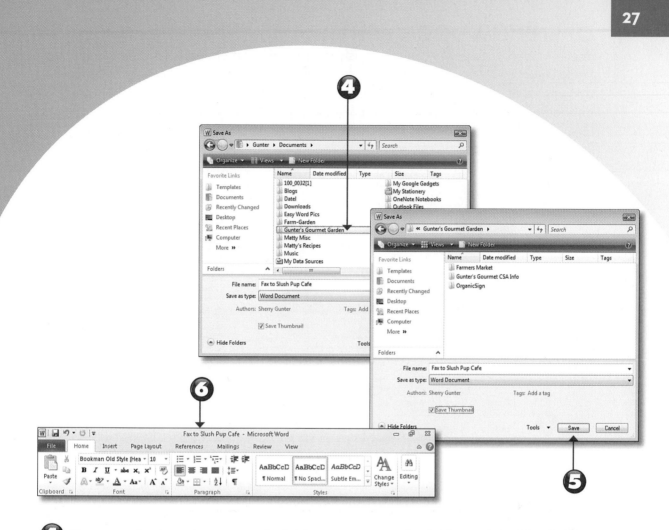

4 To save a document to a specific folder, navigate to the folder and double-click it.

5 Click **Save**.

6 The new document name appears on the Title bar.

End

TIP

Save an Existing File with a New Filename To duplicate a file and give it a new name, click the **File** tab and then click **Save As**. This opens the Save As dialog box, and you can type a new name for the document and save it. ■

TIP

The File Tab You can also access the Save As dialog box through Backstage view. Click the **File** tab and then click **Save As**. ■

OPENING A DOCUMENT

You can open documents you previously saved to work on them again. You can use the Backstage view to open files through the Open options or you can view a list of recent documents and choose one from the list. You can even keep your favorite documents listed on the Recent Documents list so you can always access them quickly.

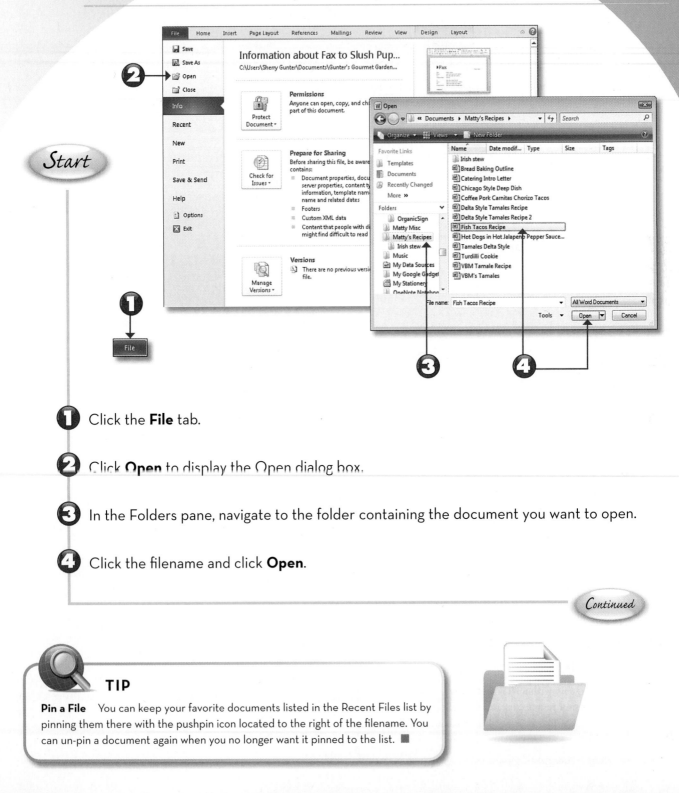

Start

1 Click the **File** tab.

2 Click **Open** to display the Open dialog box.

3 In the Folders pane, navigate to the folder containing the document you want to open.

4 Click the filename and click **Open**.

Continued

TIP

Pin a File You can keep your favorite documents listed in the Recent Files list by pinning them there with the pushpin icon located to the right of the filename. You can un-pin a document again when you no longer want it pinned to the list. ∎

5 Click the **File** tab.

6 Click **Recent**.

7 Click the document you want to open.

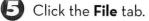

End

TIP

Shortcut Idea If you get tired of opening the File tab to the Backstage view every time you want to open a file, you can add the Open command to your Quick Access toolbar to save yourself a step. See the task "Customizing the Quick Access Toolbar" in Chapter 1, "Getting Started with Word," to learn more. ■

PRINTING A DOCUMENT

When you're ready to print a document, you can choose from a range of printing options through the Backstage view as well as preview the document page by page. You can control the number of copies you print, the page orientation, and the printer you use.

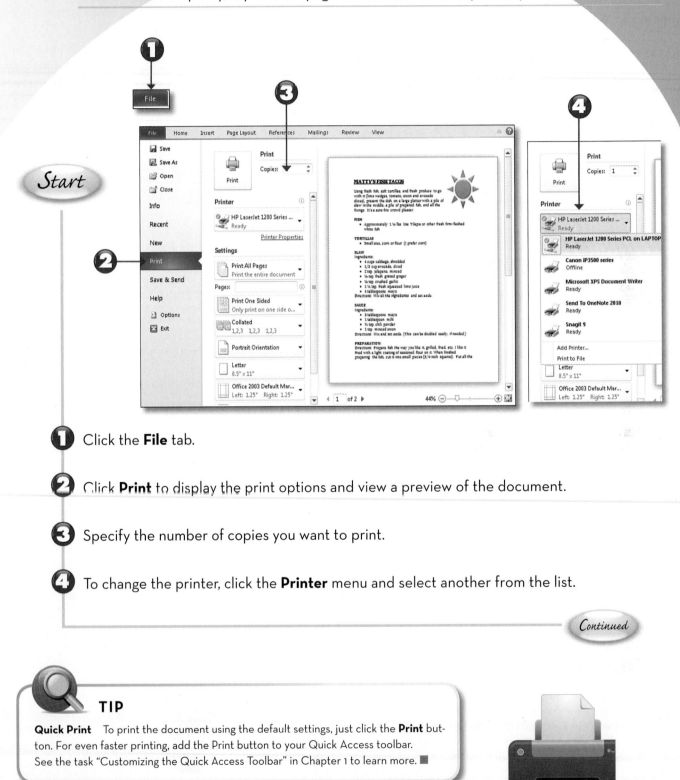

1 Click the **File** tab.

2 Click **Print** to display the print options and view a preview of the document.

3 Specify the number of copies you want to print.

4 To change the printer, click the **Printer** menu and select another from the list.

Continued

TIP

Quick Print To print the document using the default settings, just click the **Print** button. For even faster printing, add the Print button to your Quick Access toolbar. See the task "Customizing the Quick Access Toolbar" in Chapter 1 to learn more. ■

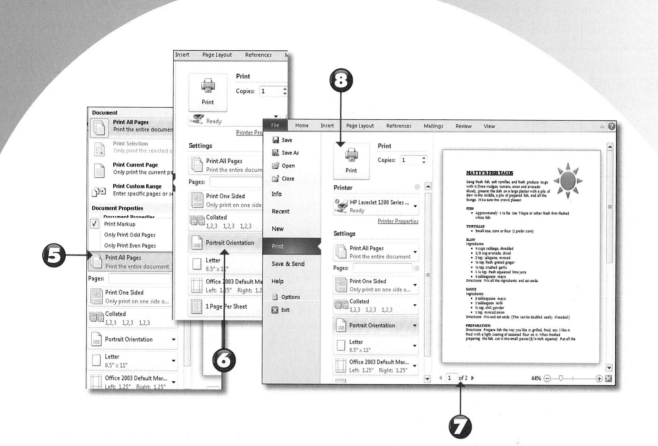

⑤ Click here to specify whether you want to print the whole document, selected text, the current page, or a custom range. You can also specify a range of pages to print.

⑥ Scroll down to view settings for choosing paper orientation, paper size, margins, and collating documents. Simply click the menu item you want to change and make your selections.

⑦ If your document has more than one page, you can click the page buttons to view each page before printing.

⑧ Click the **Print** button to print the document.

End

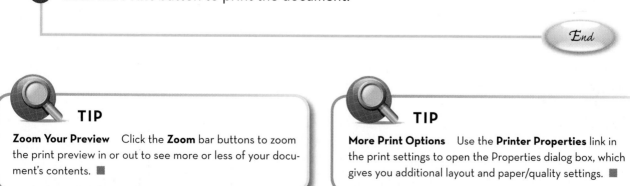

TIP

Zoom Your Preview Click the **Zoom** bar buttons to zoom the print preview in or out to see more or less of your document's contents. ■

TIP

More Print Options Use the **Printer Properties** link in the print settings to open the Properties dialog box, which gives you additional layout and paper/quality settings. ■

VIEWING MULTIPLE DOCUMENTS

You can open and work with multiple documents in Word. For example, you might want to open two documents and compare them side by side. When you open two or more documents, you can use the View tools to control how you view them.

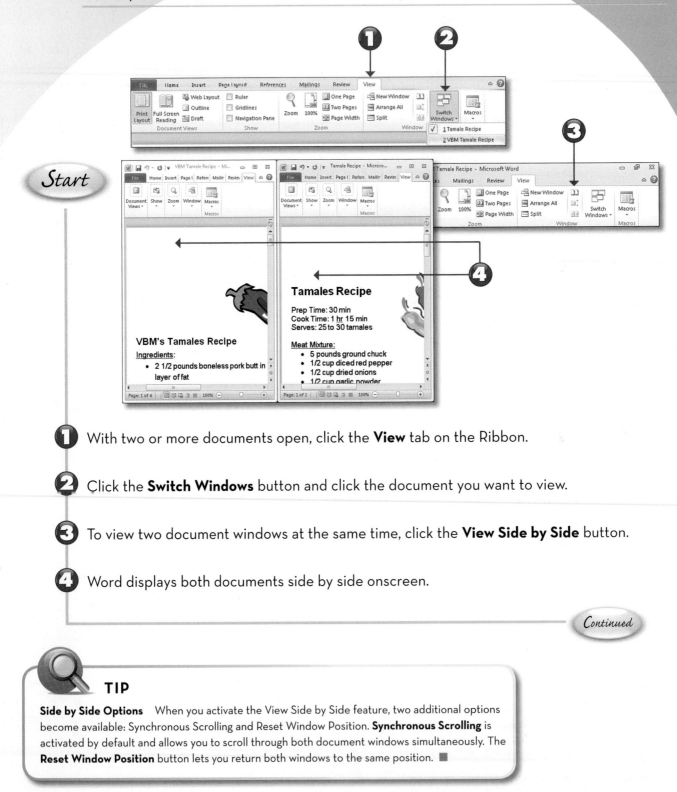

1 With two or more documents open, click the **View** tab on the Ribbon.

2 Click the **Switch Windows** button and click the document you want to view.

3 To view two document windows at the same time, click the **View Side by Side** button.

4 Word displays both documents side by side onscreen.

Continued

TIP

Side by Side Options When you activate the View Side by Side feature, two additional options become available: Synchronous Scrolling and Reset Window Position. **Synchronous Scrolling** is activated by default and allows you to scroll through both document windows simultaneously. The **Reset Window Position** button lets you return both windows to the same position. ■

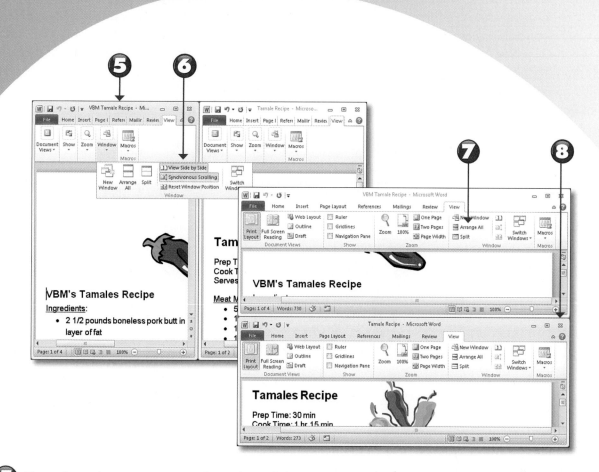

5 To make a document active for edits, click the document's title bar.

6 To turn off side by side viewing, click the **View Side by Side** button located under the **Window** options on the shortened Ribbon.

7 To view multiple documents tiled horizontally instead of vertically, click the **Arrange All** button.

8 Click the **Close** button to close a document at any time, or click the **Maximize** button to return a document to its full window again.

End

TIP

Split a Window   You can split the current document window into two scrollable parts. For example, if you're making a long table, you might want the top of the table with all the headings to stay in view while adding additional content at the bottom of the table. Click the **Split** button on the View tab to keep the top portion onscreen and then click on the document where you want the split to occur. Click the **Remove Split** button to toggle the feature off. ■

ASSIGNING DOCUMENT PASSWORDS

You can assign a password to a document to prevent unauthorized access to the file. It's crucial when creating a password to make sure you keep it in a safe place. If you forget it, you will not be able to recover the document. Word passwords are case-sensitive, and, as with any passwords you assign, stronger passwords include both numbers and letters.

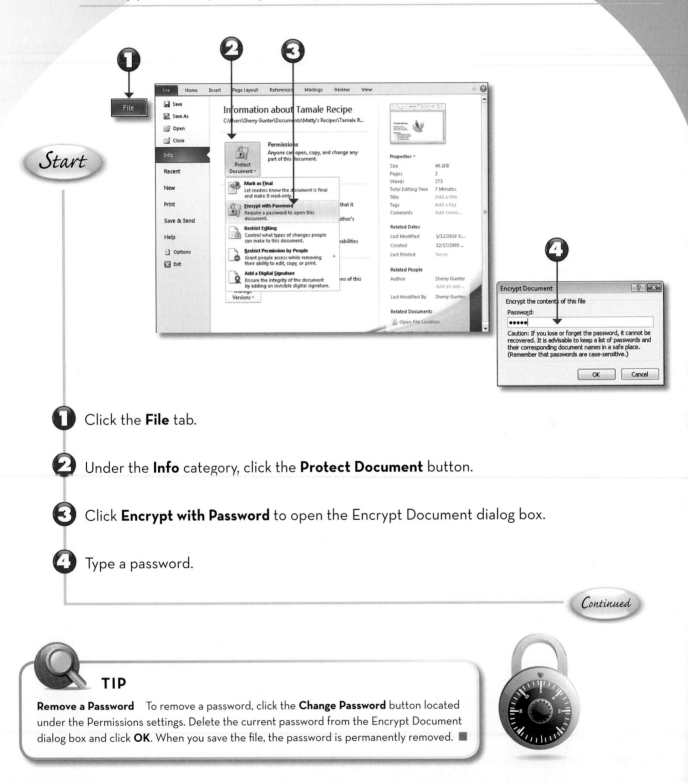

1 Click the **File** tab.

2 Under the **Info** category, click the **Protect Document** button.

3 Click **Encrypt with Password** to open the Encrypt Document dialog box.

4 Type a password.

Continued

TIP

Remove a Password   To remove a password, click the **Change Password** button located under the Permissions settings. Delete the current password from the Encrypt Document dialog box and click **OK**. When you save the file, the password is permanently removed. ■

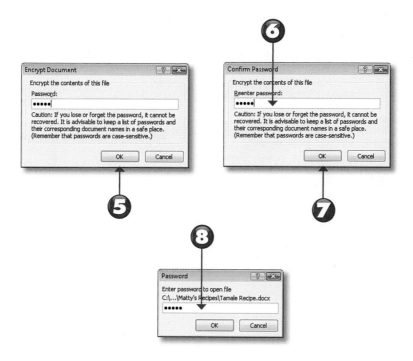

5 Click **OK** and the Confirm Password dialog box opens.

6 Retype the password.

7 Click **OK**. Be sure to save your file before closing it or the password will not be saved as part of the document.

8 The next time you open the file, a Password prompt box appears. Type the password you assigned and click **OK**.

End

TIP

Add a Digital Signature   You can add a digital signature to a Word document to ascertain its authenticity. Click the **Protect Document** button and click **Add a Digital Signature**. Click **OK** in the prompt box that appears and follow the instructions for adding or creating a digital signature. ■

APPLYING A TEMPLATE

Word installs with a variety of ready-made, pre-formatted templates you can use to create all kinds of documents, from brochures and business cards to calendars and budgets. With an online connection, you can find even more on the Office.com website. By default, Backstage view displays both installed templates and online templates. Most templates include placeholder text and graphical elements that can be replaced by your own text. Depending on the template you select in Backstage view, you might first need to download it from the Office website in order to apply it to a document.

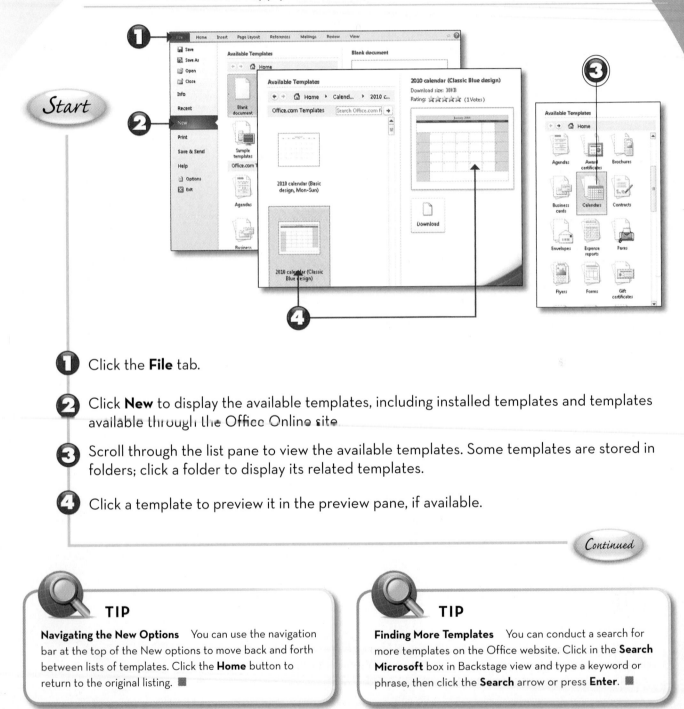

1 Click the **File** tab.

2 Click **New** to display the available templates, including installed templates and templates available through the Office Online site.

3 Scroll through the list pane to view the available templates. Some templates are stored in folders; click a folder to display its related templates.

4 Click a template to preview it in the preview pane, if available.

Continued

TIP

Navigating the New Options You can use the navigation bar at the top of the New options to move back and forth between lists of templates. Click the **Home** button to return to the original listing. ■

TIP

Finding More Templates You can conduct a search for more templates on the Office website. Click in the **Search Microsoft** box in Backstage view and type a keyword or phrase, then click the **Search** arrow or press **Enter**. ■

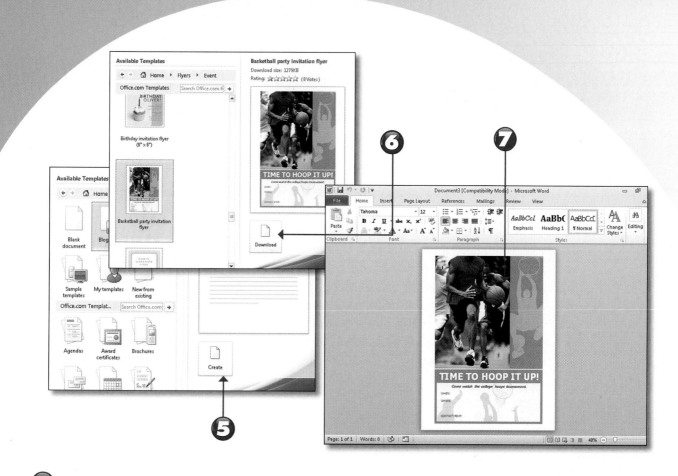

5 When you find a template you like, click the **Create** button to apply it to the document.

6 Some templates may need to be downloaded first; click the **Download** button to add it to your computer.

7 After you've applied a template, you can replace the placeholder text or graphics with your own.

End

TIP

Create Your Own Template   You can save an existing document as a template file to reuse to build other documents. Click the **File** tab and then click **Save As**. In the Save As dialog box, assign a unique name to the file, then click the **Save as Type** menu and choose **Word Template** as the file type. Click **Save** and the new template is created. By default, Word saves templates in the Templates folder for easy access unless directed otherwise. ■

Chapter 3

ENTERING TEXT

To start building a document, begin by entering your text. Word is set up so you can start typing right away in a fresh, new document file. A blinking cursor marks your current location in a document. You can click anywhere in a document and start typing from that point onward. As you type, the cursor marks your spot on the page. In this chapter, you'll learn the basics for adding text, including how to insert special symbols, select text, move and copy text, and use pre-built text elements.

Use the Document area to add and edit text.

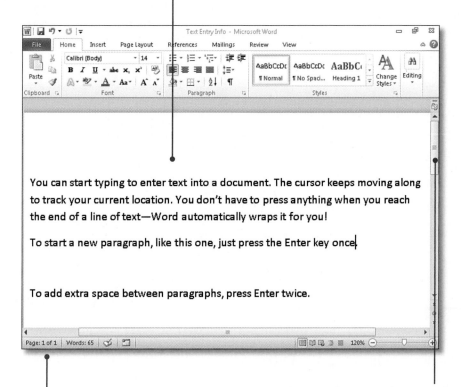

Keep track of document length here.

As your document grows in length, you can use the scrollbar to move up and down to view the document.

TYPING AND EDITING TEXT

To add text to a document, just start typing. If you want to add text in a certain spot on the page, click the area to move the cursor and type in your text. The cursor, the blinking line on your document page, marks your current location in the document. This blinking cursor is also called the insertion point. When you reach the end of a line, Word automatically wraps the text to the next line for you. Default margins are already in place and Word makes sure your lines of text fit within those margins.

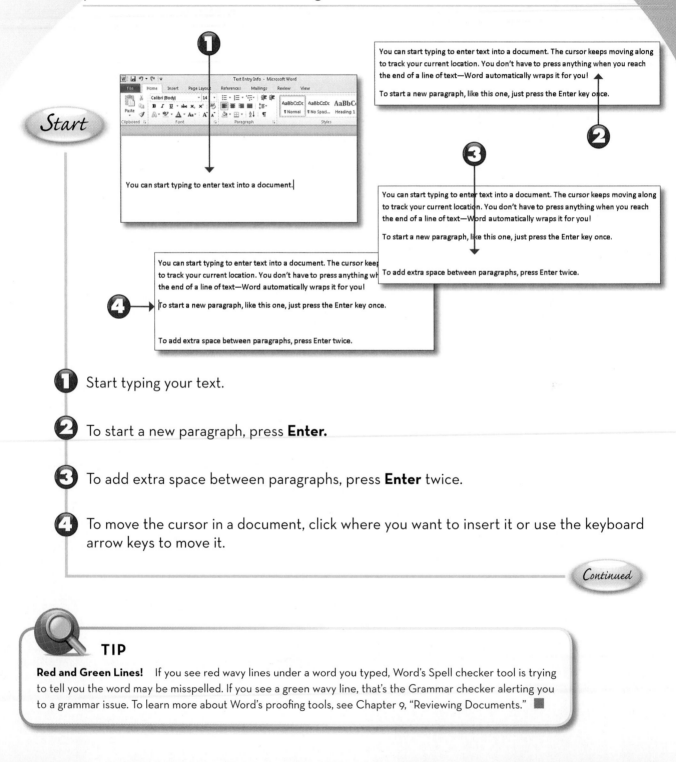

1 Start typing your text.

2 To start a new paragraph, press **Enter.**

3 To add extra space between paragraphs, press **Enter** twice.

4 To move the cursor in a document, click where you want to insert it or use the keyboard arrow keys to move it.

Continued

TIP

Red and Green Lines! If you see red wavy lines under a word you typed, Word's Spell checker tool is trying to tell you the word may be misspelled. If you see a green wavy line, that's the Grammar checker alerting you to a grammar issue. To learn more about Word's proofing tools, see Chapter 9, "Reviewing Documents." ■

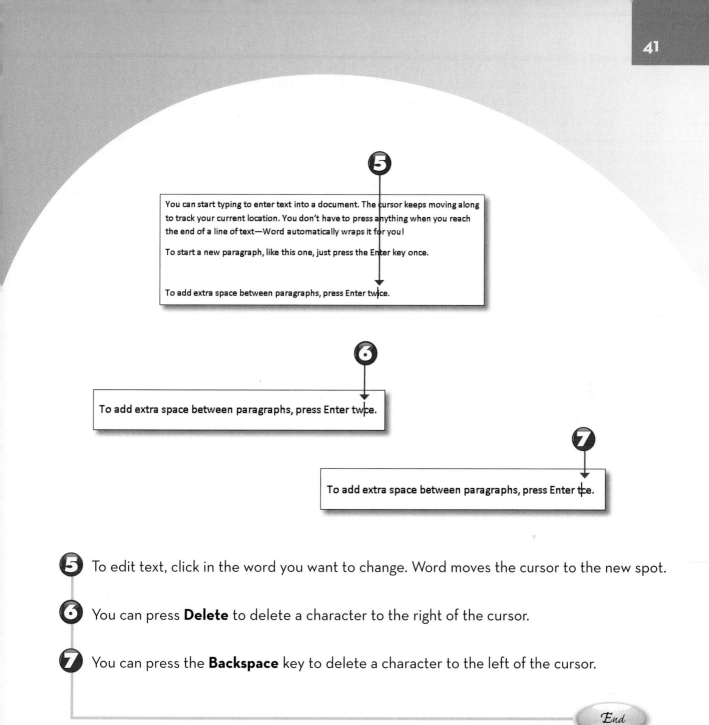

You can start typing to enter text into a document. The cursor keeps moving along to track your current location. You don't have to press anything when you reach the end of a line of text—Word automatically wraps it for you!

To start a new paragraph, like this one, just press the Enter key once.

To add extra space between paragraphs, press Enter twice.

To add extra space between paragraphs, press Enter twice.

To add extra space between paragraphs, press Enter tce.

5 To edit text, click in the word you want to change. Word moves the cursor to the new spot.

6 You can press **Delete** to delete a character to the right of the cursor.

7 You can press the **Backspace** key to delete a character to the left of the cursor.

End

TIP

Insert and Overtype   You can switch between two modes of text entry when working on a document: Insert and Overtype. Insert mode is the default mode, and anywhere you click the cursor you can start typing and any existing text moves over to make room for new text. When Overtype mode is turned on, existing text is replaced by whatever you type. In Word 2010, you can turn the Insert key on your keyboard into a toggle to switch between the two modes. To do so, click the **File** tab and click **Options**. Under Advanced options, click the **Use the Insert Key to Control Overtype Mode** check box. ■

SELECTING TEXT

To edit your text and assign various formatting, you must first learn how to select the text you want to modify. Selecting text is as easy as clicking or dragging, or a combination of both. There are a variety of text selection techniques you can apply, whether you're selecting a single character, a word, a sentence, a paragraph, or even an entire document.

Start

Selecting Text

You can use the click and drag technique to select text, or you can use some clicking techniques with the or an entire paragraph. Anything y on the Word screen.

Selecting Text

You can use the click and drag technique to select text, or you can use some clicking techniques to select a word, a sentence, or an entire paragraph. Anything you select appears highlighted in blue on the screen.

Selecting Text

You can use the click and drag technique to select text, or you can use some clicking techniques to select a word, a sentence, or an entire paragraph. Anything you select appears highlighted in blue on the screen.

① To select by dragging, click and drag across the character, word, or paragraph you want to select.

② Selected text appears highlighted in the document.

③ You can double-click within a word to select a single word in the document.

④ To select a paragraph, triple-click anywhere in the paragraph.

Continued

abc

Selecting Text

You can use the click and drag technique to select text, or you can use some clicking techniques to select a word, a sentence, or an entire paragraph. Anything you select appears highlighted in blue on the screen.

5 You can use the document margin to quickly select lines of text, paragraphs, or the entire document.

Selecting Text

You can use the click and drag technique to select text, or you can use some clicking techniques to select a word, a sentence, or an entire paragraph. Anything you select appears highlighted in blue on the screen.

6 You can use the document margin to quickly select paragraphs, or the entire document.

7

Selecting Text

You can use the click and drag technique to select text, or you can use some clicking techniques to select a word, a sentence, or an entire paragraph. Anything you select appears highlighted in blue on the screen.

You can use the document margin to quickly select lines of text, paragraphs, or the entire document.

5 You can also select text by clicking in the margin. To select a line of text, click in the margin directly left of the line.

6 To select a paragraph, double-click in the margin.

7 To select the entire document, triple-click in the margin.

End

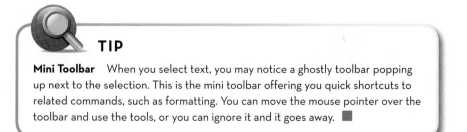

TIP

Mini Toolbar When you select text, you may notice a ghostly toolbar popping up next to the selection. This is the mini toolbar offering you quick shortcuts to related commands, such as formatting. You can move the mouse pointer over the toolbar and use the tools, or you can ignore it and it goes away. ■

MOVING AND COPYING TEXT

You can easily move and copy text in a document, and paste it wherever you want it to go, including into other documents. Using the Cut, Copy, and Paste commands, you can edit and rearrange text and other elements you insert into a document. You can drag and drop text to move it, or use the Cut and Paste technique. When copying text, you're making a duplicate of the original.

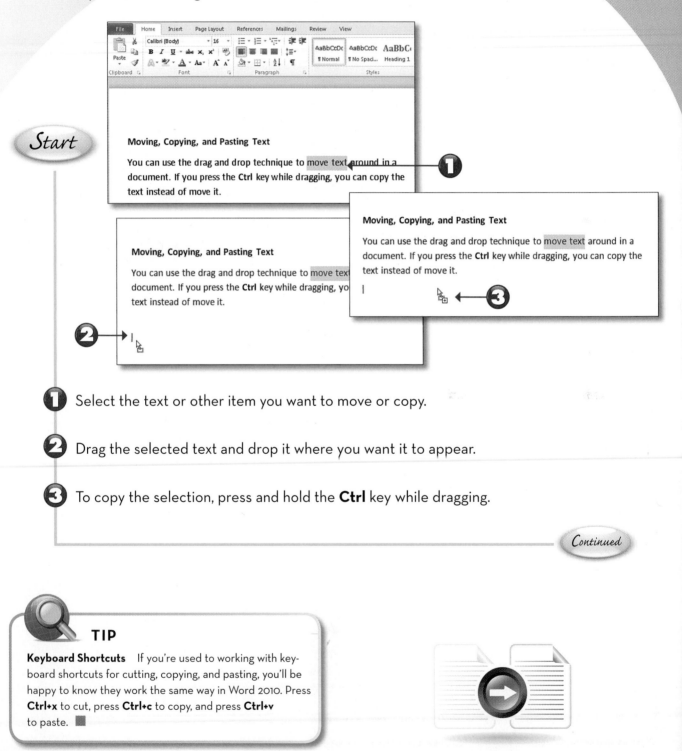

Start

Moving, Copying, and Pasting Text

You can use the drag and drop technique to move text around in a document. If you press the **Ctrl** key while dragging, you can copy the text instead of move it.

① Select the text or other item you want to move or copy.

② Drag the selected text and drop it where you want it to appear.

③ To copy the selection, press and hold the **Ctrl** key while dragging.

Continued

TIP

Keyboard Shortcuts If you're used to working with keyboard shortcuts for cutting, copying, and pasting, you'll be happy to know they work the same way in Word 2010. Press **Ctrl+x** to cut, press **Ctrl+c** to copy, and press **Ctrl+v** to paste. ■

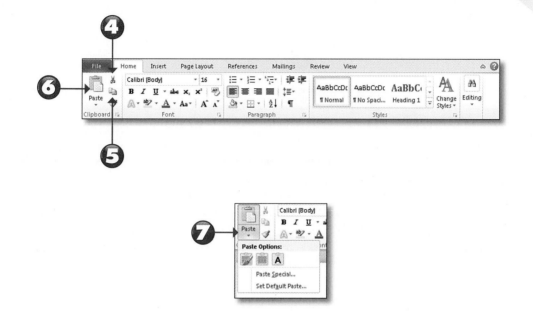

4 To move selected text with the Cut command, click the **Cut** button on the Home tab of the Ribbon.

5 To copy selected text with the Copy command, click the **Copy** button.

6 To paste the cut or copied text, click where you want it to go and click the **Paste** button.

7 To control paste options, click the **Paste** menu button and choose an option.

End

TIP

Paste Options New to Word 2010, you can right-click after cutting or copying an item and choose from several paste options. You can choose to keep the original formatting of the item you're pasting, merge the formatting, or paste only the text without the formatting. You can also find these three options through the **Paste** menu on the Home tab. ■

INSERTING QUICK PARTS

Word's Quick Parts offers you dozens of pre-made content elements, called building blocks, you can insert into your documents. Building blocks include headers that appear at the top of each page, salutations to end letters, and page numbers. Word's Building Blocks Organizer holds a vast array of reusable Quick Parts elements you can choose from, and you can add your own to the mix. You can turn any text into a building block that appears in the Quick Part Gallery to reuse over and over again.

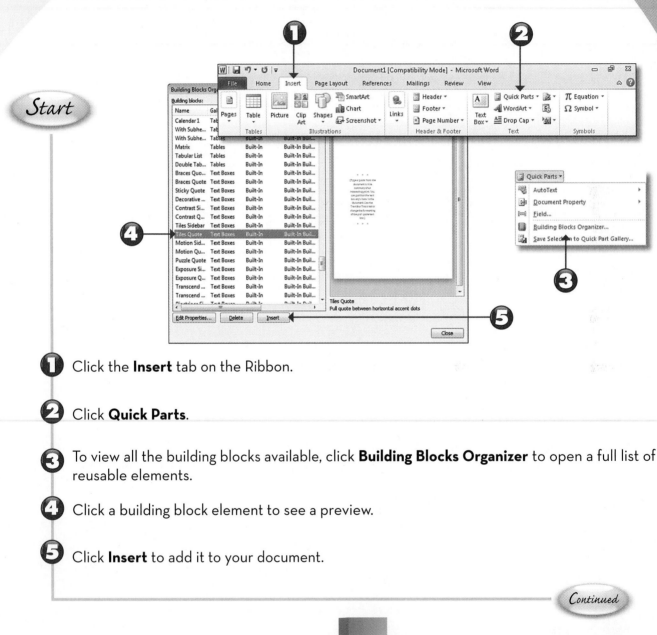

1 Click the **Insert** tab on the Ribbon.

2 Click **Quick Parts**.

3 To view all the building blocks available, click **Building Blocks Organizer** to open a full list of reusable elements.

4 Click a building block element to see a preview.

5 Click **Insert** to add it to your document.

Continued

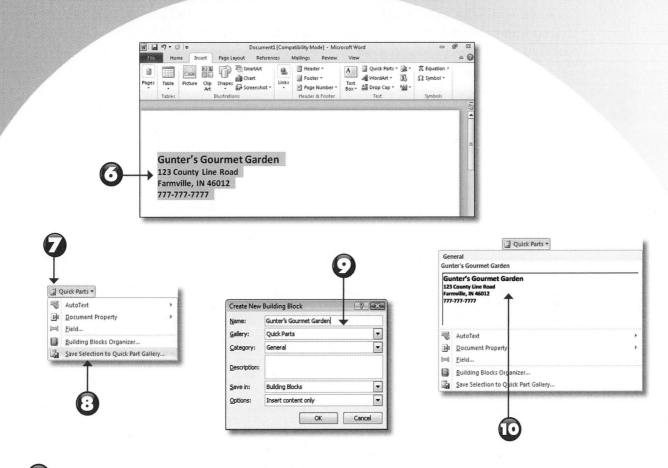

6 To turn text into a building block, first select the text in the document.

7 Click **Quick Parts**.

8 Click **Save Selection to Quick Part Gallery**.

9 Fill out any details you want to save along with the text element and click **OK**.

10 Word displays the text in the gallery the next time you click **Quick Parts**.

End

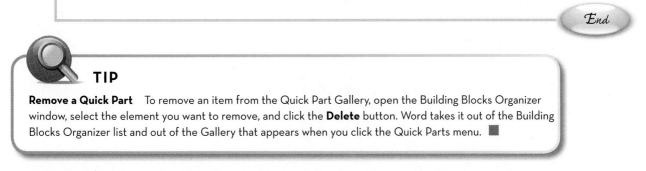

TIP

Remove a Quick Part To remove an item from the Quick Part Gallery, open the Building Blocks Organizer window, select the element you want to remove, and click the **Delete** button. Word takes it out of the Building Blocks Organizer list and out of the Gallery that appears when you click the Quick Parts menu. ■

INSERTING SYMBOLS

If you ever need to insert a special symbol or character into your document, such as a copyright symbol or a paragraph mark, you can open the Symbol dialog box. This dialog box offers a library of special symbols and characters ranging from mathematical symbols to special quote marks.

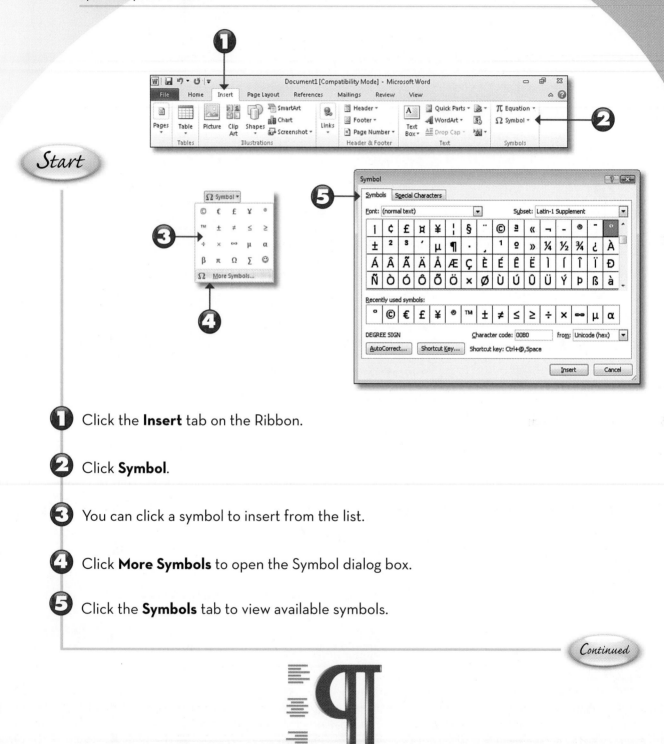

1 Click the **Insert** tab on the Ribbon.

2 Click **Symbol**.

3 You can click a symbol to insert from the list.

4 Click **More Symbols** to open the Symbol dialog box.

5 Click the **Symbols** tab to view available symbols.

Continued

6 Click the **Special Characters** tab to view characters.

7 Click the symbol or character you want to insert.

8 Click **Insert** to insert the symbol into the document. The dialog box remains open in case you want to insert more symbols. Click **Close** to exit.

End

TIP

Even More Symbols If you don't see the symbol you're looking for in the Symbols tab of the Symbols dialog box, try switching to another font or symbol subset using the drop-down arrows. ■

TIP

Symbol Shortcuts Some symbols have their own shortcut keys you can press to quickly insert the symbol. To learn the shortcut, select the symbol in the Symbol dialog box and look for the shortcut key combination listed at the bottom. ■

Chapter 4

FORMATTING TEXT

After taking the time to type up your document text, the next phase is to make it all look nice—that's where formatting comes into play. Formatting is the application of various commands to control the appearance of text in your document. Formatting includes controlling the font and size of your text, the position of it on the page, the color of the text, and much more. There are several default settings at play when you start any document in Word, including font, font size, and alignment. You can change any of these settings using Word's formatting controls. The Home tab on the Ribbon features most of the font and paragraph controls you can use to format a document. In this chapter, you learn about basic formatting controls.

The Home tab on the Ribbon is the place to go to find basic formatting controls.

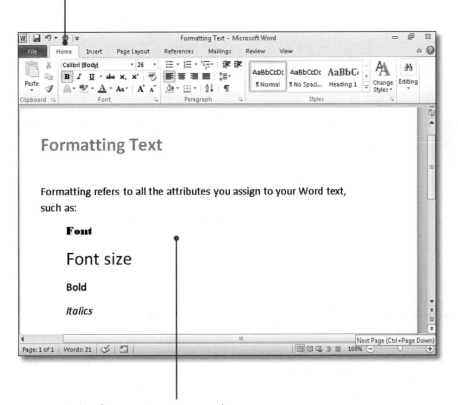

The formatting you apply appears in the Document area.

ASSIGNING BOLD, ITALIC, AND UNDERLINING

The most basic of all formatting you can apply boils down to three tried-and-true controls: bold, italic, and underlining. When you apply bold to text, the font takes on a darker, thicker appearance. When you apply italic, the text appears slanted slightly. Lastly, when you apply underlining, the text features an underscore, or line, under the characters. All three types are easy ways to add emphasis to your text, whether it's a single character, a word, or an entire sentence.

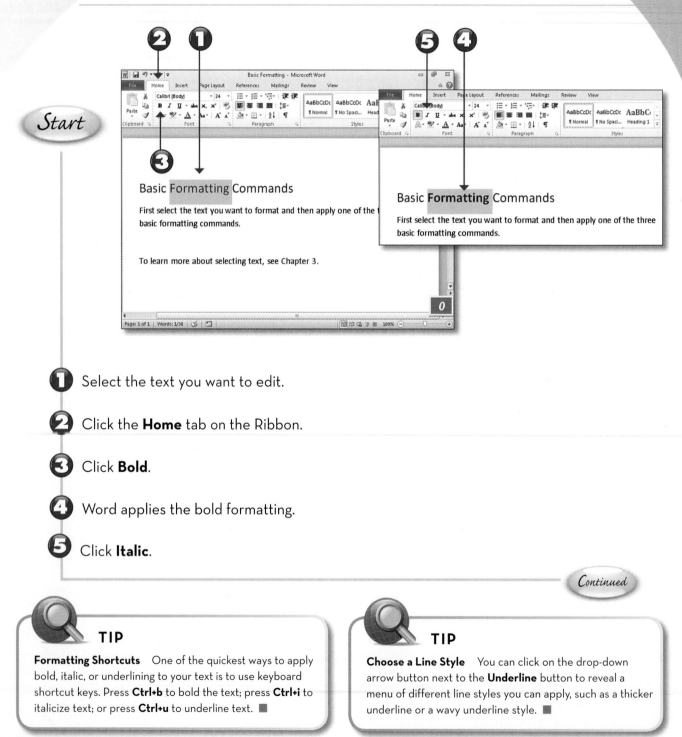

① Select the text you want to edit.

② Click the **Home** tab on the Ribbon.

③ Click **Bold**.

④ Word applies the bold formatting.

⑤ Click **Italic**.

Continued

TIP

Formatting Shortcuts   One of the quickest ways to apply bold, italic, or underlining to your text is to use keyboard shortcut keys. Press **Ctrl+b** to bold the text; press **Ctrl+i** to italicize text; or press **Ctrl+u** to underline text. ■

TIP

Choose a Line Style   You can click on the drop-down arrow button next to the **Underline** button to reveal a menu of different line styles you can apply, such as a thicker underline or a wavy underline style. ■

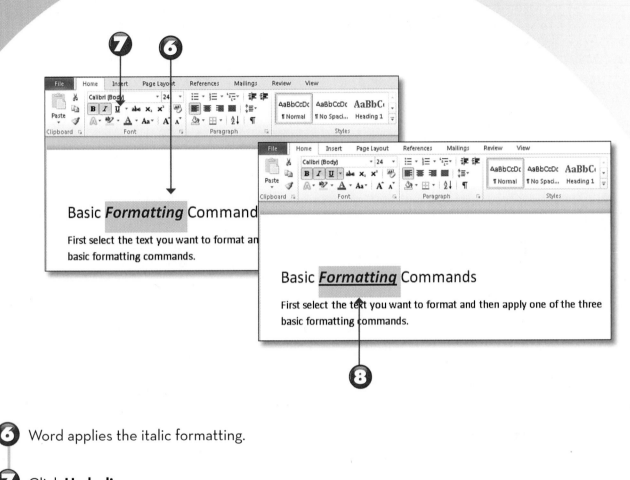

Basic *Formatting* Commands

First select the text you want to format and then apply one of the three basic formatting commands.

6 Word applies the italic formatting.

7 Click **Underline**.

8 Word applies the underlining to your text.

End

TIP

Font Dialog Box You can also assign basic formatting through the Font dialog box. To open the box, click the tiny **Font** dialog box icon located in the bottom right corner of the Font group of commands on the Ribbon. In the dialog box, you can find bold and italic listed under the Font Style options. The underlining command is listed under the Underline Style setting; click the drop-down arrow to display a menu of underlining styles you can apply. Simply make your changes in the dialog box and then click **OK** to apply them to the text. ■

USING THE MINI TOOLBAR

Whenever you select text in a Word document, a ghostly pop-up toolbar appears next to the text. This is the Mini Toolbar, offering easy access to common commands, such as bold, italic, and underlining. You can choose to use the toolbar right away, or just ignore it, which makes it fade away. If you move the mouse pointer over the toolbar, its buttons are fully displayed and you can click which one you want to apply to the selected text.

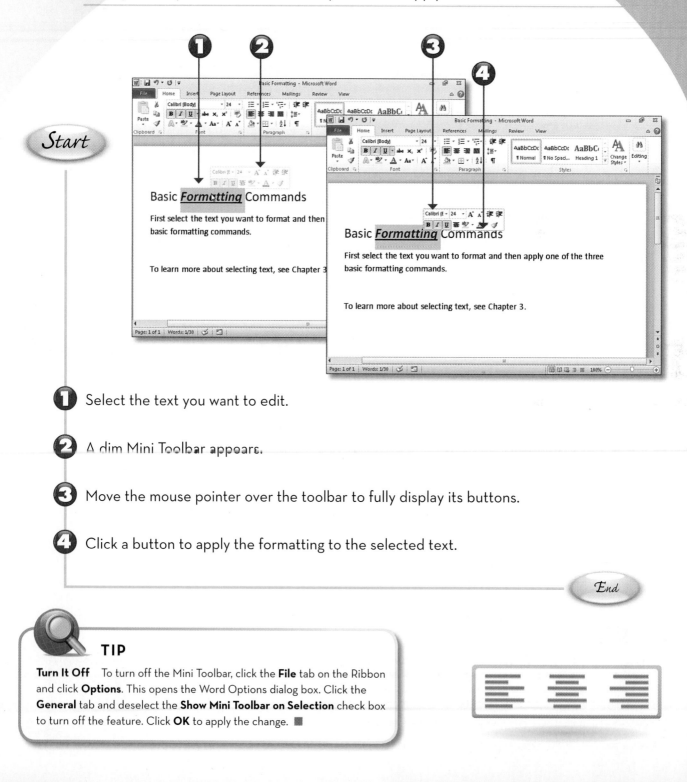

Start

1 Select the text you want to edit.

2 A dim Mini Toolbar appears.

3 Move the mouse pointer over the toolbar to fully display its buttons.

4 Click a button to apply the formatting to the selected text.

End

TIP

Turn It Off   To turn off the Mini Toolbar, click the **File** tab on the Ribbon and click **Options**. This opens the Word Options dialog box. Click the **General** tab and deselect the **Show Mini Toolbar on Selection** check box to turn off the feature. Click **OK** to apply the change. ■

CHANGING THE FONT

A font is the style of characters applied to your text, also called a typeface. Word features a wide variety of fonts to choose from, ranging from sleek and simple to frilly and fanciful. You can use the Font drop-down menu on the Home tab to change the font style. The font menu displays the fonts just as they appear in the document. With the Live Preview feature, which is turned on by default, you can hover your mouse pointer over a font name in the menu list and see the selected text in the document with the font applied. Additionally, you can also open the Font dialog box to peruse fonts and set more font formatting controls.

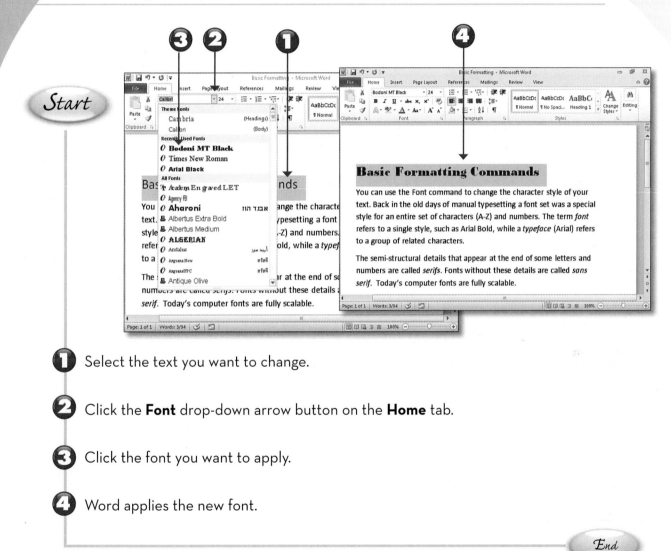

1 Select the text you want to change.

2 Click the **Font** drop-down arrow button on the **Home** tab.

3 Click the font you want to apply.

4 Word applies the new font.

End

TIP

Or Use the Mini Toolbar You can also use the Mini Toolbar that appears when you select text to change the font or font size. Just move the mouse pointer over the toolbar to display it fully, then look for the **Font** drop-down menu for easy font changes, or use the **Font Size** drop-down menu to change the font size. ■

CHANGING THE FONT SIZE

Font size formatting refers to the size of type in a document. Font size is measured in points, a throwback measurement to the days of manual typesetting. By default, Word uses 11-point type. You can set a specific font size using the Font Size formatting option.

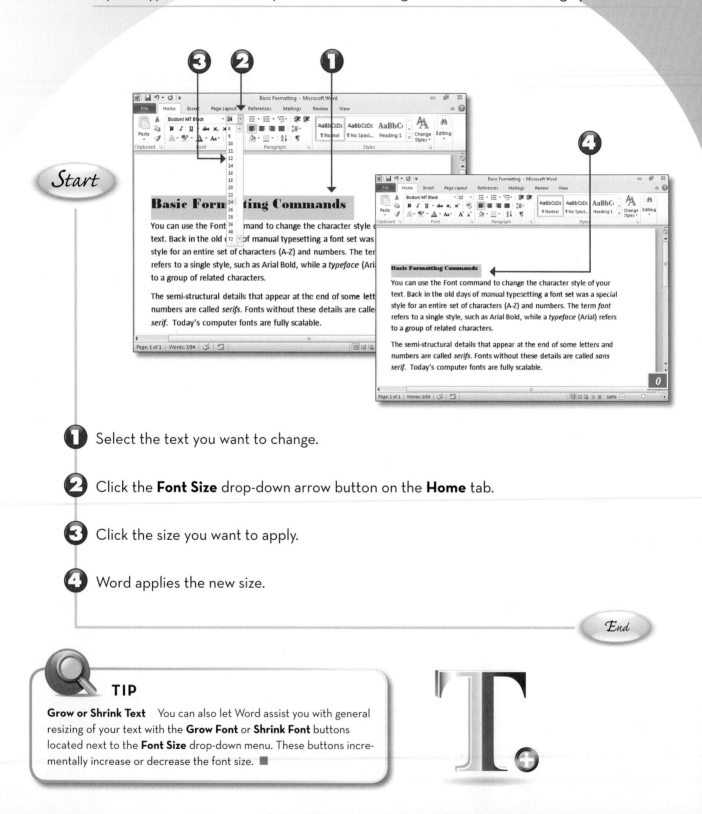

Start

1. Select the text you want to change.

2. Click the **Font Size** drop-down arrow button on the **Home** tab.

3. Click the size you want to apply.

4. Word applies the new size.

End

TIP

Grow or Shrink Text You can also let Word assist you with general resizing of your text with the **Grow Font** or **Shrink Font** buttons located next to the **Font Size** drop-down menu. These buttons incrementally increase or decrease the font size. ∎

ADDING COLOR TO TEXT

You can apply color to your Word text through Font Color formatting. You can choose from a palette of colors that are theme-related or from Word's Standard Colors. Based on the theme you apply, the palette displays colors designed to work with that particular motif. The Standard Colors are basic colors, such as red and yellow. Always keep legibility in mind when choosing font colors.

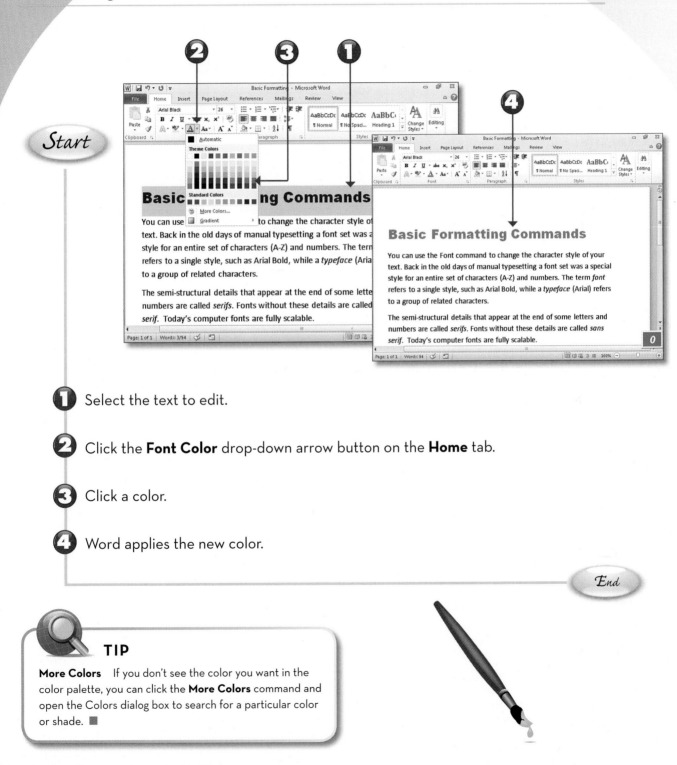

Start

1. Select the text to edit.

2. Click the **Font Color** drop-down arrow button on the **Home** tab.

3. Click a color.

4. Word applies the new color.

End

TIP

More Colors If you don't see the color you want in the color palette, you can click the **More Colors** command and open the Colors dialog box to search for a particular color or shade. ■

ALIGNING TEXT

You can control the placement of text within a document using Word's alignment commands. The horizontal alignment commands control how text is aligned horizontally across the page: Align Text Left, Center, Align Text Right, and Justify. By default, Word applies left alignment unless you specify otherwise.

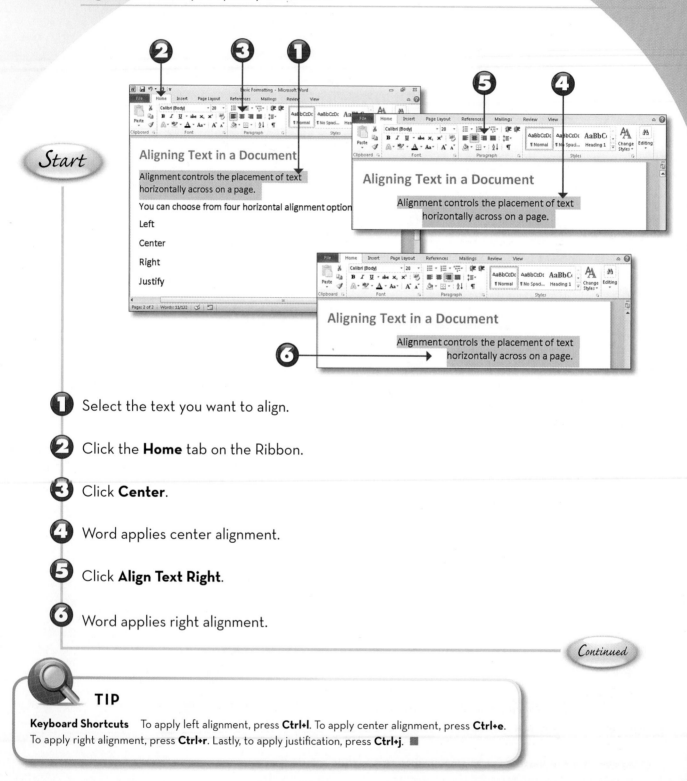

1 Select the text you want to align.

2 Click the **Home** tab on the Ribbon.

3 Click **Center**.

4 Word applies center alignment.

5 Click **Align Text Right**.

6 Word applies right alignment.

Continued

TIP

Keyboard Shortcuts   To apply left alignment, press **Ctrl+l**. To apply center alignment, press **Ctrl+e**. To apply right alignment, press **Ctrl+r**. Lastly, to apply justification, press **Ctrl+j**. ■

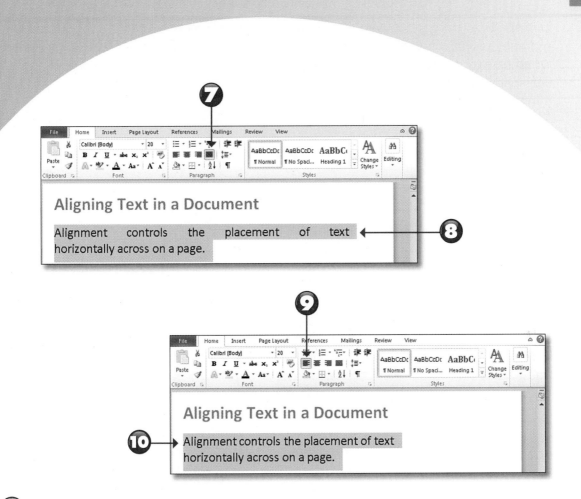

7 Click **Justify**.

8 Word justifies the text so it aligns at the margins on both the left and right sides of the page. This command only works when you have enough text to space evenly between the two margins.

9 Click **Align Text Left**.

10 Word applies the left alignment.

End

TIP

Vertical Alignment You can also control the vertical alignment of text on a page. To do so, click the **Page Layout** tab on the Ribbon and click the **Align** button located on the far right side of the Ribbon. Vertical alignment options include **Align Top**, **Align Middle**, and **Align Bottom**. ■

SETTING LINE SPACING

Line spacing refers to the amount of space between lines of text and paragraphs. For example, you might want a business letter to show single line spacing, or you might want a typed research paper to display double line spacing. You can choose from several preset line spacing amounts. By default, Multiple spacing is assigned until you change it to something else.

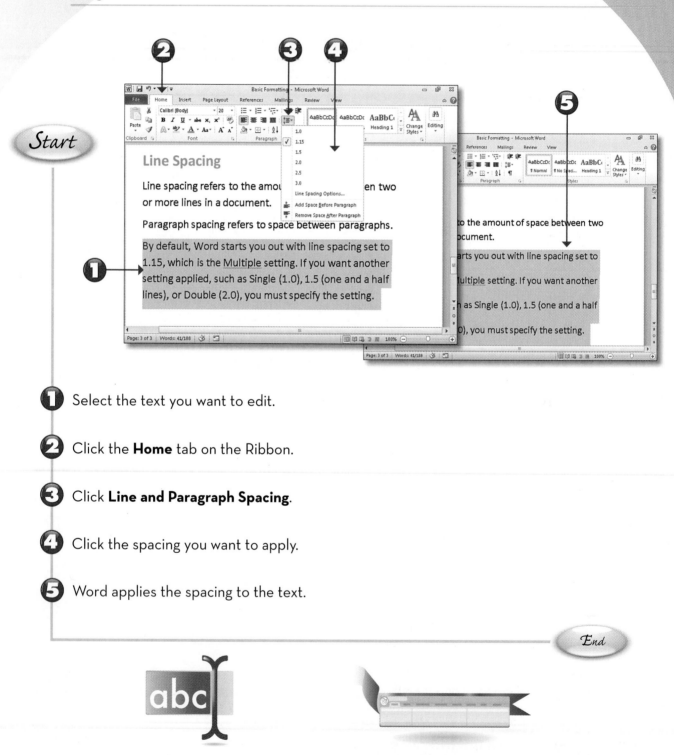

1 Select the text you want to edit.

2 Click the **Home** tab on the Ribbon.

3 Click **Line and Paragraph Spacing**.

4 Click the spacing you want to apply.

5 Word applies the spacing to the text.

End

SETTING CHARACTER SPACING

Character spacing refers to the amount of space between characters. Sometimes called tracking, character spacing can help you place typed characters closer together or further apart. You can find character spacing controls among the Advanced options available in the Font dialog box.

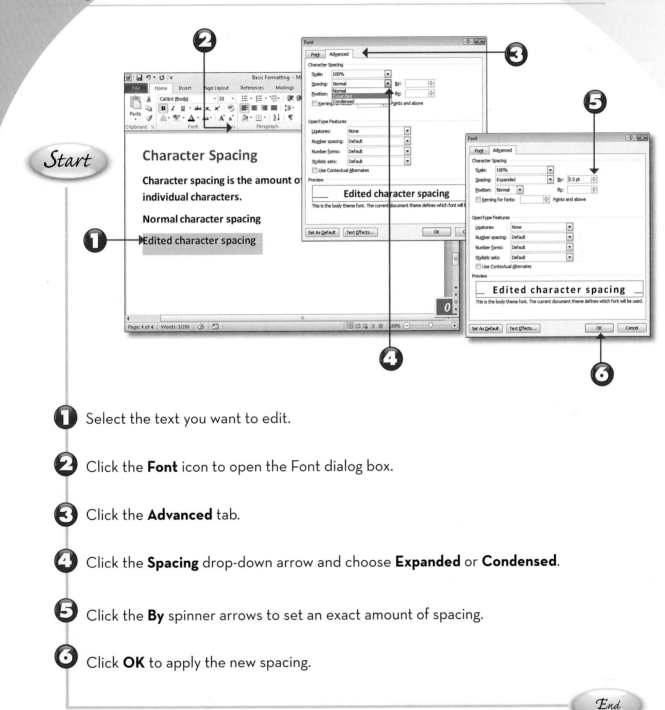

1 Select the text you want to edit.

2 Click the **Font** icon to open the Font dialog box.

3 Click the **Advanced** tab.

4 Click the **Spacing** drop-down arrow and choose **Expanded** or **Condensed**.

5 Click the **By** spinner arrows to set an exact amount of spacing.

6 Click **OK** to apply the new spacing.

COPYING FORMATTING

After you have formatted text in one area of your document, you can easily apply the same formatting to another. You can do this without having to repeat all the same steps again. Instead, you can use Word's handy Format Painter tool. The Format Painter copies formatting either by selecting text and then clicking the button or dragging it over the text you want to format.

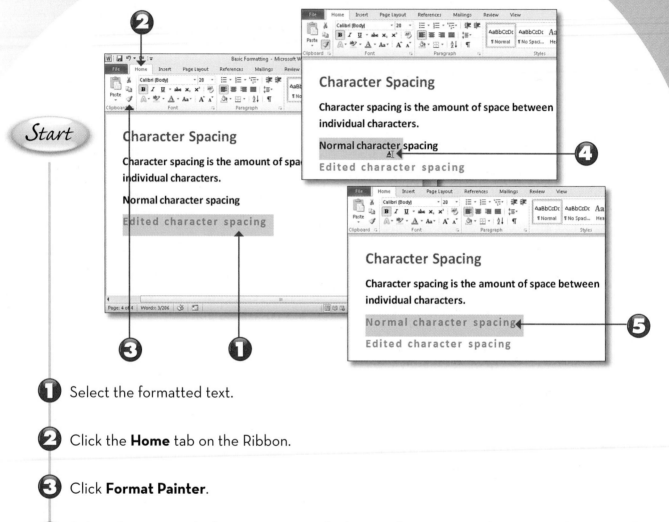

1 Select the formatted text.

2 Click the **Home** tab on the Ribbon.

3 Click **Format Painter**.

4 Select the text to which you want to apply the new formatting or drag across the text with the Format Painter icon.

5 Word immediately applies the same formatting to the new text.

REMOVING FORMATTING

Word makes it easy to remove formatting from your text and return it to its default condition. You can apply the Clear Formatting command. Use this command any time you need to strip out the formatting but keep the text intact.

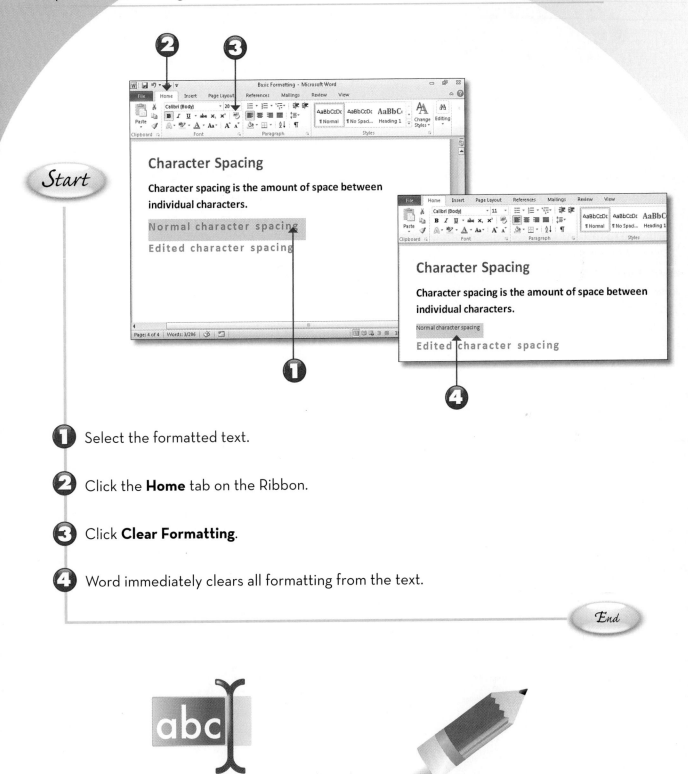

1. Select the formatted text.

2. Click the **Home** tab on the Ribbon.

3. Click **Clear Formatting**.

4. Word immediately clears all formatting from the text.

Chapter 5

FORMATTING PARAGRAPHS AND PAGES

In the previous chapter, you learned some basic techniques for applying formatting to text. Now you're ready to take formatting to the next level and start applying it to paragraphs and pages. Word offers all kinds of commands for controlling the placement and positioning of text in a document, as well as features for adding page elements. For example, you can indent text, apply tabs to create columns, and turn text into a bulleted or numbered list. You can also add page numbers, section breaks, and headers or footers. Word groups paragraph commands in a section on the Ribbon's Home tab labeled Paragraph. You can also find another group of Paragraph commands on the Page Layout tab. The Page Layout tab is the place to go for general page features.

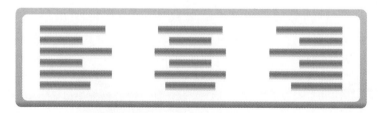

You can also find paragraph and page formatting controls on the Page Layout tab.

The Home tab on the Ribbon features some basic paragraph formatting controls.

Click the Paragraph icon to open a dialog box full of paragraph formatting options.

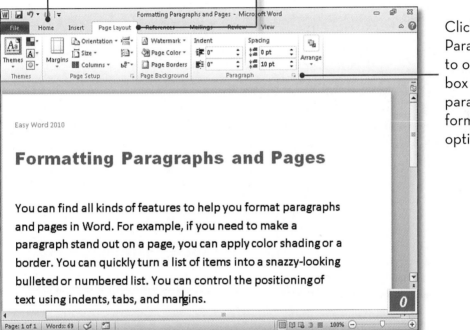

ADDING INDENTS

You can use indents to move text horizontally from the page margin to set it apart from surrounding text. The Increase Indent and Decrease Indent commands create left indents in increments. You can find these two commands on the Home tab. You can set more precise indent controls on the Page Layout tab, which includes a setting for specifying left and right indents on a page.

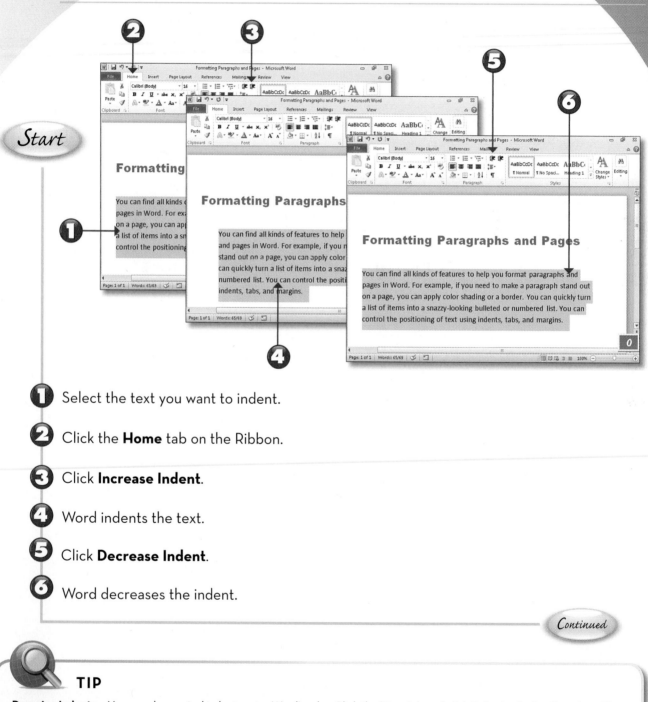

① Select the text you want to indent.

② Click the **Home** tab on the Ribbon.

③ Click **Increase Indent**.

④ Word indents the text.

⑤ Click **Decrease Indent**.

⑥ Word decreases the indent.

Continued

TIP

Dragging Indents   You can also control indents using Word's ruler. Click the **View** tab and click **Ruler** to display the rulers. The top horizontal ruler has indent and margin markers you can drag to new locations to set new indents and margins for a page. ■

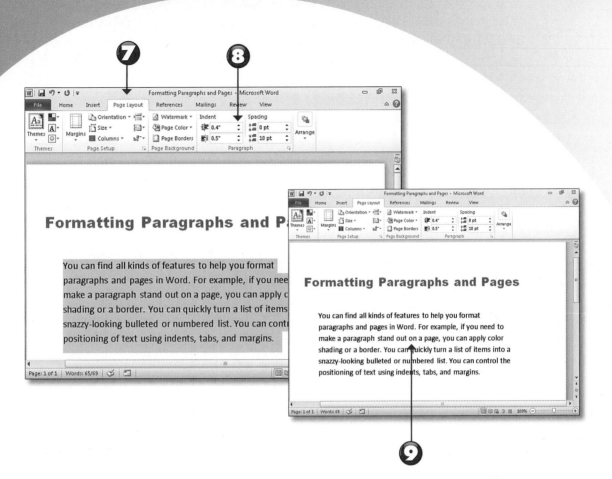

7 Click the **Page Layout** tab.

8 Click the spinner arrows for the **Left** or **Right** indents to specify an indentation amount.

9 Word applies the indent to your text.

End

TIP

Paragraph Spacing Next door to the Indent spinner arrows on the Page Layout tab are spacing controls to specify how much space you want to add before and after paragraphs. Paragraph spacing controls allow you to add some extra space between paragraphs without inserting extra lines of text. ■

TIP

Ruler Indents You can use Word's ruler to add First Line and Hanging Indents. A first line indent moves the first line of a paragraph only, while a hanging indent indents everything except the first line of text in a paragraph. To view the ruler, click the **View** tab and click **Ruler**. Click the **Tab** stop icon until you see the indent you want to set and then click where you want the indent to appear on the ruler. ■

SETTING TABS

You can use tab stops to line up text in a document or create columns of text. By default, Word's tabs indent text by half an inch. You can use a default tab stop simply by pressing the Tab key. To define your own tab stops, you can use Word's ruler. You can apply tabs before you type or to selected text in a document.

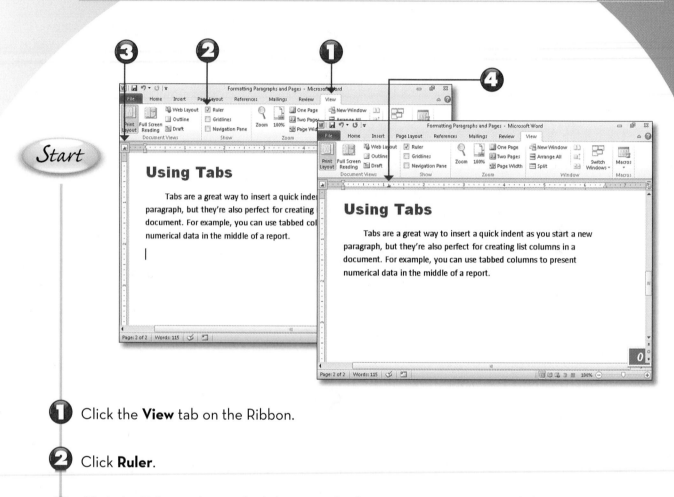

1. Click the **View** tab on the Ribbon.

2. Click **Ruler**.

3. Click the **Tab** icon box to find the type of tab you want to set. Keep clicking to view all the different tab types: Left, Center, Right, Decimal, and Bar.

4. Click on the ruler where you want to add a tab stop.

Continued

TIP

Paragraph Dialog Box You can also define your own tab stops using the Tabs dialog box. To find your way there, click the **Paragraph** icon on the Home tab or on the Page Layout tab. This opens the Paragraph dialog box. Click the **Tabs** button. This opens a dialog box where you can add and edit tab stops, set tab stop alignments, and specify special tab leader characters. ■

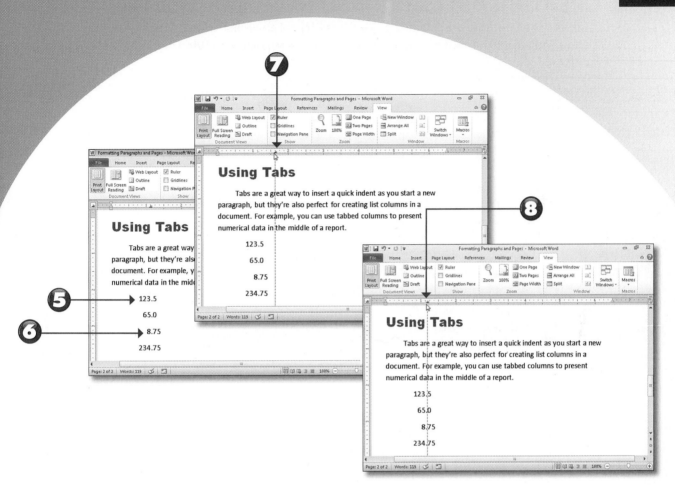

⑤ Press **Tab** and type your text.

⑥ Continue adding as many tab stops as you need and entering your tabbed text. In this example, a Decimal tab is applied, causing all the decimals to line up in the column.

⑦ To move the tab, drag it to a new location on the ruler.

⑧ To remove a tab stop, drag it off the ruler.

End

TIP

Leader Characters Leader characters are simply characters that appear between tab stops. Dots, for example, are a common leader character used, or a dash or solid line. Leader characters extend from one tabbed column to the next, filling in the extra space between columns. You can set leader characters through the Tabs dialog box described in the previous tip. ■

CREATING BULLETED AND NUMBERED LISTS

Bulleted and numbered lists are a great way to organize list text in a document and make it stand out from the rest of the text. You can even specify a style to use for your bullets or numbers.

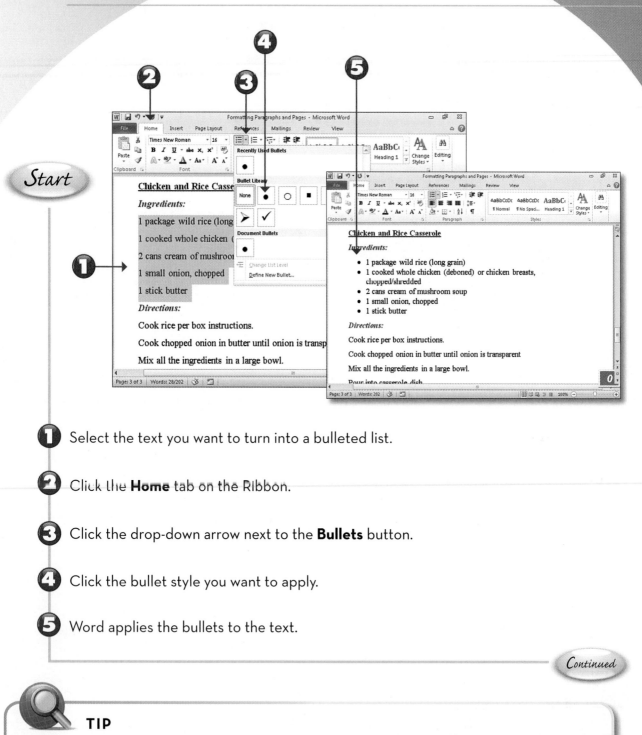

Start

1 Select the text you want to turn into a bulleted list.

2 Click the **Home** tab on the Ribbon.

3 Click the drop-down arrow next to the **Bullets** button.

4 Click the bullet style you want to apply.

5 Word applies the bullets to the text.

Continued

TIP

Quick Bullets or Numbers You don't have to open the bullets or numbering menus to create a list. You can just click the **Bullets** button to assign the default bullet style, or click the **Numbering** button to apply the default number style. ■

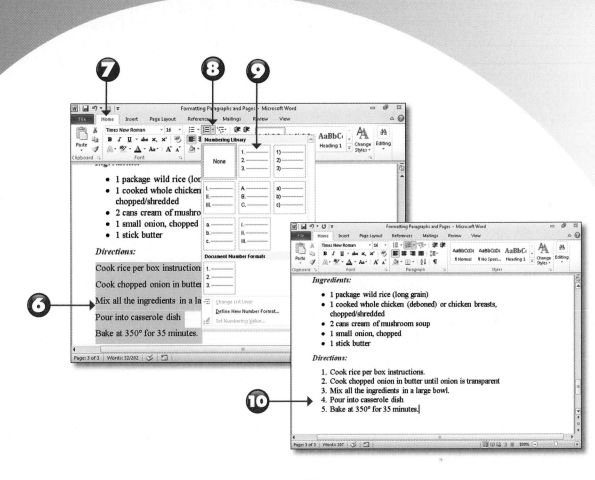

6 Select the text you want to turn into a numbered list.

7 Click the **Home** tab on the Ribbon.

8 Click the drop-down arrow next to the **Numbering** button.

9 Click the number style you want to apply.

10 Word applies the numbers to the text.

End

TIP

Continued List After you assign bullets or numbers to selected text, any new lines you add below the list are also assigned bullet or numbering status. To turn this off, just press **Ctrl+z** or click the **Undo** button on the Quick Access toolbar. ■

CONTROLLING PARAGRAPH SPACING

By default, Word adds extra space below every paragraph. You can control the spacing to suit your own document needs. For example, if you are typing up a letter or a report, you might want normal spacing between paragraphs. You can specify how much space to include before and after paragraphs.

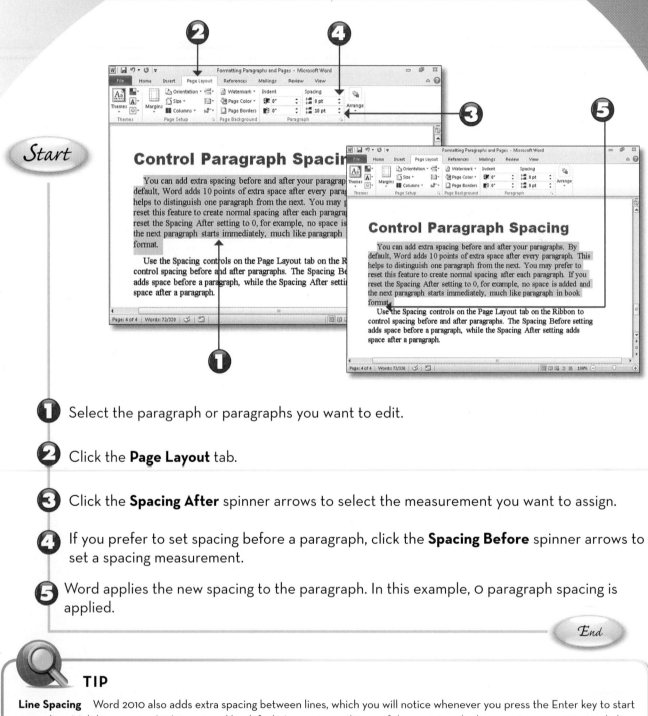

1. Select the paragraph or paragraphs you want to edit.

2. Click the **Page Layout** tab.

3. Click the **Spacing After** spinner arrows to select the measurement you want to assign.

4. If you prefer to set spacing before a paragraph, click the **Spacing Before** spinner arrows to set a spacing measurement.

5. Word applies the new spacing to the paragraph. In this example, 0 paragraph spacing is applied.

TIP

Line Spacing   Word 2010 also adds extra spacing between lines, which you will notice whenever you press the Enter key to start a new line. Multiline spacing (1.15) is assigned by default. In previous editions of the program, the line spacing was set to single line (1.0). To assign single line spacing in Word 2010, click the **Home** tab, click the **Line and Paragraph Spacing** button and click **1.0**. ■

SETTING MARGINS

Word's default margins are set to 1-inch on all sides of the page. You can change these margins to suit your document needs. Word includes several preset margins you can apply, or you can create your own custom margins.

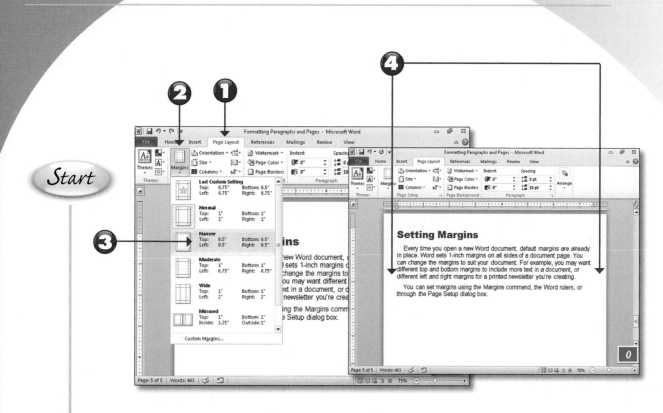

Start

1. Click the **Page Layout** tab.

2. Click **Margins**.

3. Click the margins setting you want to apply.

4. Word applies the new margins to the document pages.

End

TIP

Custom Margins You can use the Page Layout dialog box to set customized margins for your document. Click **Margins**, **Custom Margins** to open the dialog box to the Margins tab. Here you can set Top, Left, Bottom, and Right margins. Measurements are specified in inches from the edge of the page. Your last custom margins always appear listed at the top of the Margins menu list so you can easily apply them again. ■

TIP

Ruler Margins You can use Word's horizontal and vertical rulers to check out your page margins. You can also use the margin markers on the rulers to reset margins simply by dragging them to a new position on the ruler. To turn on the Ruler, click the **View** tab and click the **Ruler** check box. ■

CREATING COLUMNS

You can turn your Word text into columns much like those found in a newspaper or magazine. With the column feature, text snakes from column to column on a page. Columns are perfect for newsletters, bulletins, and other publications.

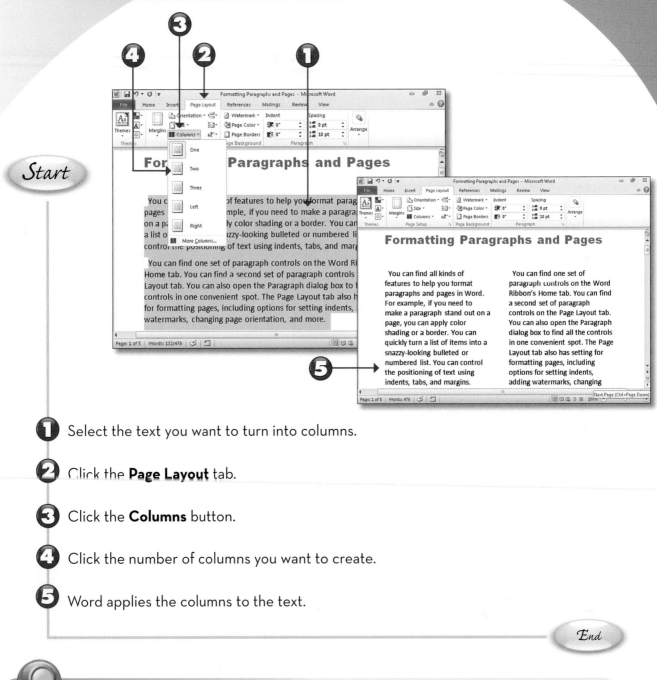

Start

End

① Select the text you want to turn into columns.

② Click the **Page Layout** tab.

③ Click the **Columns** button.

④ Click the number of columns you want to create.

⑤ Word applies the columns to the text.

TIP

Custom Columns You can create custom columns with a little help from the Columns dialog box. To display the dialog box, click the **Columns** button and click **More Columns**. You can set a specific measurement for each column and set the amount of spacing that appears between the columns. ■

ADDING A PARAGRAPH BORDER

One way to set off a paragraph in a document is to add a border surrounding the text. You might use this technique to set apart a quote or important fact in the middle of a report, for example. You can customize paragraph borders to include all four sides, or just one or two sides, and so on.

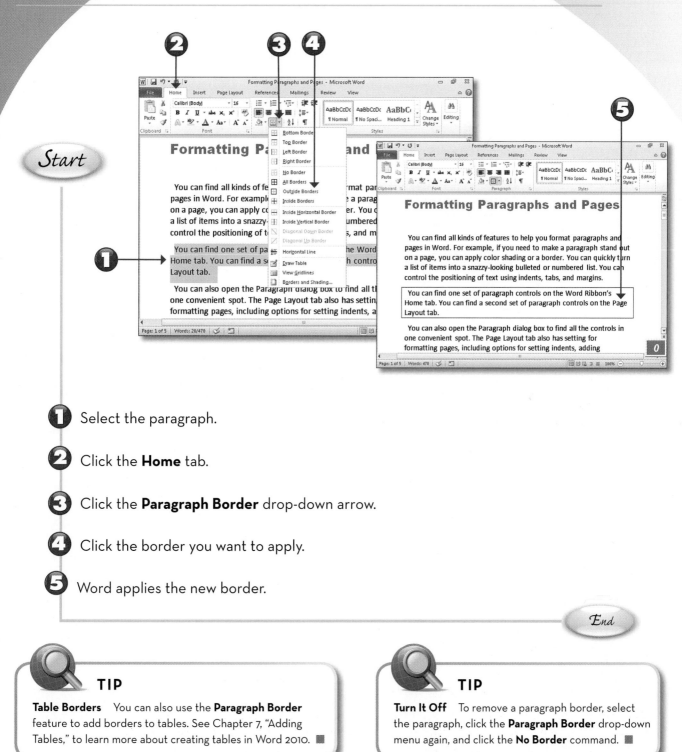

Start

1. Select the paragraph.

2. Click the **Home** tab.

3. Click the **Paragraph Border** drop-down arrow.

4. Click the border you want to apply.

5. Word applies the new border.

End

TIP

Table Borders You can also use the **Paragraph Border** feature to add borders to tables. See Chapter 7, "Adding Tables," to learn more about creating tables in Word 2010. ∎

TIP

Turn It Off To remove a paragraph border, select the paragraph, click the **Paragraph Border** drop-down menu again, and click the **No Border** command. ∎

ADDING SHADING TO A PARAGRAPH

Along with paragraph borders, you can also set off a paragraph with color shading. For example, you might add a light color shading behind paragraph text detailing a note in the middle of your report or brochure. Word's color palettes include a theme-based palette as well as a standard color palette from which you can choose just the right color for your document.

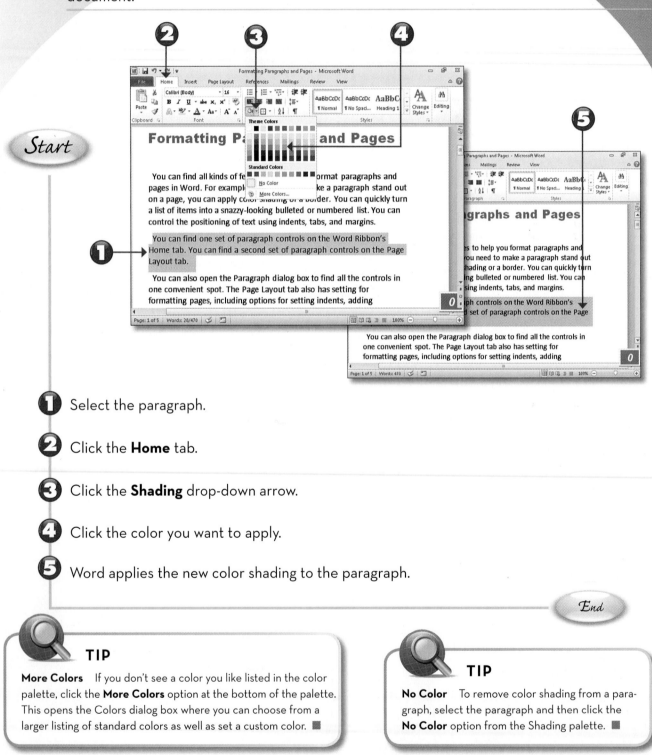

Start

1 Select the paragraph.

2 Click the **Home** tab.

3 Click the **Shading** drop-down arrow.

4 Click the color you want to apply.

5 Word applies the new color shading to the paragraph.

End

TIP

More Colors If you don't see a color you like listed in the color palette, click the **More Colors** option at the bottom of the palette. This opens the Colors dialog box where you can choose from a larger listing of standard colors as well as set a custom color. ■

TIP

No Color To remove color shading from a paragraph, select the paragraph and then click the **No Color** option from the Shading palette. ■

INSERTING PAGE NUMBERS

It's easy to add page numbers to longer documents you create in Word. You can choose to insert page numbers at the top or bottom of your pages. Page numbers are part of Word's Header and Footers feature. As such, you can choose from a variety of preset page number styles, each with a different appearance or positioning on the page.

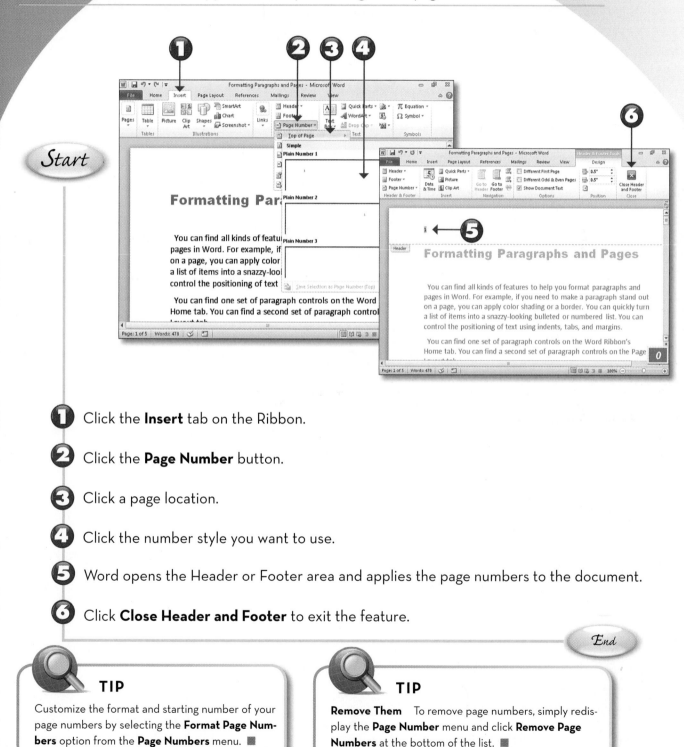

1 Click the **Insert** tab on the Ribbon.

2 Click the **Page Number** button.

3 Click a page location.

4 Click the number style you want to use.

5 Word opens the Header or Footer area and applies the page numbers to the document.

6 Click **Close Header and Footer** to exit the feature.

TIP

Customize the format and starting number of your page numbers by selecting the **Format Page Numbers** option from the **Page Numbers** menu. ■

TIP

Remove Them To remove page numbers, simply redisplay the **Page Number** menu and click **Remove Page Numbers** at the bottom of the list. ■

ADDING HEADERS AND FOOTERS

You can use headers and footers in Word to add extra text in the top and bottom margin areas. A header appears at the top of every page, while a footer appears at the bottom. You can use headers and footers to display the document title, name of your organization, your name, date, and so on. Word offers a wide variety of preset headers and footers you can use, or you can create your own. This task shows a header added to a document, but you can use the same steps to add a footer instead.

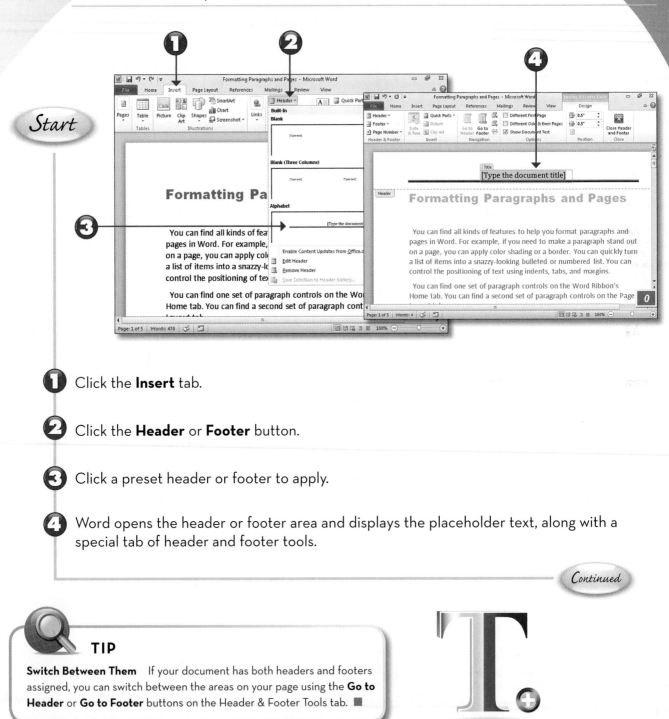

1 Click the **Insert** tab.

2 Click the **Header** or **Footer** button.

3 Click a preset header or footer to apply.

4 Word opens the header or footer area and displays the placeholder text, along with a special tab of header and footer tools.

Continued

TIP

Switch Between Them If your document has both headers and footers assigned, you can switch between the areas on your page using the **Go to Header** or **Go to Footer** buttons on the Header & Footer Tools tab. ∎

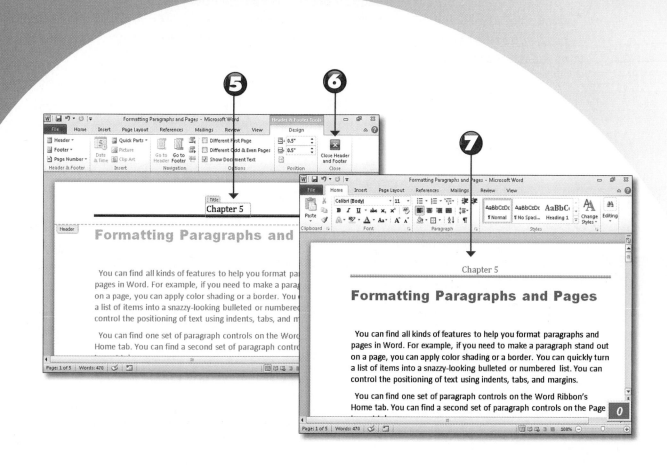

5 Replace the header or footer text with your own text.

6 Click the **Close Header and Footer** button to return to the document.

7 Word displays the header or footer text at the top or bottom of the page.

End

TIP

Customize It You can create your own custom headers and footers and add them to Word's Headers and Footers gallery. Simply select all the elements that comprise the header or footer you've customized, click the **Insert** tab, click the **Header** or **Footer** drop-down arrow, and then click **Save Selection to Header Gallery** or **Save Selection to Footer Gallery**. The Create New Building Block dialog box opens and you can give the header or footer a unique name. Click **OK** and it's added to the gallery. ■

INSERTING PAGE AND SECTION BREAKS

You can use page breaks and section breaks to control how your pages are laid out in a document. By default, Word breaks your document into pages for you. You can force a page break whenever you want to start a new page yourself. You can use section breaks to start new sections of your document.

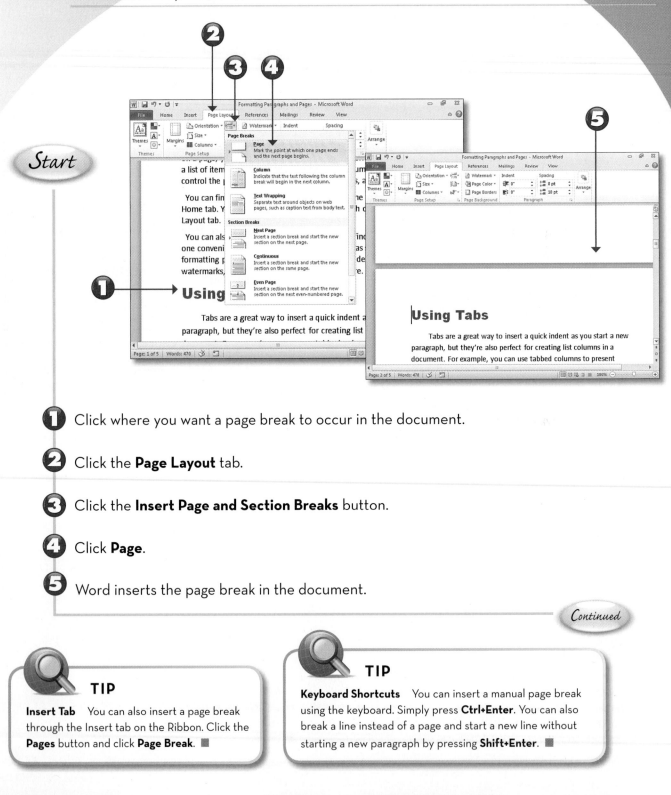

Start

1. Click where you want a page break to occur in the document.

2. Click the **Page Layout** tab.

3. Click the **Insert Page and Section Breaks** button.

4. Click **Page**.

5. Word inserts the page break in the document.

Continued

TIP

Insert Tab   You can also insert a page break through the Insert tab on the Ribbon. Click the **Pages** button and click **Page Break**. ■

TIP

Keyboard Shortcuts   You can insert a manual page break using the keyboard. Simply press **Ctrl+Enter**. You can also break a line instead of a page and start a new line without starting a new paragraph by pressing **Shift+Enter**. ■

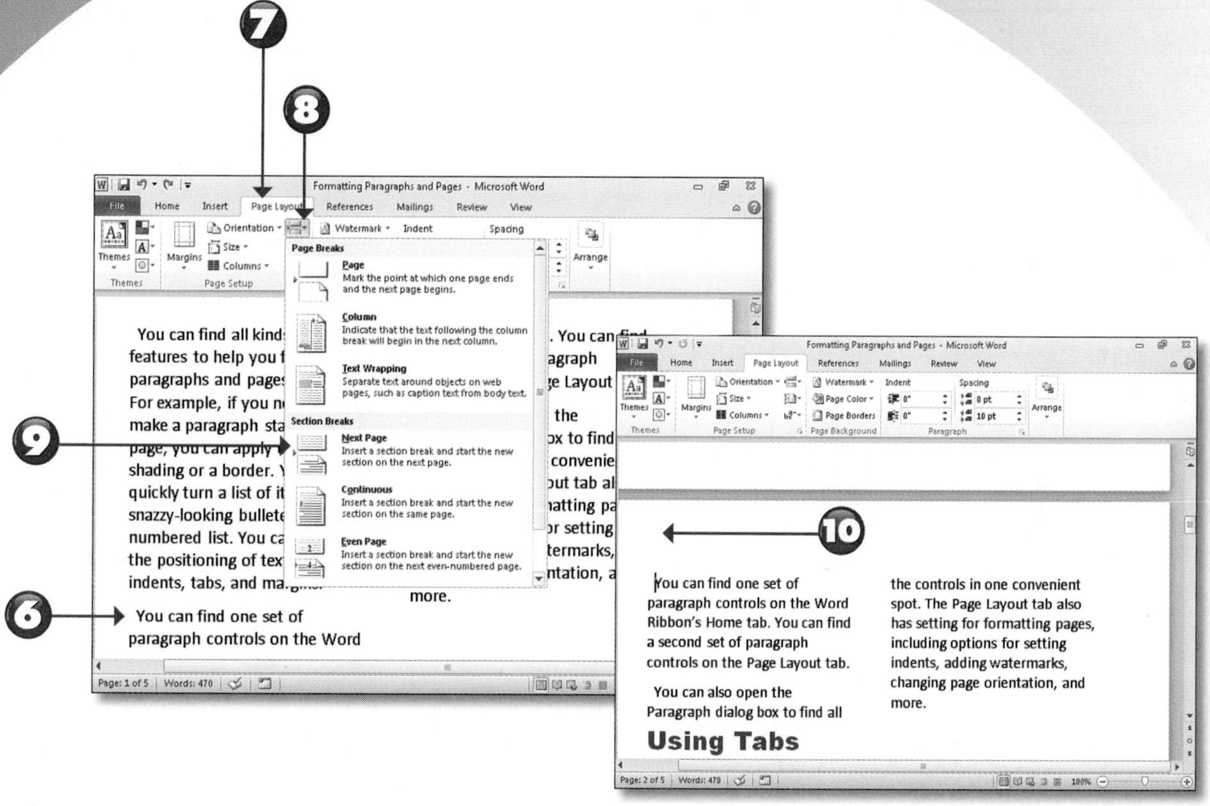

6 Click where you want a section break to occur in the document.

7 Click the **Page Layout** tab.

8 Click the **Insert Page and Section Breaks** button.

9 Click the type of section break you want to insert.

10 Word adds the section break to the document.

End

TIP

Column Breaks You can control where the column breaks and where a new column starts. Click where you want the break to occur and then click the **Insert Page and Section Breaks** button and click **Column**. ■

TIP

Section Breaks A **Next Page** break starts the next section on a new page. A **Continuous** section break starts a new section on the same page. An Even Page or Odd page break starts the new section on the next even- or odd-numbered page. ■

ADDING A WATERMARK

Watermarks are images, patterns, or text that appear behind text on the page's background. Watermarks are often used to mark a document's importance, such as Confidential, Draft, or Urgent. You might also use a company logo as a watermark. Because they appear in the background, watermarks are typically faded out so you can still read any text that appears on top of the image. Word has several preset watermarks you can choose from, or you can create your own.

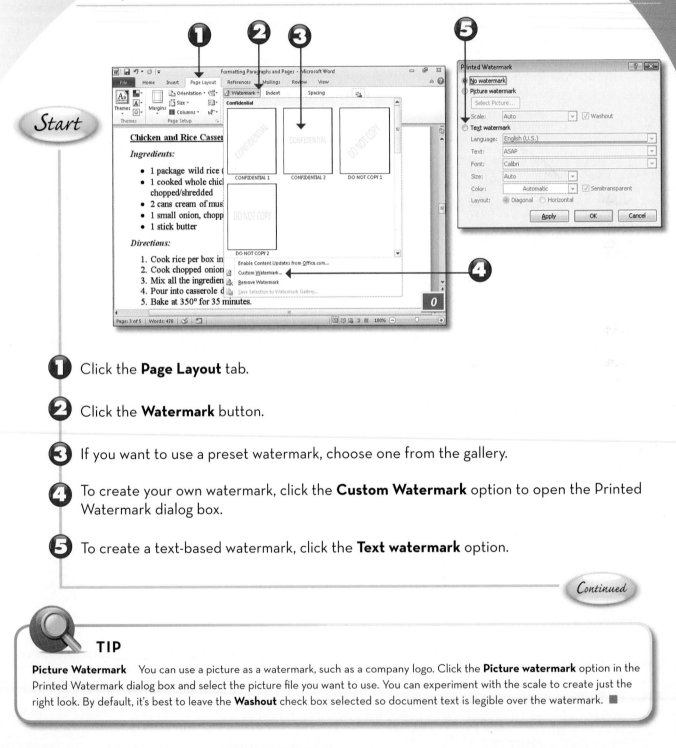

1 Click the **Page Layout** tab.

2 Click the **Watermark** button.

3 If you want to use a preset watermark, choose one from the gallery.

4 To create your own watermark, click the **Custom Watermark** option to open the Printed Watermark dialog box.

5 To create a text-based watermark, click the **Text watermark** option.

Continued

TIP

Picture Watermark   You can use a picture as a watermark, such as a company logo. Click the **Picture watermark** option in the Printed Watermark dialog box and select the picture file you want to use. You can experiment with the scale to create just the right look. By default, it's best to leave the **Washout** check box selected so document text is legible over the watermark. ∎

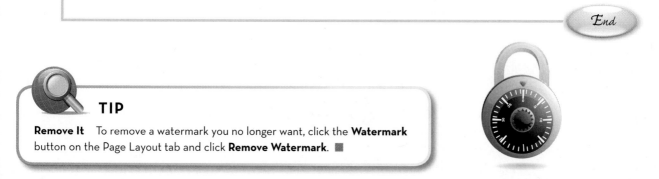

6 Click the **Text** drop-down arrow and choose the text you want to use or type in your own text.

7 Use the formatting drop-down arrows to further customize the font, size, and color of the watermark.

8 Choose whether you want to display the watermark diagonally or horizontally across the page.

9 Click **OK**.

10 Word applies the watermark to the page.

End

TIP

Remove It   To remove a watermark you no longer want, click the **Watermark** button on the Page Layout tab and click **Remove Watermark**. ■

Chapter 6

ADDING ADVANCED FORMATTING

The number of formatting features available in Word seem endless. You can apply formatting features to text, paragraphs, and entire pages. You can change the appearance of text, change the positioning of text and paragraphs, add page elements, and much more. In this chapter, you'll learn about a few of Word's more advanced formatting features. Some of these features can be real timesavers. For example, you can save yourself some effort in formatting your documents by applying a preset style or theme. You can also dress up your text further by using features like drop caps or Word's text effects.

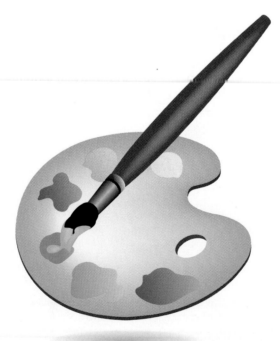

You can find all kinds of formatting controls to give your Word documents visual impact, such as text effects found on the Home tab.

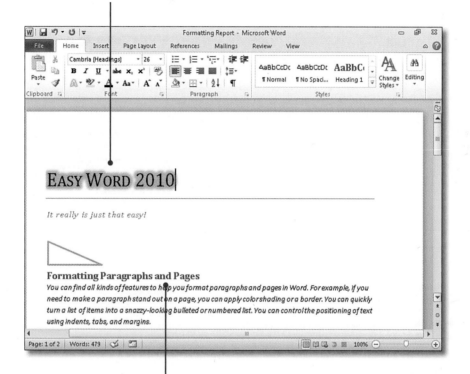

Styles can help your document appear cohesive and professional.

APPLYING STYLES

Styles are a great way to apply a collection of formatting attributes to a document and create a uniform look and feel. Word has a wide variety of preset styles you can use, or you can create your own. For example, rather than reapplying formatting each time a heading appears in your document, you can assign a heading style to apply with a simple click. You can use styles to quickly format body text, captions, and more. You can use the Quick Styles gallery to quickly insert a style, or you can change the style set shown in the gallery.

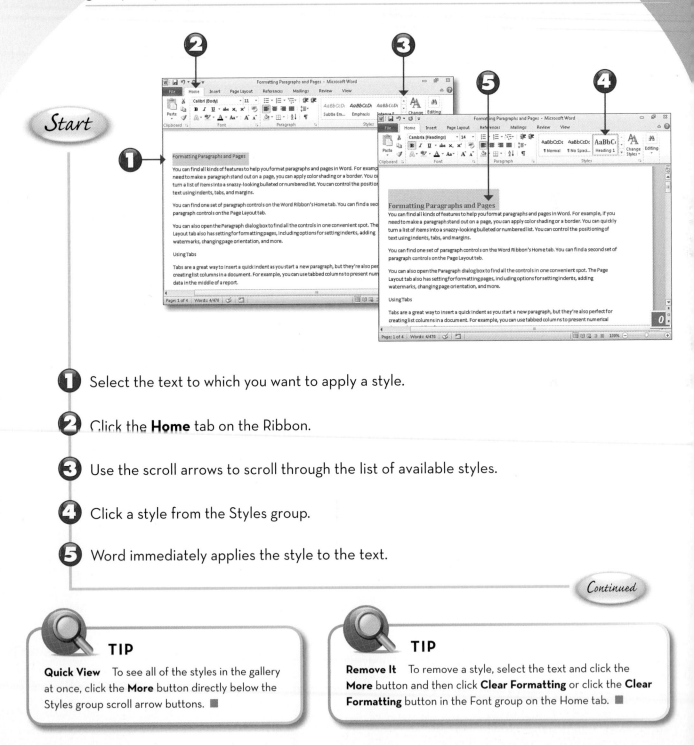

Start

1 Select the text to which you want to apply a style.

2 Click the **Home** tab on the Ribbon.

3 Use the scroll arrows to scroll through the list of available styles.

4 Click a style from the Styles group.

5 Word immediately applies the style to the text.

Continued

TIP

Quick View   To see all of the styles in the gallery at once, click the **More** button directly below the Styles group scroll arrow buttons. ■

TIP

Remove It   To remove a style, select the text and click the **More** button and then click **Clear Formatting** or click the **Clear Formatting** button in the Font group on the Home tab. ■

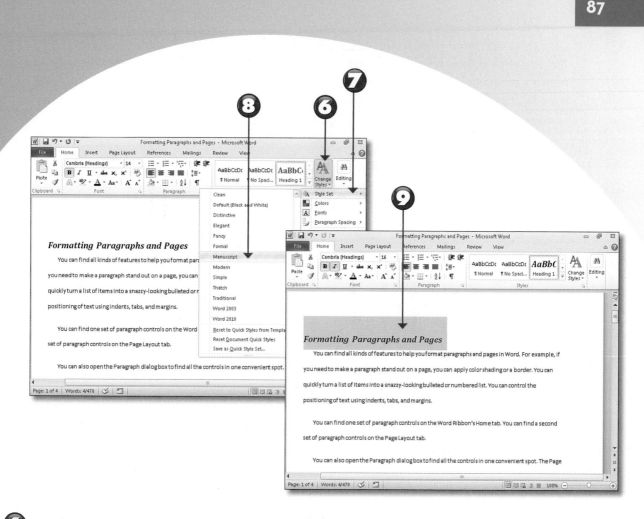

6 To change the style set, click the **Change Styles** button.

7 Click **Style Set**.

8 Click another style set from the list.

9 Word applies the style set to the Quick Styles gallery and to any styles you have already assigned in the document.

End

TIP

Make Your Own Style Format the text just the way you want it, then select it. Next, click the **More** button and click **Save Selection as a New Quick Style**. This opens the Create New Style from Formatting dialog box where you can name the style. ■

TIP

Open the Style Pane You can also open Word's Style pane to view and select styles. Click the **Styles** icon in the lower-right corner of the Styles group on the Home tab. ■

APPLYING THEMES

Themes are another way you can apply a common look and feel to your Word documents along with styles. Themes include a set of coordinating colors, fonts, and effects you can apply to make sure your documents share a professional appearance. You can choose from a variety of preset themes or browse for more themes from Office.com. Themes work best with styles you have already assigned to the document.

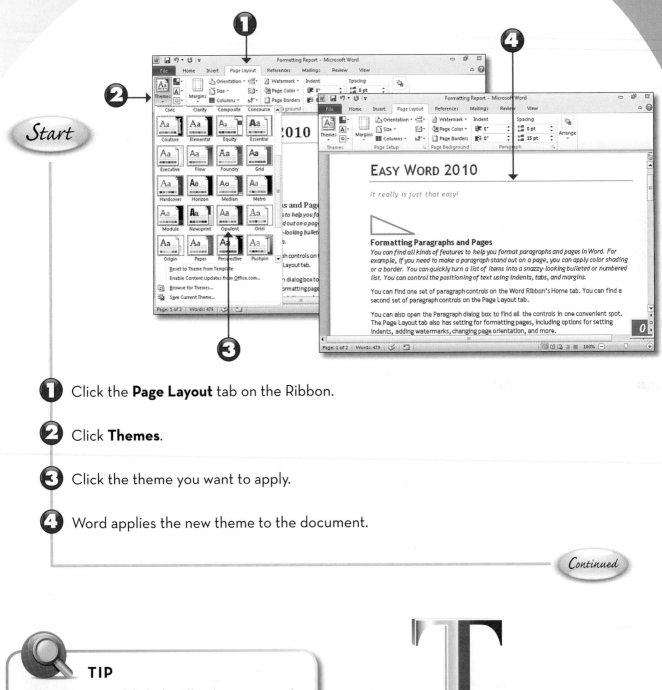

Start

1. Click the **Page Layout** tab on the Ribbon.

2. Click **Themes**.

3. Click the theme you want to apply.

4. Word applies the new theme to the document.

Continued

TIP

Office Theme By default, the Office theme is assigned to any new document you create in Word. ■

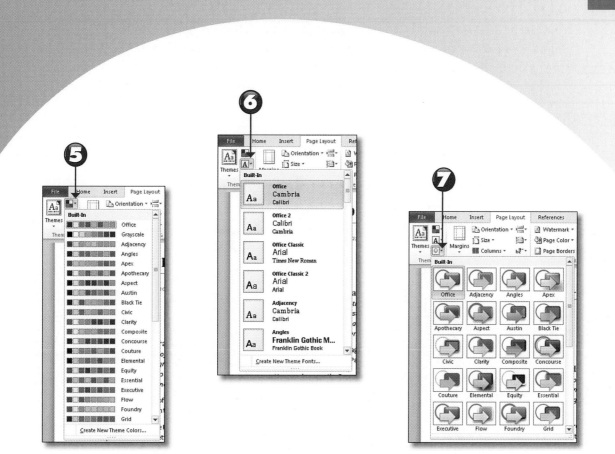

5 Click the **Theme Colors** drop-down arrow to change the color scheme associated with the theme.

6 Click the **Theme Fonts** drop-down arrow to change the fonts associated with the theme.

7 Click the **Theme Effects** drop-down arrow to change the effects.

End

TIP

What's in a Theme?   When you assign a theme, Word looks for and replaces the formats of each of the styles to the document elements. A theme includes fonts for any headings and body text assigned, including color, type style, and spacing. Themes also include 3D effects, shadows, and lighting effects. ■

TIP

Looking for More Themes   You can browse your computer or network for more themes. To browse for more themes, click the **Themes** button and click **Browse for Themes**. ■

ADDING BORDERS

You learned how to add borders to paragraphs in Chapter 5, "Formatting Paragraphs and Pages." You can also add borders to entire pages in your Word document. You can choose from several border styles, including a shadow or 3D border.

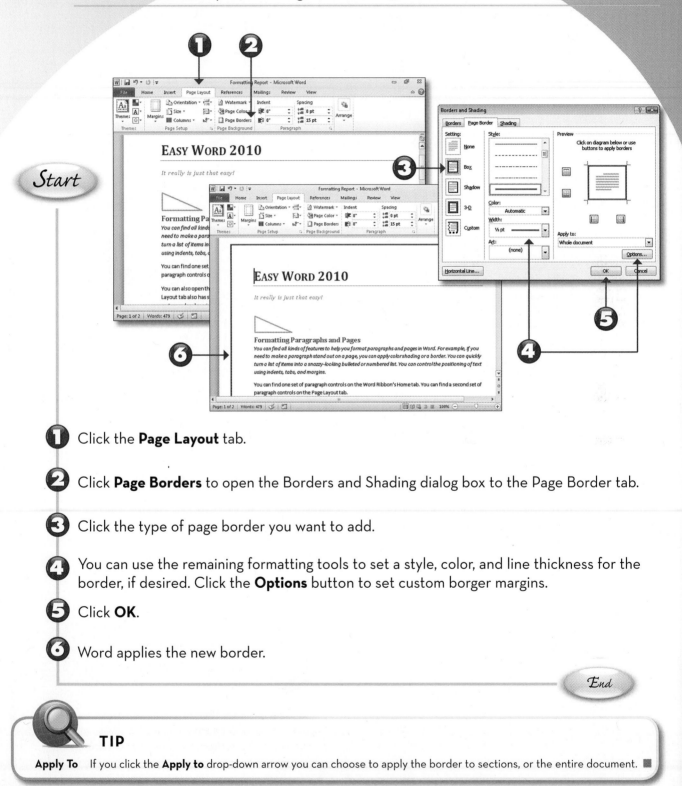

1 Click the **Page Layout** tab.

2 Click **Page Borders** to open the Borders and Shading dialog box to the Page Border tab.

3 Click the type of page border you want to add.

4 You can use the remaining formatting tools to set a style, color, and line thickness for the border, if desired. Click the **Options** button to set custom borger margins.

5 Click **OK**.

6 Word applies the new border.

TIP

Apply To   If you click the **Apply to** drop-down arrow you can choose to apply the border to sections, or the entire document. ▪

ADDING DROP CAPS

You can apply drop caps to add visual interest to a paragraph, creating a rather dramatic effect. A drop cap is a large initial or capital letter that appears at the start of the paragraph and seems to drop below the baseline into the rest of the paragraph. Drop caps can also appear offset in the margin.

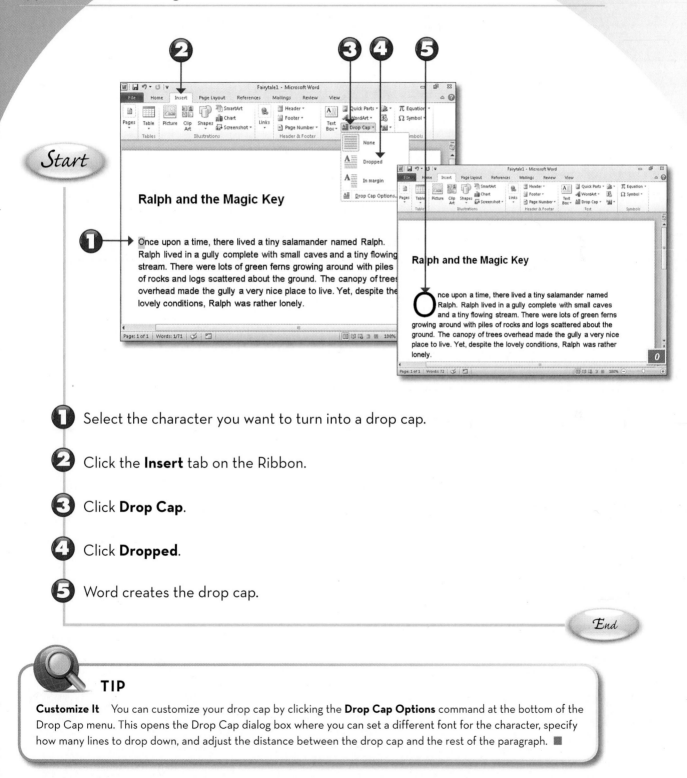

1. Select the character you want to turn into a drop cap.

2. Click the **Insert** tab on the Ribbon.

3. Click **Drop Cap**.

4. Click **Dropped**.

5. Word creates the drop cap.

TIP

Customize It   You can customize your drop cap by clicking the **Drop Cap Options** command at the bottom of the Drop Cap menu. This opens the Drop Cap dialog box where you can set a different font for the character, specify how many lines to drop down, and adjust the distance between the drop cap and the rest of the paragraph. ■

APPLYING TEXT EFFECTS

Word offers a gallery of decorative text effects you can apply to give your document more impact. Text effects include outlines, shadows, glows, and reflections.

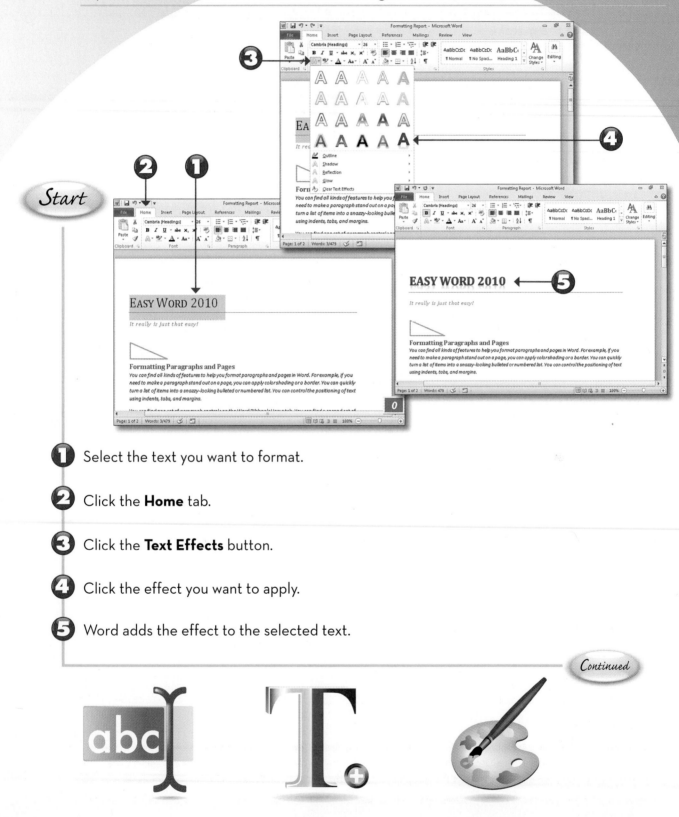

Start

1. Select the text you want to format.

2. Click the **Home** tab.

3. Click the **Text Effects** button.

4. Click the effect you want to apply.

5. Word adds the effect to the selected text.

Continued

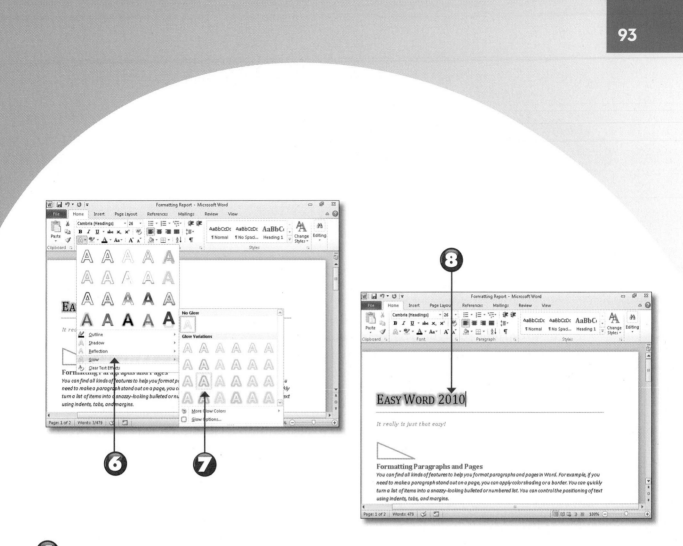

6 To view additional choices for any text effect, click the name to view a submenu of effects.

7 Click an effect.

8 Word applies the effect to your text.

End

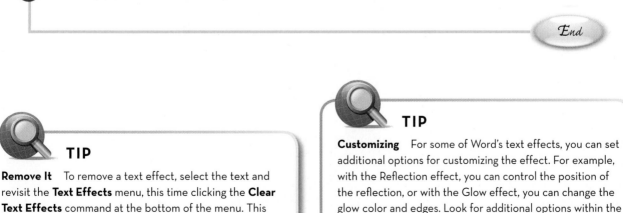

TIP

Remove It To remove a text effect, select the text and revisit the **Text Effects** menu, this time clicking the **Clear Text Effects** command at the bottom of the menu. This returns your text to its original setting. ■

TIP

Customizing For some of Word's text effects, you can set additional options for customizing the effect. For example, with the Reflection effect, you can control the position of the reflection, or with the Glow effect, you can change the glow color and edges. Look for additional options within the effect's submenu. ■

ADDING TABLES

Tables are a great way to organize data and other types of information in a document. Their structure, based on columns and rows that intersect to form cells, make tables ideal for listing and organizing text, pictures, or even creating page layouts. By default, tables do not print with any borders, but you can choose to add them to give your tables even more visual impact. Word's tables are incredibly flexible, and you can easily add and subtract columns and rows as you need. You can also dress up your tables with formatting to make them attractive and complementary to the rest of your Word document. This chapter shows you all the ins and outs of building tables.

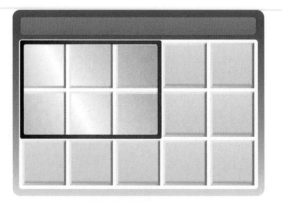

The Design tab offers tools for controlling the appearance of your table, such as applying styles, shading, and borders.

Word displays two new tabs when you add a table to a document.

The Layout tab offers tools for adding and subtracting columns and rows, resizing cells, changing cell alignment, and more.

your table, or draw your own custom table. You can also choose from several pre-set tables that install with Word 2010, called Quick Tables. You can even tap into Excel's spreadsheet power to create a spreadsheet within Word.

Class	Teacher	Room
English 1	Evalene Janese	112
English 2	Sue Lewis	220
English 3-A	Matt Wallace	302
Algebra 1	Melissa Cannon	114
Algebra 2	Jeramiah Gunter	203
Algebra 3-A	Melissa Cannon	308
History – American	Rick Isom	107
History – World	Jared Privett	218
Geography 1	Candace Noland	116
Geography 2	Kathy Privett	205

Once you have inserted a table, you can add text,

format the table, add and delete columns and rows, and merge and split cells.

INSERTING A TABLE

You can use tables to organize text and other elements you add to your Word documents. Tables are built on rows and columns that intersect to form cells. Cells are where you enter your text. When creating a table, you can specify exactly how many columns and rows you need. Once you create your table, you can click in a cell and start typing your text.

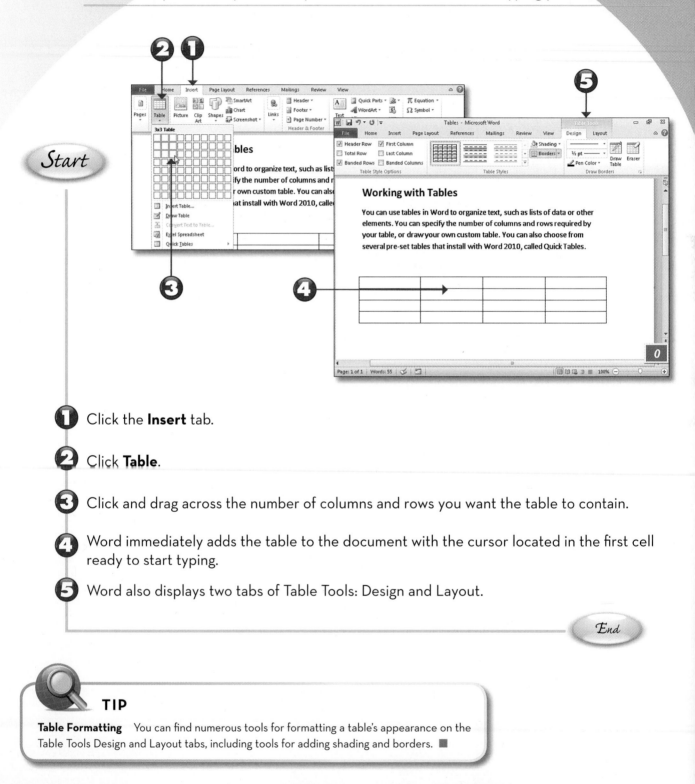

1 Click the **Insert** tab.

2 Click **Table**.

3 Click and drag across the number of columns and rows you want the table to contain.

4 Word immediately adds the table to the document with the cursor located in the first cell ready to start typing.

5 Word also displays two tabs of Table Tools: Design and Layout.

TIP

Table Formatting You can find numerous tools for formatting a table's appearance on the Table Tools Design and Layout tabs, including tools for adding shading and borders. ■

INSERTING QUICK TABLES

In addition to tables you create from scratch, you can also make use of a variety of built-in tables installed with Word, called Quick Tables. Quick Tables include calendars, tabular lists, tables with subheadings, and more. Once you select a preset table, you can replace the text with your own table text.

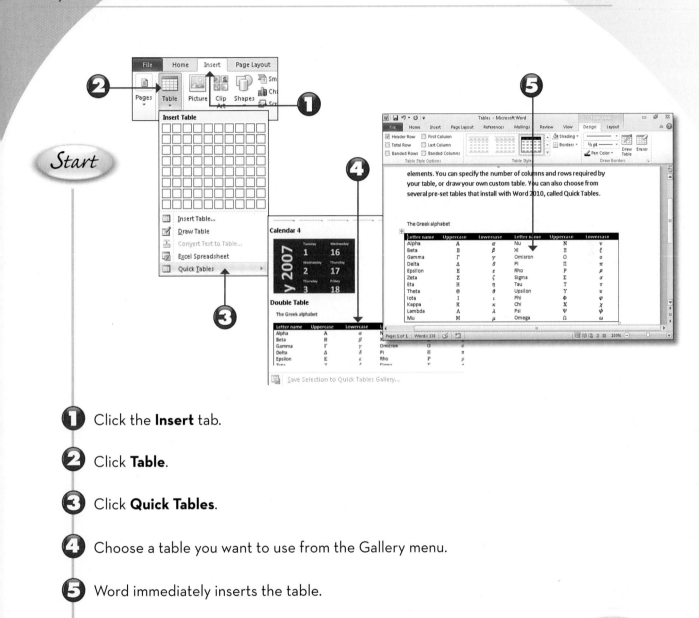

Start

1 Click the **Insert** tab.

2 Click **Table**.

3 Click **Quick Tables**.

4 Choose a table you want to use from the Gallery menu.

5 Word immediately inserts the table.

End

DRAWING YOUR OWN TABLE

You can create your own custom table by drawing the table's dimensions, columns, and rows onscreen. This technique gives you complete control over the table and allows you to create customized cell sizes to suit your needs.

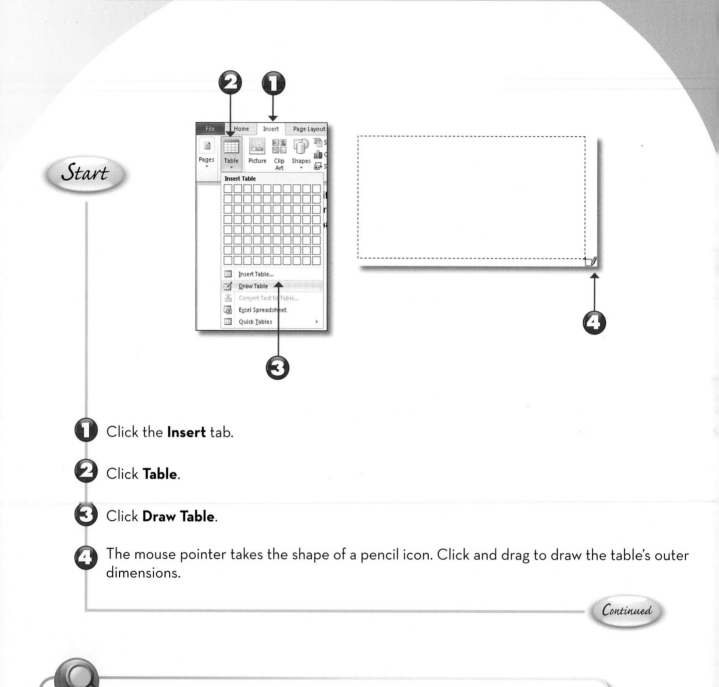

1 Click the **Insert** tab.

2 Click **Table**.

3 Click **Draw Table**.

4 The mouse pointer takes the shape of a pencil icon. Click and drag to draw the table's outer dimensions.

Continued

TIP

Adding Items   You can insert all kinds of items into your table cells, including other tables. You can use the same techniques for inserting shapes, clip art, and pictures into your documents and insert items into table cells. See Chapter 12, "Using Word's Graphics Tools," to learn more about the graphics tools in Word. ■

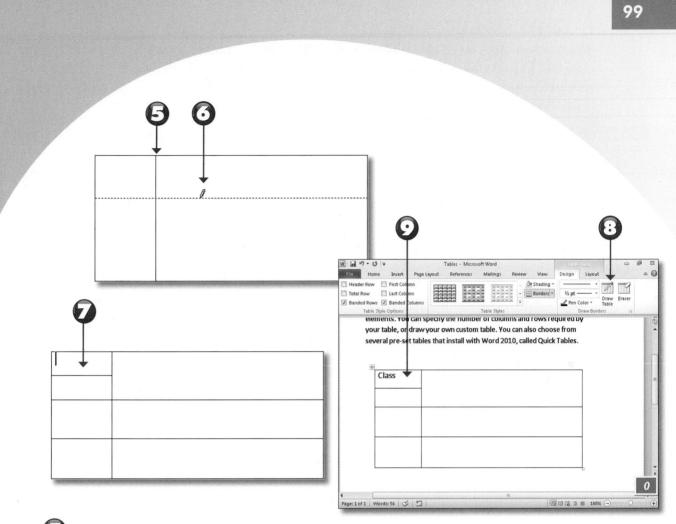

5 Click and drag to define each column in the table.

6 Click and drag to define each row in the table.

7 Continue adding lines to create your table's cells.

8 To toggle the drawing pencil off, click **Draw Table**.

9 To add text to a cell, click inside the cell and start typing.

End

TIP

Erasing Lines You can erase lines in your table by selecting the Eraser tool. On the **Design** tab, click the **Eraser** button, then click the line you want to remove from the table. Click the button again to toggle the tool off when you finish editing your table. ■

INSERT EXCEL SPREADSHEETS AS TABLES

You can tap into Excel's spreadsheet feature to help you create a table in Word. When you insert an Excel spreadsheet, Excel tools appear on the Ribbon, including tools for adding formulas and functions, sorting and filtering, and more. The Microsoft Graph feature opens if you do not have Excel installed.

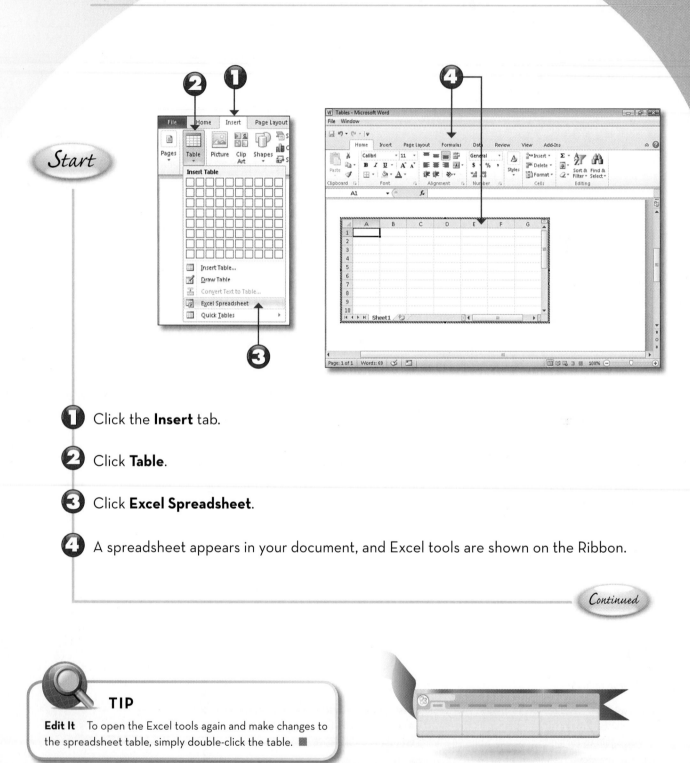

Start

1. Click the **Insert** tab.

2. Click **Table**.

3. Click **Excel Spreadsheet**.

4. A spreadsheet appears in your document, and Excel tools are shown on the Ribbon.

Continued

TIP

Edit It   To open the Excel tools again and make changes to the spreadsheet table, simply double-click the table. ■

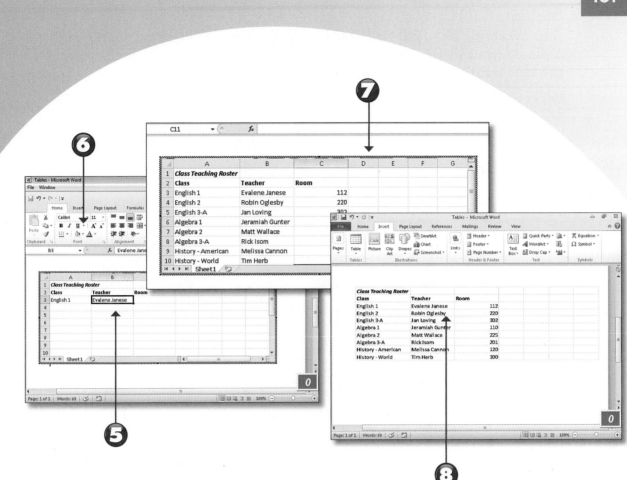

5 Click inside a worksheet cell and enter your table data.

6 You can use the formatting tools on the Home tab to format cell data.

7 When finished entering your data, click outside the datasheet object.

8 Word displays the new table.

End

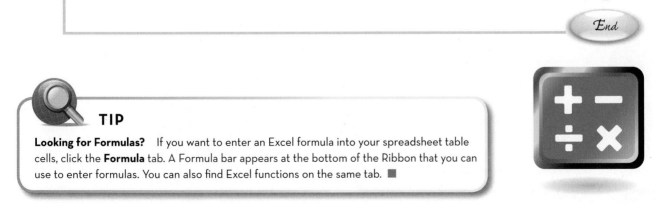

TIP

Looking for Formulas?   If you want to enter an Excel formula into your spreadsheet table cells, click the **Formula** tab. A Formula bar appears at the bottom of the Ribbon that you can use to enter formulas. You can also find Excel functions on the same tab. ■

SELECTING TABLE CELLS AND DATA

After creating a table, you may need to select columns, rows, or cells to format them. An obvious technique for selecting table parts is to click and drag across the areas you want to select. In addition, you can click different parts of the table to select areas.

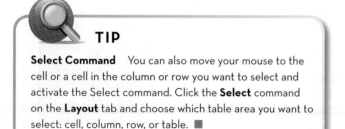

Start

1 To select a column in your table, click the top of the column.

2 To select a row, double-click the left side of the row.

3 To select multiple columns or rows, click and drag over the columns or rows you want to select.

Continued

TIP

Select Command   You can also move your mouse to the cell or a cell in the column or row you want to select and activate the Select command. Click the **Select** command on the **Layout** tab and choose which table area you want to select: cell, column, row, or table. ■

Class Teacher Roster		
Class	Teacher	Room
English 1	Evalene Janese	112
English 2	Sue Lewis	220
English 3-A	Matt Wallace	302
Algebra 1	Melissa Cannon	114
Algebra 2	Jeramiah Gunter	203
Algebra 3-A	Melissa Cannon	308
History – American	Rick Isom	107
History – World	Jared Privett	218
Geography 1	Candace Noland	116
Geography 2	Kathy Privett	205

5

4

Class Teacher Roster		
Class	Teacher	
English 1	Evalene Janese	
English 2	Sue Lewis	220
English 3-A	Matt Wallace	302
Algebra 1	Melissa Cannon	114
Algebra 2	Jeramiah Gunter	203
Algebra 3-A	Melissa Cannon	308
History – American	Rick Isom	107
History – World	Jared Privett	218
Geography 1	Candace Noland	116
Geography 2	Kathy Privett	205

4 To select a single cell, double-click inside the cell.

5 To select the entire table, click the **Table** icon in the upper-left corner of the table.

End

TIP

Finding Formatting   You can use all the same text formatting commands on the Home tab to apply formatting to your table text. To find table-specific formatting commands, click the table and then click the **Design** tab. Here you'll find table style options, styles, borders, and shading you can apply. ■

CHANGING COLUMN WIDTH AND ROW HEIGHT

As you fill your table cells with data, you may find yourself needing to resize a column or row to fit your text or to make the table more visually appealing. You can easily resize tables manually by clicking and dragging a border or with the resizing commands for auto-fitting the text.

Start

1. To manually resize a column, move the mouse pointer over the border of the column you want to resize, then click and drag to resize the column width.

2. To manually resize a row, move the mouse pointer over the border of the row you want to resize, then click and drag to resize the row height.

3. To set a precise column width, click inside the column you want to change and set a new value in the **Table Column Width** box. You can either click the spinner arrows or type in a value.

4. To set a precise row height, click inside the row you want to change and set a new value in the **Table Row Height** box. You can either click the spinner arrows or type in a value.

Continued

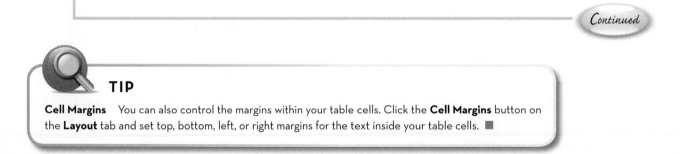

TIP

Cell Margins   You can also control the margins within your table cells. Click the **Cell Margins** button on the **Layout** tab and set top, bottom, left, or right margins for the text inside your table cells. ■

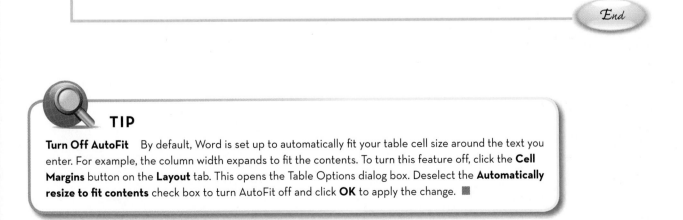

5 To automatically fit the column width to the text, click the **AutoFit** button and click **AutoFit Contents**.

6 To distribute rows equally in height, click **Distribute Rows**.

7 To distribute columns equally in width, click **Distribute Columns**.

End

TIP

Turn Off AutoFit By default, Word is set up to automatically fit your table cell size around the text you enter. For example, the column width expands to fit the contents. To turn this feature off, click the **Cell Margins** button on the **Layout** tab. This opens the Table Options dialog box. Deselect the **Automatically resize to fit contents** check box to turn AutoFit off and click **OK** to apply the change. ■

ADDING COLUMNS AND ROWS

It's easy to add more columns and rows to your Word tables, and you can employ several methods to do so. For example, you can use the buttons on the Layout tab or you can right-click over the table cell and choose an option.

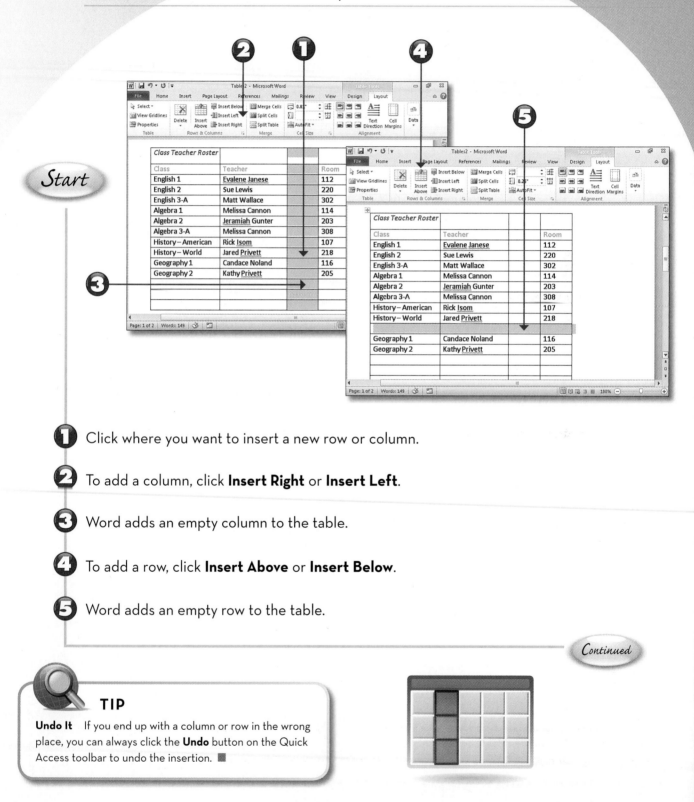

Start

1. Click where you want to insert a new row or column.

2. To add a column, click **Insert Right** or **Insert Left**.

3. Word adds an empty column to the table.

4. To add a row, click **Insert Above** or **Insert Below**.

5. Word adds an empty row to the table.

Continued

TIP

Undo It If you end up with a column or row in the wrong place, you can always click the **Undo** button on the Quick Access toolbar to undo the insertion.

6 To use the right-click method, right-click in the table where you want to insert a column or row.

7 Click **Insert**.

8 Choose how you want to insert the column or row: left, right, above, or below.

9 Word inserts the column or row as specified. In this example, a new row is added.

End

TIP

Adding Multiple Columns and Rows You can select two or more columns before applying the Insert command on the Layout tab to add multiple columns or rows to your table. Simply drag over the number of columns or rows you want to create, then click **Insert Above** or **Insert Below** to add rows, or **Insert Left** or **Insert Right** to add columns. ■

DELETING COLUMNS AND ROWS

You can delete columns and rows you no longer need or want in your Word table. When you delete a column or row, any data contained within the cells is deleted as well. You can use the Delete tool on the Layout tab, or you can use the shortcut menu that appears when you right-click on a table cell. When you remove a column or row, Word moves the adjacent columns or rows over or up to fill the void.

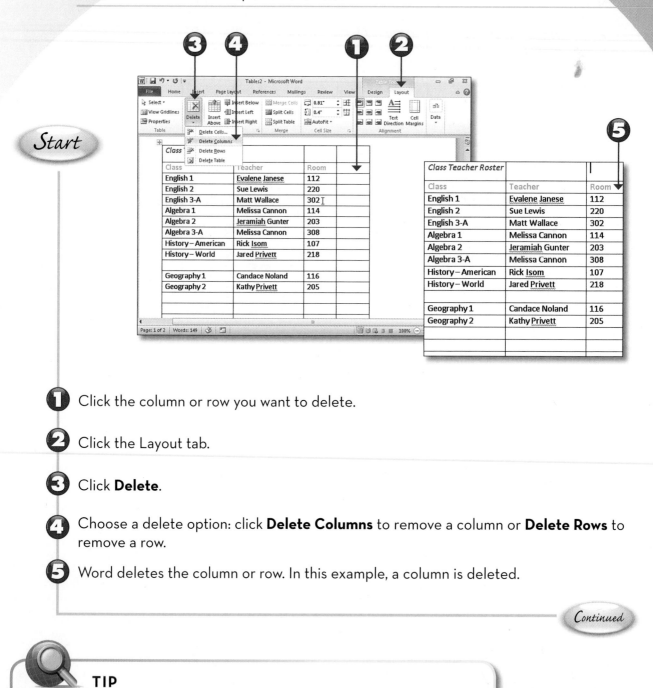

Start

1 Click the column or row you want to delete.

2 Click the Layout tab.

3 Click **Delete**.

4 Choose a delete option: click **Delete Columns** to remove a column or **Delete Rows** to remove a row.

5 Word deletes the column or row. In this example, a column is deleted.

Continued

TIP

Deleting Multiples   To remove more than one column or row in your table, select the columns or rows you want to remove before applying the Delete command. ■

The following table appears in the screenshot:

Class Teacher Roster		
Class	Teacher	Room
English 1	Evalene Janese	112
English 2	Sue Lewis	220
English 3-A	Matt Wallace	302
Algebra 1	Melissa Cannon	114
Algebra 2	Jeramiah Gunter	203
Algebra 3-A	Melissa Cannon	308
History – American	Rick Isom	107
History – World	Jared Privett	218
Geography 1	Candace Noland	116
Geography 2	Kathy Privett	205

6 Select the row or column you want to remove.

7 Right-click the column or row.

8 Click **Delete Rows** or **Delete Columns**.

9 Word removes the column or row. In this example, a row is removed.

End

TIP

Deleting Cells You can also delete cells in your table. See the task "Deleting Cells" later in this chapter to learn more. ■

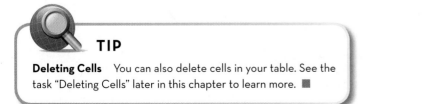

MERGING CELLS

You can merge cells in a table to create a larger cell. For example, you might combine two side-by-side cells to create a large cell for a title or combine two cells vertically to insert artwork.

Start

1 Select the cells you want to merge.

2 Click the **Layout** tab.

3 Click **Merge Cells**.

4 Word merges the cells.

End

SPLITTING CELLS

You can split cells to create two or more additional cells in the same space.

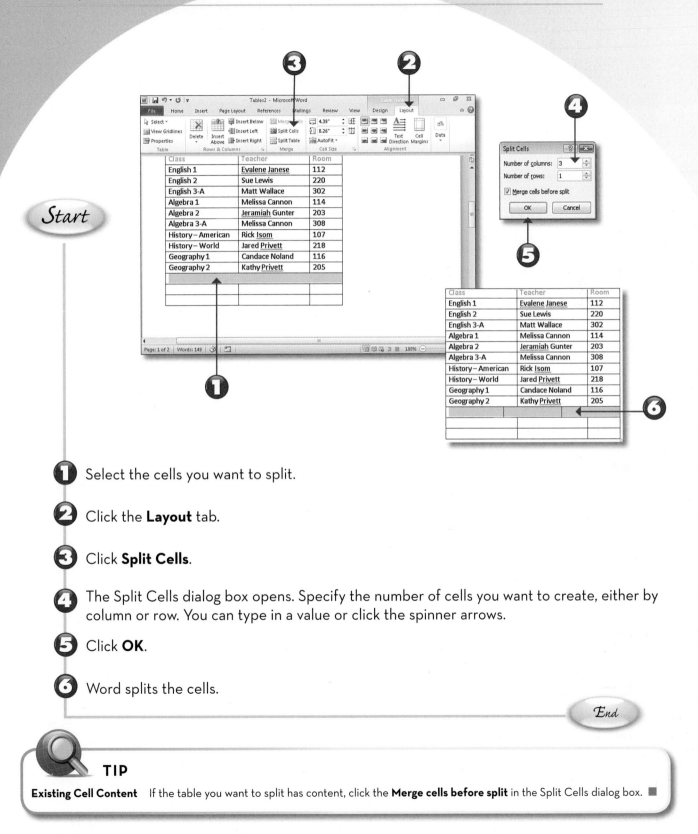

1 Select the cells you want to split.

2 Click the **Layout** tab.

3 Click **Split Cells**.

4 The Split Cells dialog box opens. Specify the number of cells you want to create, either by column or row. You can type in a value or click the spinner arrows.

5 Click **OK**.

6 Word splits the cells.

Start

End

TIP

Existing Cell Content   If the table you want to split has content, click the **Merge cells before split** in the Split Cells dialog box. ■

DELETING CELLS

You can remove cells from a table with a little help from the Delete Cells dialog box. When you remove cells, Word shifts the other cells up or over to fill the void.

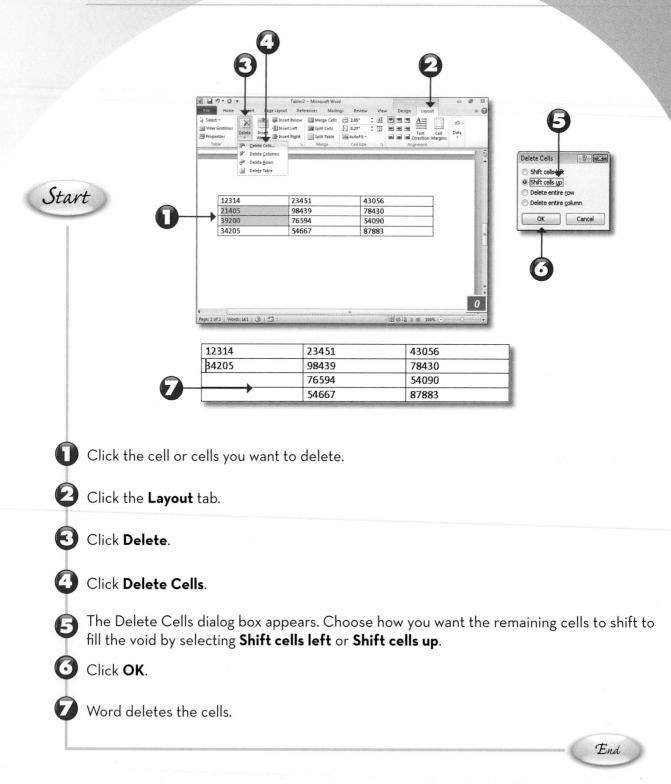

Start

1 Click the cell or cells you want to delete.

2 Click the **Layout** tab.

3 Click **Delete**.

4 Click **Delete Cells**.

5 The Delete Cells dialog box appears. Choose how you want the remaining cells to shift to fill the void by selecting **Shift cells left** or **Shift cells up**.

6 Click **OK**.

7 Word deletes the cells.

End

DELETING TABLES

You can delete a table you no longer need. You can use the Delete tool on the Layout tab.

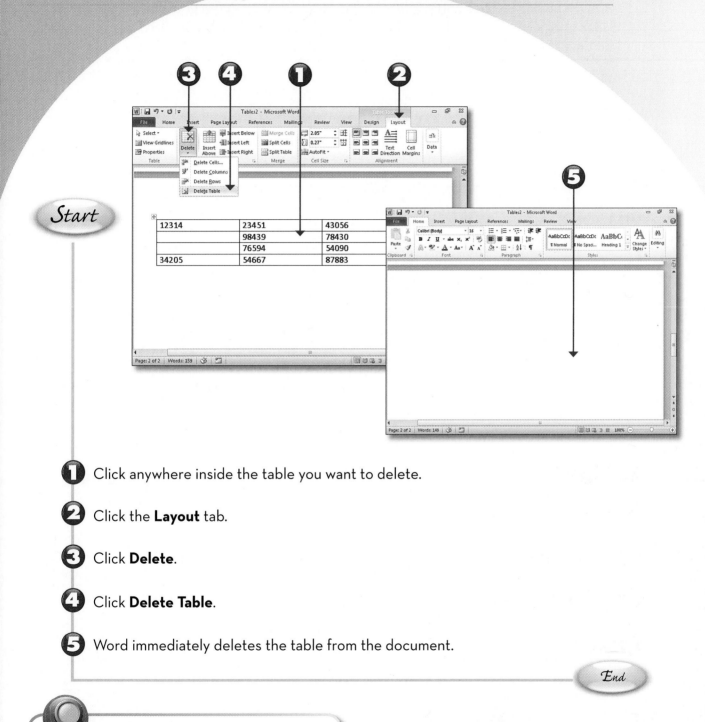

Start

① Click anywhere inside the table you want to delete.

② Click the **Layout** tab.

③ Click **Delete**.

④ Click **Delete Table**.

⑤ Word immediately deletes the table from the document.

End

TIP

What About the Delete Key? If you just select the table and press the **Delete** key on the keyboard, Word only deletes the table contents, not the table. ■

ASSIGNING TABLE STYLES

You can format your tables to make them more visually appealing by changing fonts, sizes, or even adding borders and shading. Rather than applying all the formatting yourself, consider using one of Word's built-in table styles instead. Styles allow you to dress up a table in no time at all. A style is preset formatting that includes colors, borders, fonts, and font sizes.

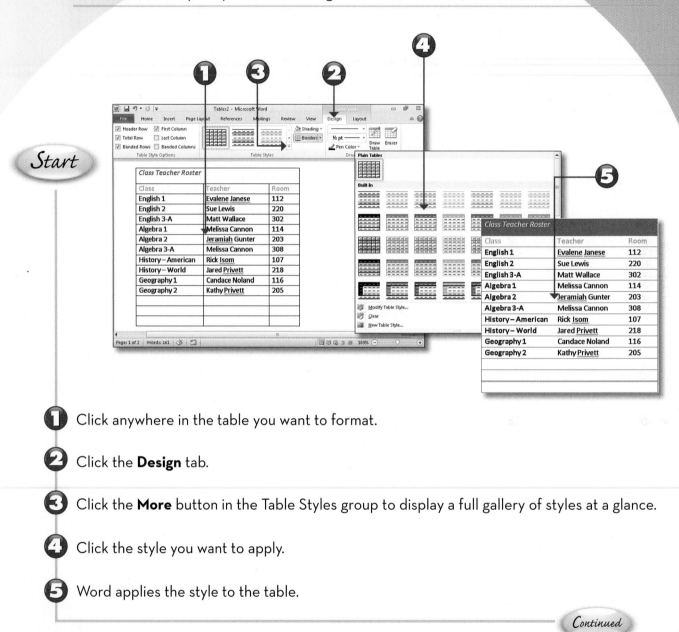

Start

1. Click anywhere in the table you want to format.

2. Click the **Design** tab.

3. Click the **More** button in the Table Styles group to display a full gallery of styles at a glance.

4. Click the style you want to apply.

5. Word applies the style to the table.

Continued

TIP

Plain Tables   When it comes to plain table formatting, you can choose **Table Grid**, which is the default style that places a border around every cell. You can choose the style in the Table Styles gallery. ■

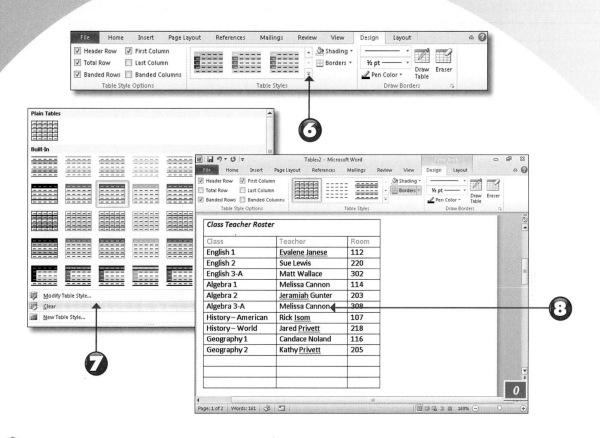

6 To remove a style from a table, click the **More** button again.

7 Click **Clear**.

8 Word removes the table formatting.

End

TIP

Save a Style If you've taken the time to format a table and want to reuse the formatting again for future tables, you can save the table as a table style in the Table Styles Gallery. Select the finished table, click the **More** button, and then click **New Table Style**. Give the table a new name in the Create New Style from Formatting dialog box and click **OK**. The new style is added to the Gallery. ■

TIP

Modify It You can customize any table preset style you apply and save it as a new style. To do so, click the Table Styles **More** button and click **Modify Table Styles**. This opens the Modify Style dialog box where you can change the font, line style, font color, line color, and more. ■

CHANGING CELL ALIGNMENT

You can change the alignment of text within the table cells. Like paragraph alignment, you can align text horizontally to the left, center, or right side of cells. You can also align text vertically, choosing from top, center, or bottom. By default, text is aligned top left. You can find all of the alignment options on the Layout tab in the Alignment group of tools.

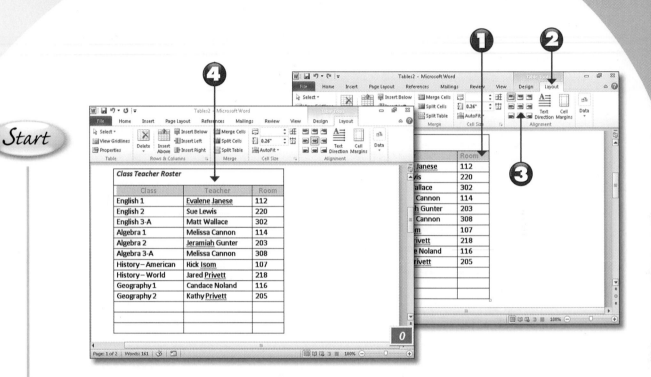

Start

1 Select the cell or cells you want to edit.

2 Click the **Layout** tab.

3 Click an alignment option.

4 Word applies the alignment to the selected cell(s).

End

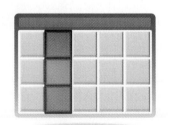

CHANGING TEXT DIRECTION

Table cells present a unique opportunity to align text in different directions. For example, you might want to use a column as a row heading and display the label running vertically in the space, as shown in this task.

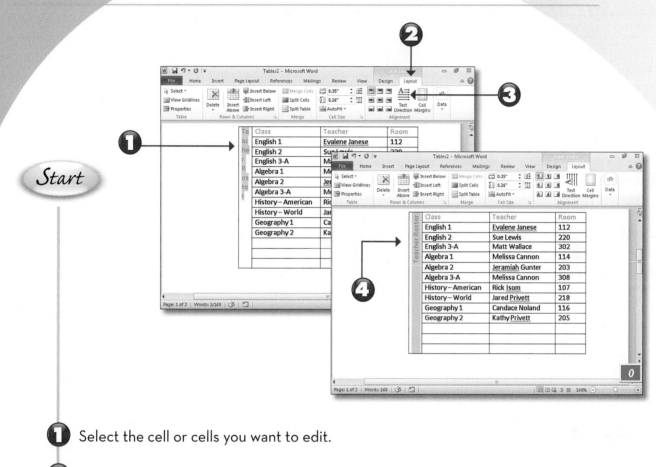

Start

1 Select the cell or cells you want to edit.

2 Click the **Layout** tab.

3 Click **Text Direction**. Keep clicking the button to achieve the desired text direction.

4 Word rotates the text.

End

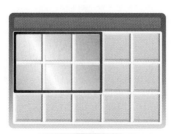

REPOSITIONING AND RESIZING A TABLE

You can move and resize tables in your Word document with a few easy steps. You can click and drag the table's selection handle and place the table wherever you want in a document. You can also click and drag a table corner to resize a table.

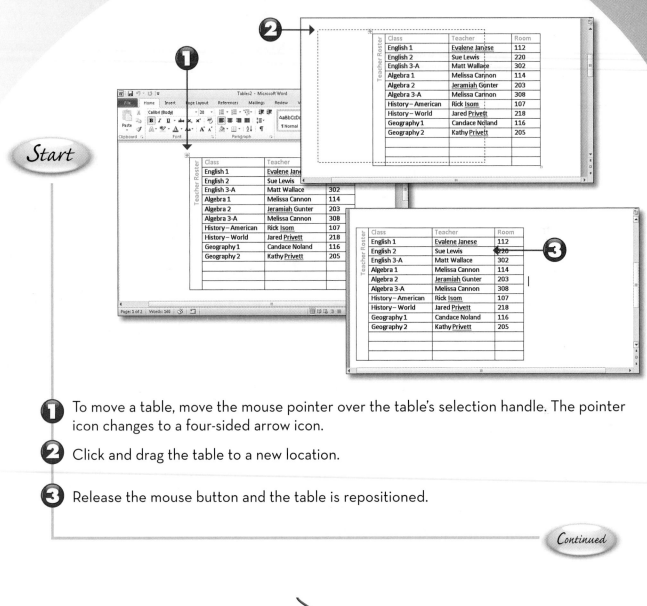

Start

1 To move a table, move the mouse pointer over the table's selection handle. The pointer icon changes to a four-sided arrow icon.

2 Click and drag the table to a new location.

3 Release the mouse button and the table is repositioned.

Continued

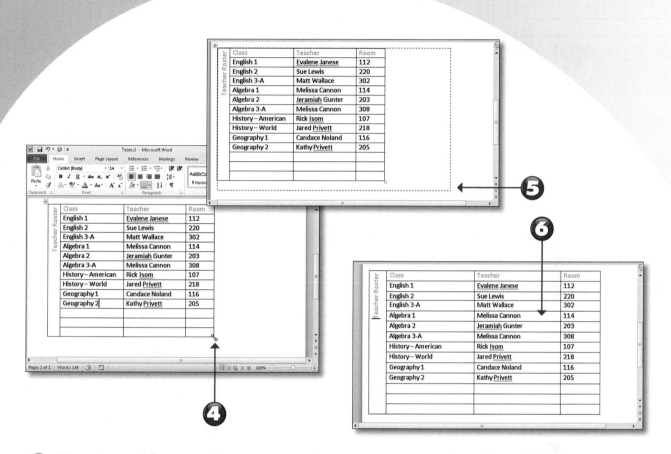

4 To resize a table, move the mouse pointer over a corner or edge of the table. The mouse pointer changes to a double-sided arrow icon.

5 Click and drag the table edge.

6 Release the mouse button and the table is resized.

End

TIP

Wrap Text   You can control how text wraps around a table just as you do with wrapping text around graphic objects (see Chapter 12 to learn more about graphic objects). Depending on your table placement in a document, Word may automatically wrap text around the table. To control text wrapping around tables, you must open the Table Properties dialog box. Click the **Properties** button on the **Layout** tab, then click the Table tab to find the two text-wrapping settings: **None** or **Around**. Click **None** to turn off the wrapping or click **Around** to make text flow around the table. ■

Chapter 8

USING WORD'S DOCUMENT AND REFERENCES TOOLS

Word offers a wide variety of research and referencing tools you can use with longer or more complex documents you create. If you're working on a research paper, for example, you can use Word's References tools to add footnotes, endnotes, cross-references, and even a table of contents. This chapter shows you how to use the various Word features to translate text, look up words in the built-in dictionaries and thesaurus, navigate long documents with the Navigation Pane and bookmarks, and even tap into Excel's spreadsheet powers to make a chart. You'll learn how to build a document using Outline View, add captions to graphic elements, and insert comments.

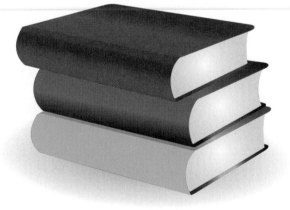

The Navigation Pane can help
you browse your document
by headings or by pages.

BUILDING DOCUMENTS WITH OUTLINE VIEW

If your document is based on headings, subheadings, and body content, you can use Word's Outline view to create and edit your pages. Outline View lets you focus on the document's structure rather than on its formatting. You can assign heading levels and change levels as needed as your document develops.

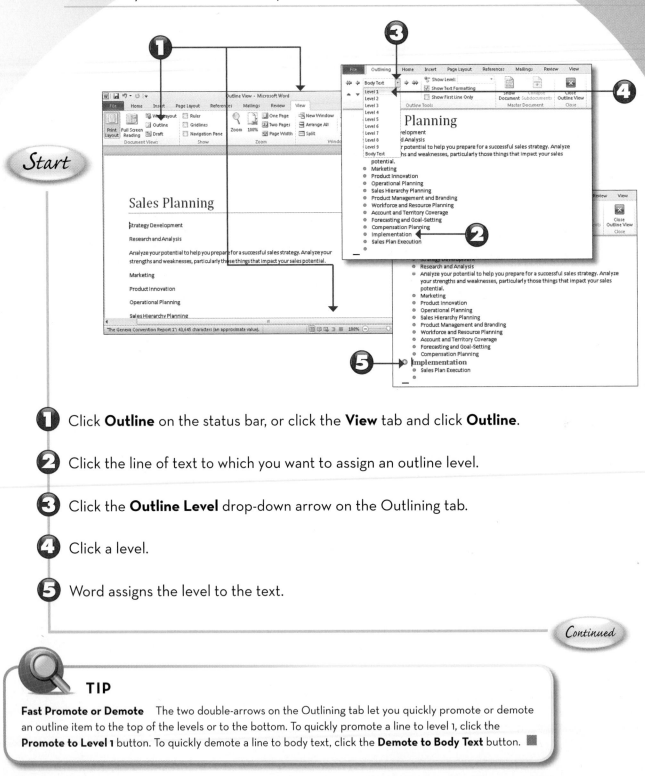

Start

1 Click **Outline** on the status bar, or click the **View** tab and click **Outline**.

2 Click the line of text to which you want to assign an outline level.

3 Click the **Outline Level** drop-down arrow on the Outlining tab.

4 Click a level.

5 Word assigns the level to the text.

Continued

TIP

Fast Promote or Demote   The two double-arrows on the Outlining tab let you quickly promote or demote an outline item to the top of the levels or to the bottom. To quickly promote a line to level 1, click the **Promote to Level 1** button. To quickly demote a line to body text, click the **Demote to Body Text** button. ■

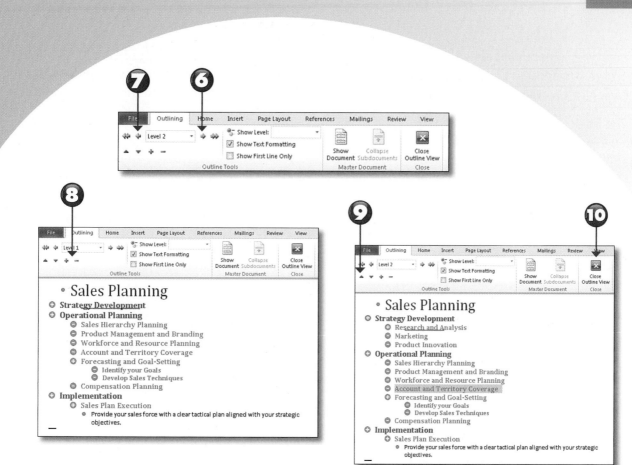

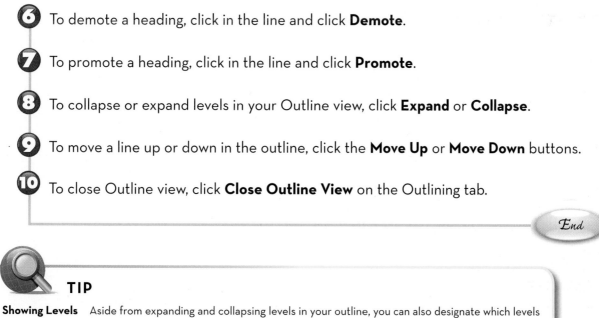

6 To demote a heading, click in the line and click **Demote**.

7 To promote a heading, click in the line and click **Promote**.

8 To collapse or expand levels in your Outline view, click **Expand** or **Collapse**.

9 To move a line up or down in the outline, click the **Move Up** or **Move Down** buttons.

10 To close Outline view, click **Close Outline View** on the Outlining tab.

End

TIP

Showing Levels Aside from expanding and collapsing levels in your outline, you can also designate which levels you want to view using the Show Level feature in the Outlining tab. Simply click the **Show Level** drop-down arrow and choose which level you want to view. ◼

NAVIGATING DOCUMENTS WITH THE NAVIGATION PANE

When navigating through longer documents, you can simplify the process of looking through pages and headings by using Word's Navigation Pane. With the Navigation Pane you can browse your pages by headings or by thumbnail icons, or you can conduct a search for a specific word or phrase.

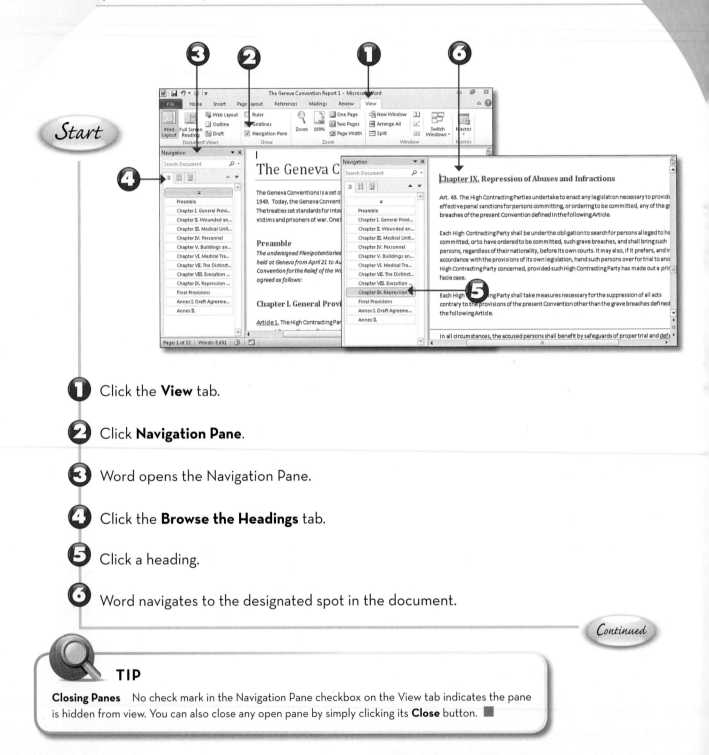

1. Click the **View** tab.

2. Click **Navigation Pane**.

3. Word opens the Navigation Pane.

4. Click the **Browse the Headings** tab.

5. Click a heading.

6. Word navigates to the designated spot in the document.

Continued

TIP

Closing Panes No check mark in the Navigation Pane checkbox on the View tab indicates the pane is hidden from view. You can also close any open pane by simply clicking its **Close** button. ∎

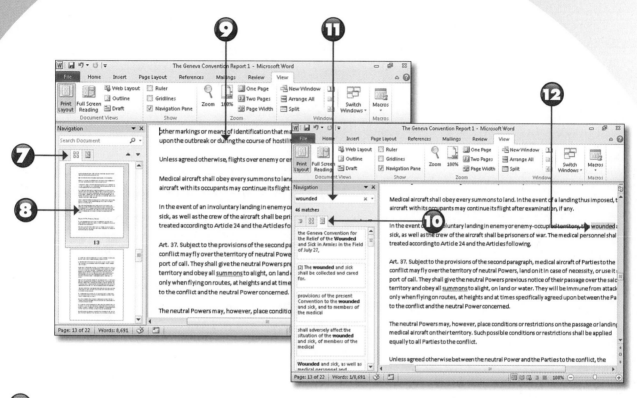

7 Click the **Browse the Pages** tab.

8 Click a page thumbnail.

9 Word navigates to the designated spot in the document.

10 Click the **Browse the Results** tab.

11 Type the word or phrase you want to search for in the document and press Enter.

12 Word highlights the first occurrence.

End

TIP

Moving Around Headings   You can click the **Previous Heading** or **Next Heading** buttons in the Navigation Pane to jump around from one heading to another. ■

TRANSLATING WORDS

You can easily translate a word in your document to help you communicate with others around the globe in languages such as Spanish, French, or Arabic. Word installs with several translation tools, such as bilingual dictionaries and access to online translation sites.

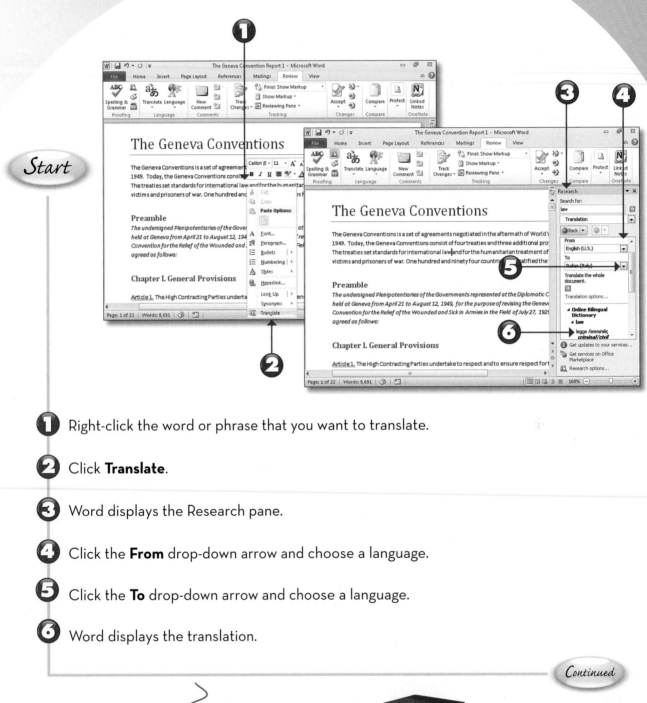

Start

1 Right-click the word or phrase that you want to translate.

2 Click **Translate**.

3 Word displays the Research pane.

4 Click the **From** drop-down arrow and choose a language.

5 Click the **To** drop-down arrow and choose a language.

6 Word displays the translation.

Continued

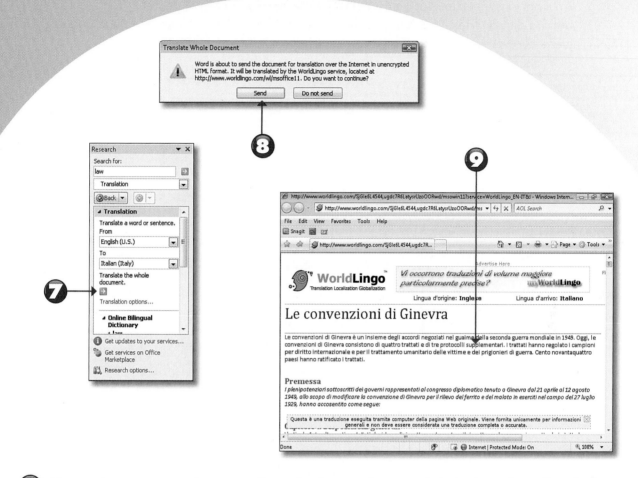

7 To translate an entire document from the Research pane, click the **Translate the whole document** arrow button.

8 Click **Send**.

9 Your default Web browser opens and displays the translation.

End

TIP

Translation Options You can choose which languages to display among Word's bilingual dictionaries. Click the **Translation Options** link in the Research pane to open the Translation Options dialog box and check or uncheck which languages you want available for translation activities. ■

TIP

Review Tab You can also use the Review tab to translate a selected word or phrase in your document. Click the **Review** tab, click the **Translate** button, and then click **Translate Selected Text**. Like the right-click method you learned about in the steps, the Research pane opens and offers you tools for translating the phrase. ■

LOOKING UP SYNONYMS AND DEFINITIONS

Another easy task in Word is the ability to look up a synonym or definition. Using Word's built-in dictionaries, you can quickly find a similar word or look up a word's meaning with just a click or two.

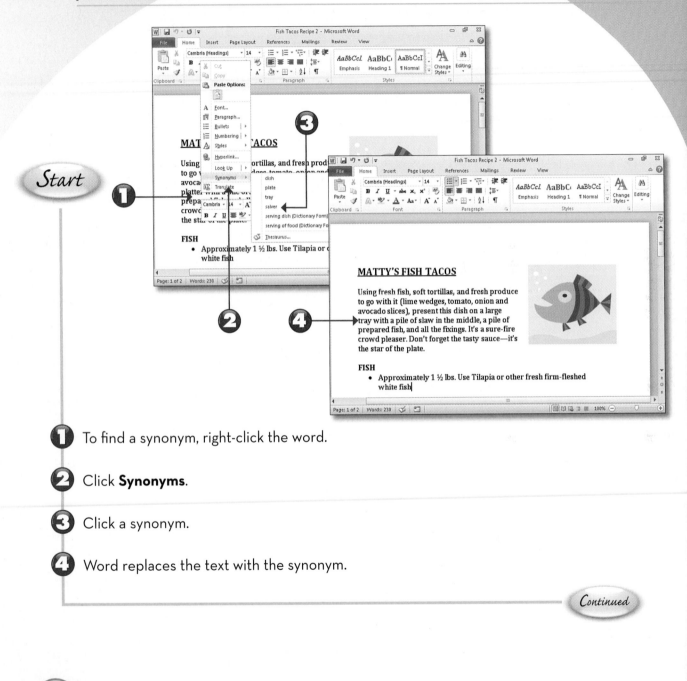

1 To find a synonym, right-click the word.

2 Click **Synonyms**.

3 Click a synonym.

4 Word replaces the text with the synonym.

Continued

TIP

Research Pane You can also open the Research Pane by clicking the **Review** tab on the Ribbon and then clicking the **Research** button located in the Proofing tools group. ■

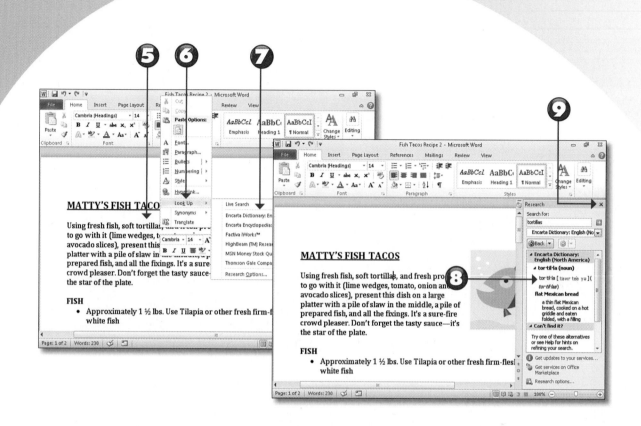

5 To look up a word's meaning, right-click the word.

6 Click **Look Up**.

7 Click a reference source, such as **Encarta Dictionary**.

8 Word opens the Research Pane and displays any matches.

9 Click here to close the pane.

End

TIP

Change Your Source To change the source you use in the Research Pane, click the drop-down arrow under the **Search for** box and select a new resource. ■

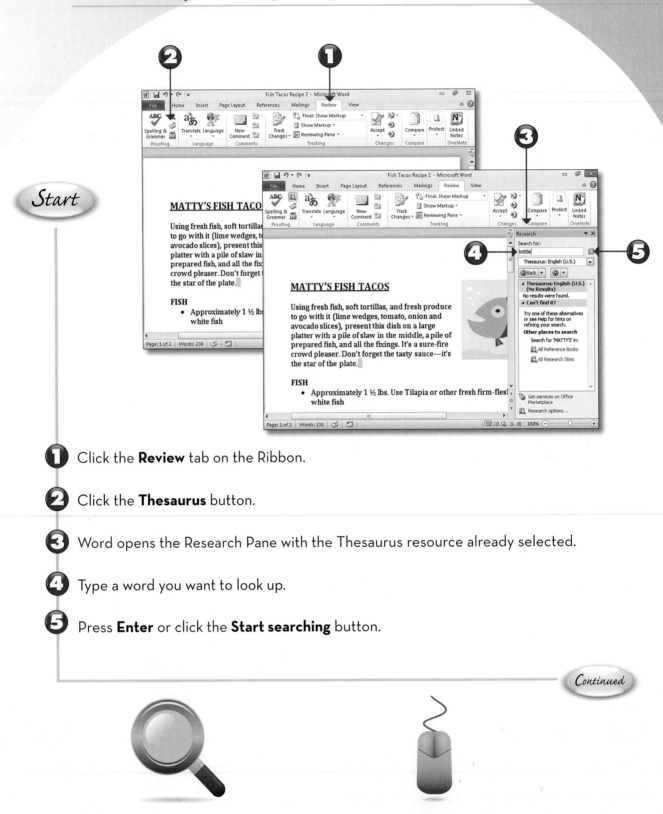

USING THE WORD THESAURUS

You can use Word's built-in Thesaurus feature, along with the Research Pane, to look up words and locate just the word you want to use.

Start

① Click the **Review** tab on the Ribbon.

② Click the **Thesaurus** button.

③ Word opens the Research Pane with the Thesaurus resource already selected.

④ Type a word you want to look up.

⑤ Press **Enter** or click the **Start searching** button.

Continued

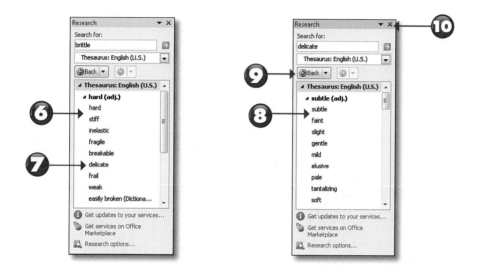

6 The pane displays any results.

7 To find more synonyms based on any word in the list, click the word.

8 The pane displays related synonyms.

9 You can click the **Back** button to return to the previous list.

10 Click **Close** to exit the Research Pane.

End

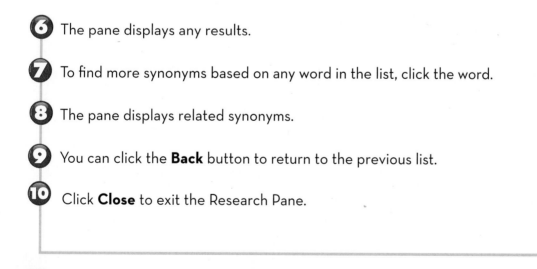

TIP

More Options You can click the **Get services on Office Marketplace** link at the bottom of the Research Pane to visit the Office Marketplace website and find more resources you can use. ■

HIGHLIGHTING TEXT

Need to bring someone's attention to text in a document? You can highlight text just like using a highlighter pen on paper. You can use Word's Highlighter Pen to drag across the text you want to draw attention to, or you can select the text first and then apply a highlighting color.

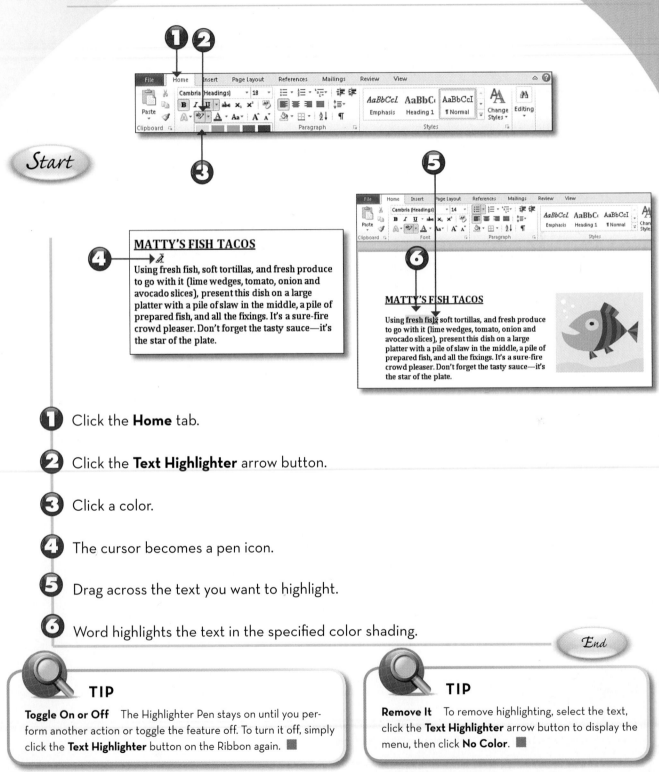

1 Click the **Home** tab.

2 Click the **Text Highlighter** arrow button.

3 Click a color.

4 The cursor becomes a pen icon.

5 Drag across the text you want to highlight.

6 Word highlights the text in the specified color shading.

Start

End

TIP

Toggle On or Off The Highlighter Pen stays on until you perform another action or toggle the feature off. To turn it off, simply click the **Text Highlighter** button on the Ribbon again. ■

TIP

Remove It To remove highlighting, select the text, click the **Text Highlighter** arrow button to display the menu, then click **No Color**. ■

INSERTING COMMENTS

You can use comments to add notations to your document that are not meant to be printed. Comments are handy when your document is being edited by multiple users, or when you want to remind yourself to revisit a section to check facts or spelling. When you insert a comment, it appears as a balloon off to the side of the document.

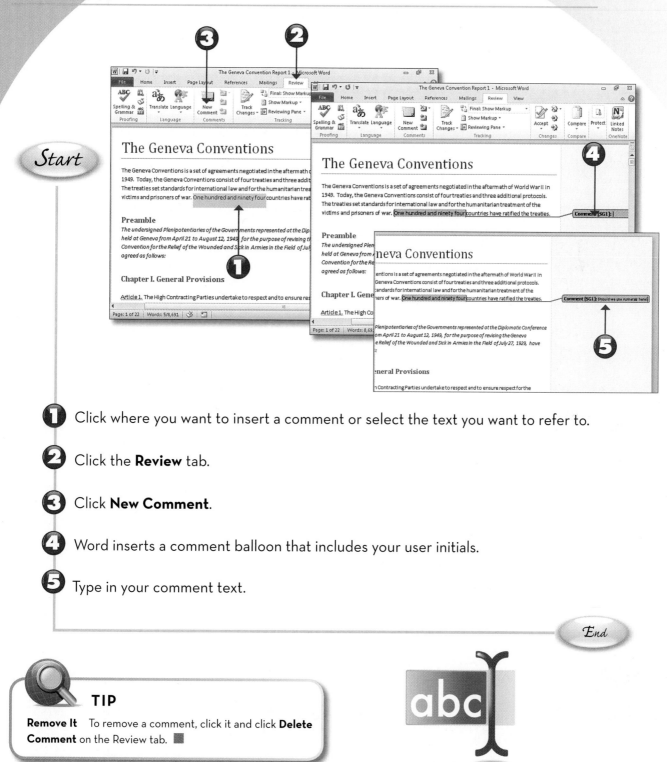

1. Click where you want to insert a comment or select the text you want to refer to.

2. Click the **Review** tab.

3. Click **New Comment**.

4. Word inserts a comment balloon that includes your user initials.

5. Type in your comment text.

TIP

Remove It   To remove a comment, click it and click **Delete Comment** on the Review tab. ■

INSERTING FOOTNOTES AND ENDNOTES

If you're working on a research paper or other document requiring resource citation, you can insert footnotes and endnotes. A footnote is an explanatory flagged note inserted at the bottom of a page to cite a source. Endnotes appear at the end of a section or document rather than at the bottom of a page.

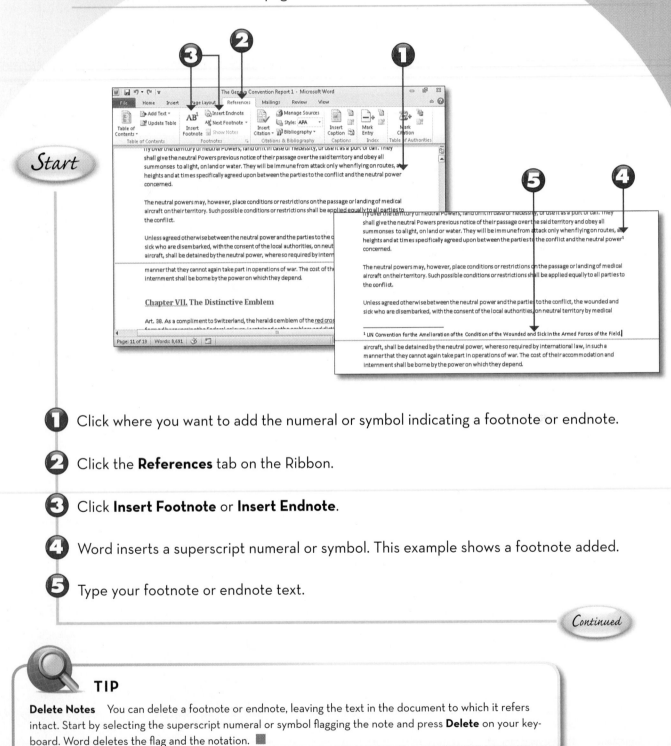

Start

1 Click where you want to add the numeral or symbol indicating a footnote or endnote.

2 Click the **References** tab on the Ribbon.

3 Click **Insert Footnote** or **Insert Endnote**.

4 Word inserts a superscript numeral or symbol. This example shows a footnote added.

5 Type your footnote or endnote text.

Continued

TIP

Delete Notes You can delete a footnote or endnote, leaving the text in the document to which it refers intact. Start by selecting the superscript numeral or symbol flagging the note and press **Delete** on your keyboard. Word deletes the flag and the notation. ▪

6 To edit footnote or endnote placement and settings, click the **Footnote and Endnote** icon in the corner of the Footnotes group of tools on the Ribbon.

7 The Footnote and Endnote dialog box opens.

8 To control where on the page the footnote or endnote should appear, click here and make a selection.

9 To change the number format, click here and select a format.

10 To control numbering, click here and choose whether the numbering should be continuous, restart at the beginning of each section, or restart at the beginning of each page.

11 Click **Apply** to apply the changes.

End

INSERTING CAPTIONS

You can add captions to pictures, charts, text boxes, and other graphic objects you place in a document. Word's captioning feature includes preset captions to use, such as Figure, Equation, or Table. Word also handles the caption numbering for you, such as Figure 1, Figure 2, and so forth.

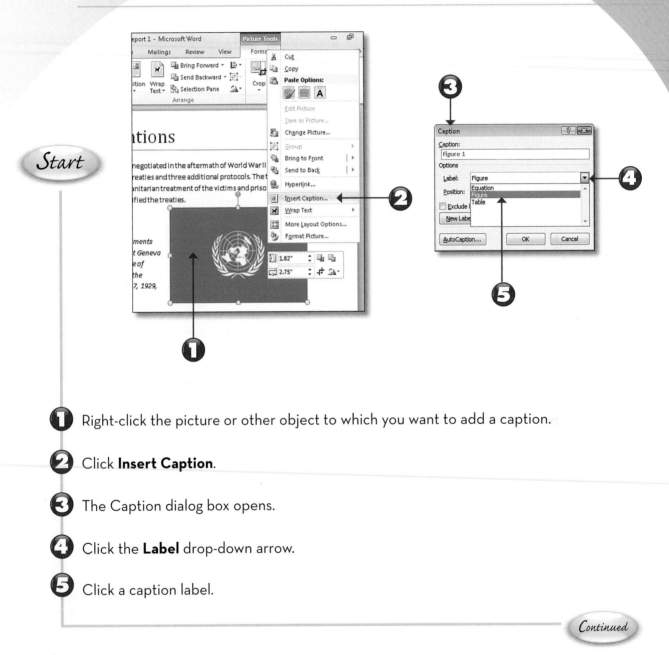

1 Right-click the picture or other object to which you want to add a caption.

2 Click **Insert Caption**.

3 The Caption dialog box opens.

4 Click the **Label** drop-down arrow.

5 Click a caption label.

Continued

TIP

New Labels You can create a new label to add it to the Caption dialog box. To create a new label, click the **New Label** button and fill out label text. To leave off the label and keep the number only, click the **Exclude label from caption** check box.

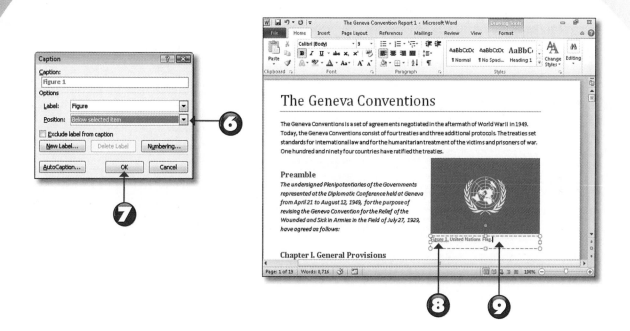

6 If you want to change the position of the caption, click here and choose another position.

7 Click **OK**.

8 Word inserts the caption.

9 Type in any additional text you want the caption to include.

End

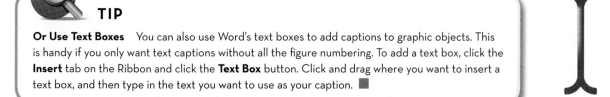

TIP

Or Use Text Boxes You can also use Word's text boxes to add captions to graphic objects. This is handy if you only want text captions without all the figure numbering. To add a text box, click the **Insert** tab on the Ribbon and click the **Text Box** button. Click and drag where you want to insert a text box, and then type in the text you want to use as your caption. ■

INSERTING CROSS-REFERENCES

You can use cross-references in your documents to refer the reader to another section of the document or refer them to additional information. You can insert cross-references to refer readers to existing text that is styled as a heading, to footnotes or endnotes, to captions and bookmarks, and even to numbered paragraphs.

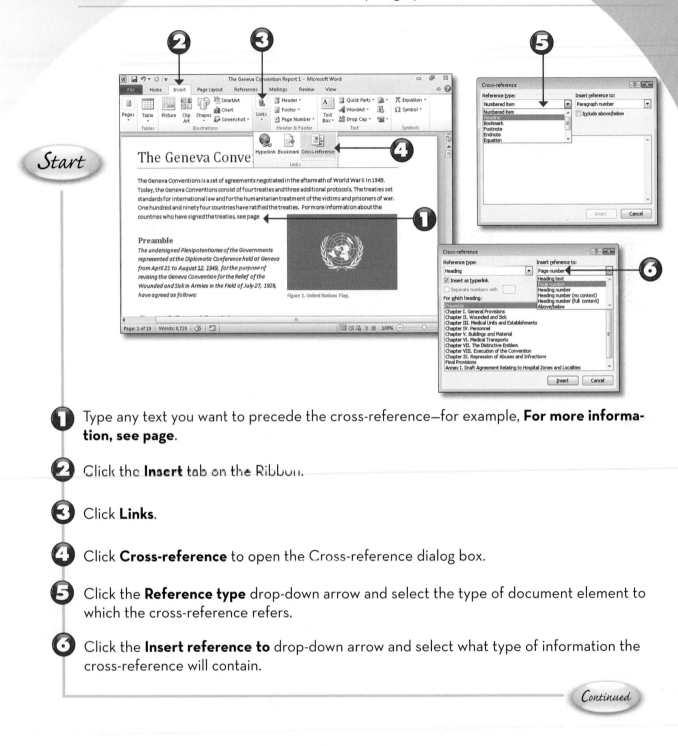

Figure 1. United Nations Flag.

① Type any text you want to precede the cross-reference—for example, **For more information, see page**.

② Click the **Insert** tab on the Ribbon.

③ Click **Links**.

④ Click **Cross-reference** to open the Cross-reference dialog box.

⑤ Click the **Reference type** drop-down arrow and select the type of document element to which the cross-reference refers.

⑥ Click the **Insert reference to** drop-down arrow and select what type of information the cross-reference will contain.

Continued

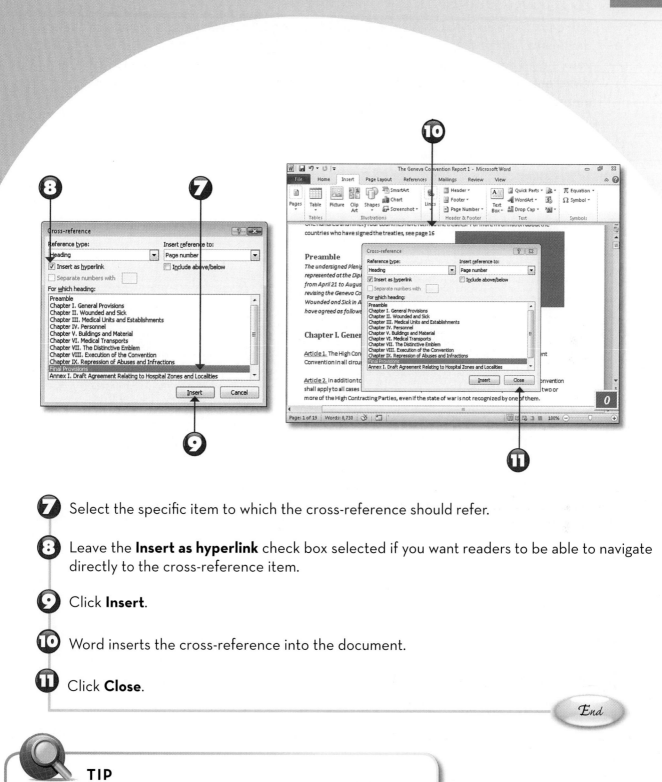

7 Select the specific item to which the cross-reference should refer.

8 Leave the **Insert as hyperlink** check box selected if you want readers to be able to navigate directly to the cross-reference item.

9 Click **Insert**.

10 Word inserts the cross-reference into the document.

11 Click **Close**.

End

🔍 **TIP**

Delete It You can remove a cross reference you no longer need. Highlight it in the document, and then press the **Delete** key. The reference is immediately deleted. ■

ADDING AN INDEX

You can create an index that contains all the marked text you want to include from your document. The process starts by marking your index words using a special XE field. Once you've marked all the index words you want to include, you can turn them into an index that Word automatically updates for you. Word's indexing feature allows you to customize your index to include leader characters and preset index designs.

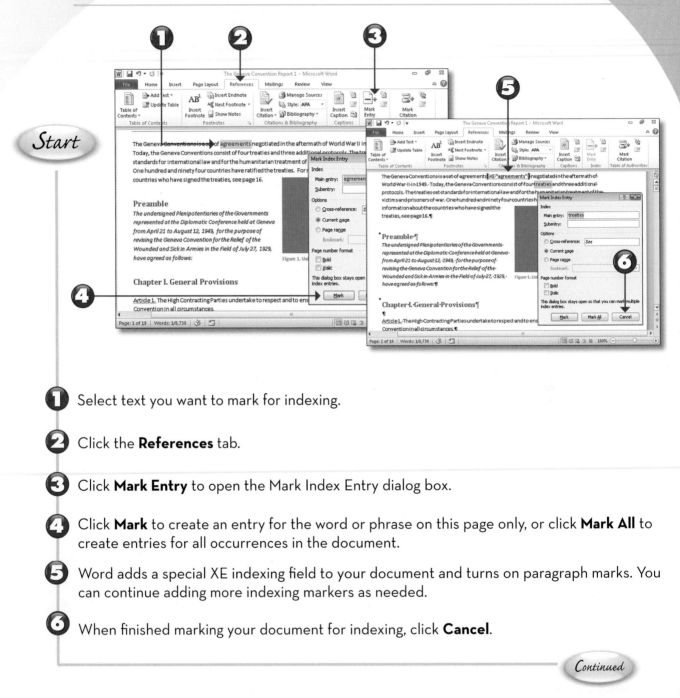

Start

1. Select text you want to mark for indexing.

2. Click the **References** tab.

3. Click **Mark Entry** to open the Mark Index Entry dialog box.

4. Click **Mark** to create an entry for the word or phrase on this page only, or click **Mark All** to create entries for all occurrences in the document.

5. Word adds a special XE indexing field to your document and turns on paragraph marks. You can continue adding more indexing markers as needed.

6. When finished marking your document for indexing, click **Cancel**.

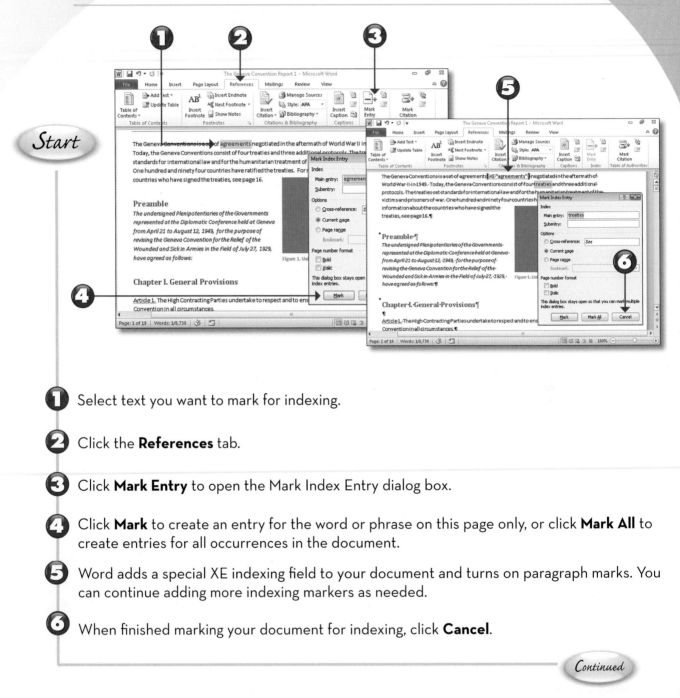

Continued

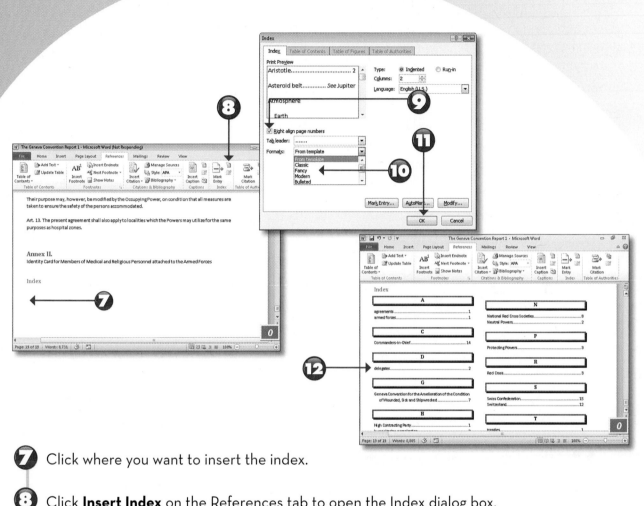

7 Click where you want to insert the index.

8 Click **Insert Index** on the References tab to open the Index dialog box.

9 Click **Right-align page numbers**.

10 Click here and select an index design.

11 Click **OK**.

12 Word generates an index.

End

TIP

Remove Indexing Fields You can delete an index entry in your document by selecting the entire XE field, including the braces ({}) that surround it, and pressing the **Delete** key on your keyboard. Then click the **Update Index** button on the References tab. ∎

ADDING A TABLE OF CONTENTS

You can instruct Word to generate a table of contents for your document. If your document uses the predefined heading styles, Word can quickly create a TOC based on the headings, and add page numbers for each.

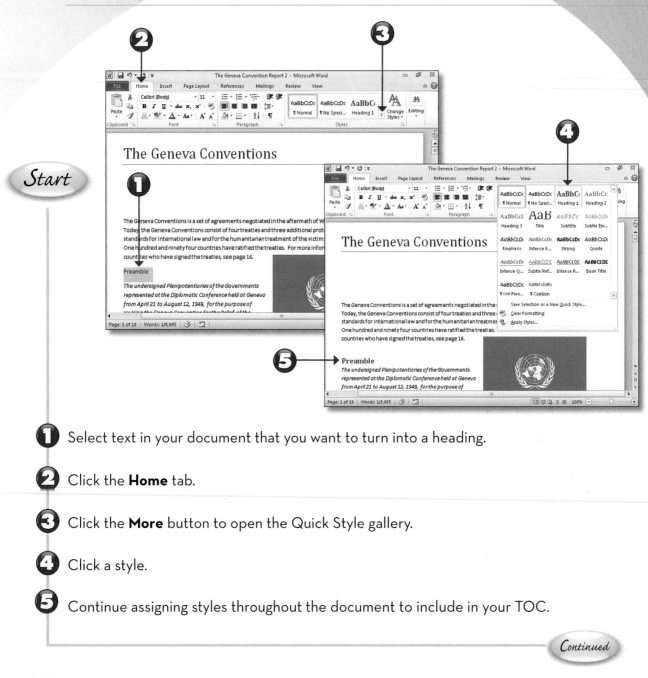

1. Select text in your document that you want to turn into a heading.

2. Click the **Home** tab.

3. Click the **More** button to open the Quick Style gallery.

4. Click a style.

5. Continue assigning styles throughout the document to include in your TOC.

Continued

TIP

Remove It To delete a TOC, click **Table of Contents** in the References tab's Table of Contents group and click **Remove Table of Contents**.

6 Click where you want to insert a TOC.

7 Click the **References** tab.

8 Click **Table of Contents**.

9 Click a TOC style.

10 Word creates a table of contents.

End

TIP

Update It If you make changes to your document's headings, you can update the table of contents to reflect the new text. On the References tab, click the **Update Table** button to open the Update Table of Contents dialog box where you can choose to update the entire table or just the page numbers.

ADDING BOOKMARKS

You can use bookmarks to navigate long documents. Digital bookmarks act a lot like actual bookmarks, allowing you to mark a location in a document for easy access later. When naming your bookmark, you must follow strict naming rules. Bookmark names must begin with a letter, and names can include numbers along with letter characters. However, no spaces are allowed in the bookmark name. If you do need to create a space, use an underscore character instead, such as Chapter_2.

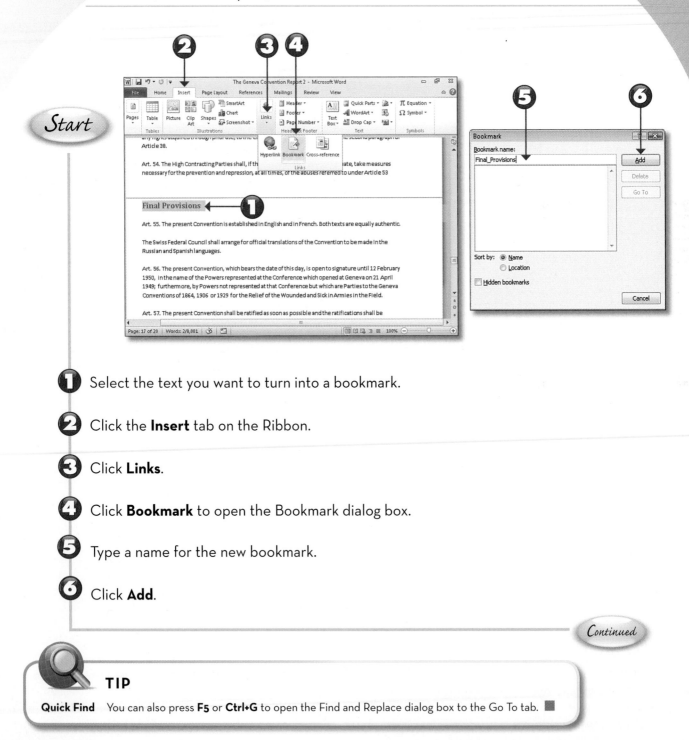

Start

1. Select the text you want to turn into a bookmark.

2. Click the **Insert** tab on the Ribbon.

3. Click **Links**.

4. Click **Bookmark** to open the Bookmark dialog box.

5. Type a name for the new bookmark.

6. Click **Add**.

Continued

TIP

Quick Find You can also press **F5** or **Ctrl+G** to open the Find and Replace dialog box to the Go To tab. ■

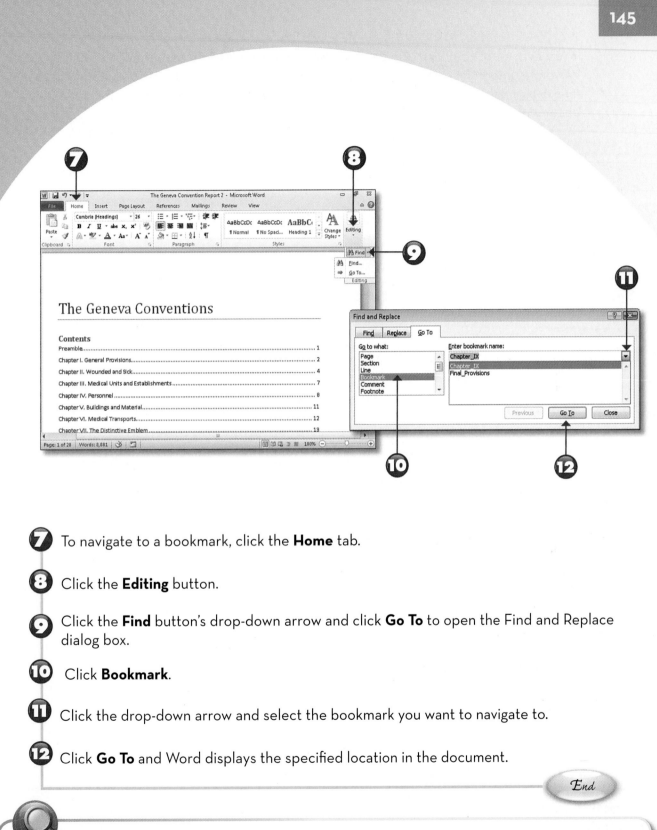

7 To navigate to a bookmark, click the **Home** tab.

8 Click the **Editing** button.

9 Click the **Find** button's drop-down arrow and click **Go To** to open the Find and Replace dialog box.

10 Click **Bookmark**.

11 Click the drop-down arrow and select the bookmark you want to navigate to.

12 Click **Go To** and Word displays the specified location in the document.

End

TIP

Delete It To remove a bookmark, open the Bookmark dialog box, select the bookmark name from the list box, and click **Delete**. ■

SUMMARIZING DATA WITH A CHART

If you ever need to utilize some spreadsheet data, you can do so without ever leaving your Word document. If you have Excel 2010 installed, you can borrow its tools and features to create a datasheet of facts and figures and turn it into a chart to display in your Word document.

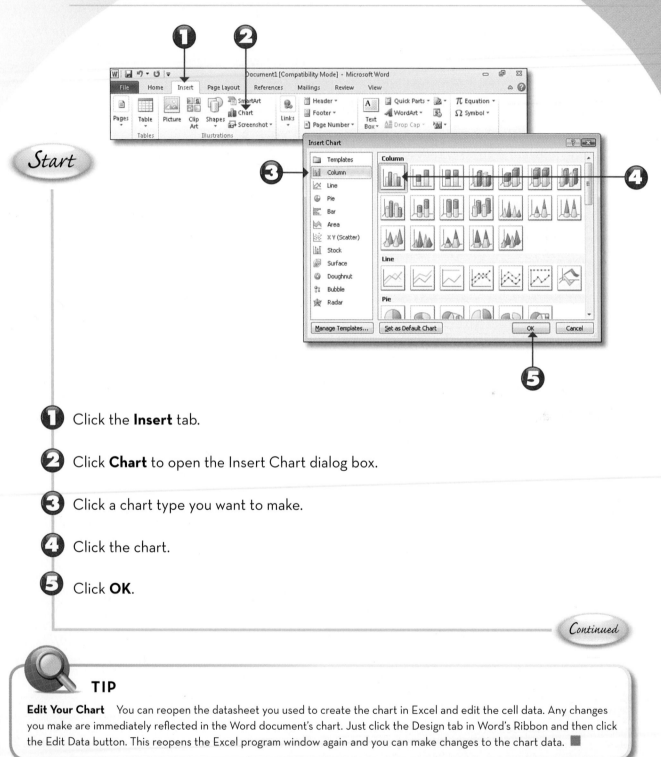

Start

1. Click the **Insert** tab.

2. Click **Chart** to open the Insert Chart dialog box.

3. Click a chart type you want to make.

4. Click the chart.

5. Click **OK**.

Continued

TIP

Edit Your Chart   You can reopen the datasheet you used to create the chart in Excel and edit the cell data. Any changes you make are immediately reflected in the Word document's chart. Just click the Design tab in Word's Ribbon and then click the Edit Data button. This reopens the Excel program window again and you can make changes to the chart data. ■

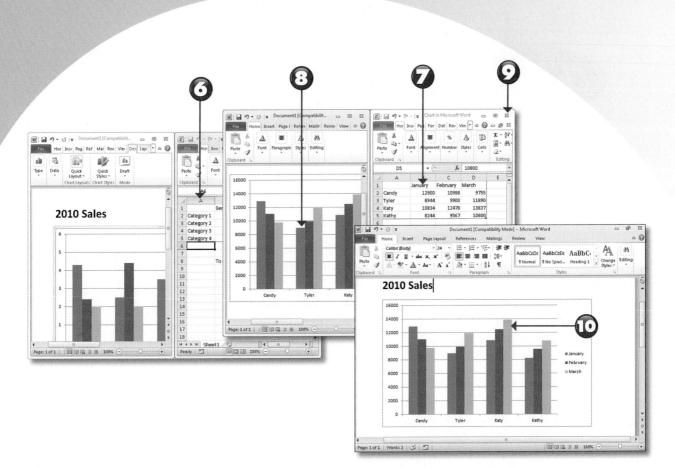

6 The Excel 2010 program window opens to a placeholder datasheet and shares onscreen space with your Word document, showing a placeholder chart.

7 Enter the data you want to chart using the worksheet cells.

8 Word updates the chart in the document as soon as you start entering data in the datasheet.

9 When done typing in your chart data, click **Close** to exit the Excel window.

10 You can now move and resize your chart on the document page, as needed.

End

TIP

No Excel? Don't worry—if you don't have Excel installed, the Microsoft Graph feature opens instead and you can create a chart using it. ■

Chapter 9

REVIEWING DOCUMENTS

Proofreading your documents is always an important step in any situation, especially when you're sharing the documents with others. Since we're not all trained editors, Word offers some handy tools to help us check over our documents for errors and tools to help us locate text and look out for hidden data. You may have already noticed Word's AutoCorrect feature kicking in whenever you misspell a common word, such as *teh* instead of *the*. AutoCorrect is turned on by default, but you can add more misspellings to its list for words you personally struggle to spell correctly.

Speaking of spelling, Word also automatically checks your document's spelling and grammar as you type. You can turn this feature off and choose to activate it only when you have a final document ready to proof. If you need to quickly replace a word with another word throughout your document, you can employ Word's Find and Replace tools. You can also check over your document for hidden personal data and remove it before sending the document off. Lastly, you can use Word's Track Changes feature to review changes from multiple authors to a single document.

You can use Word's Track Changes feature to keep track of multiple users' edits to a document.

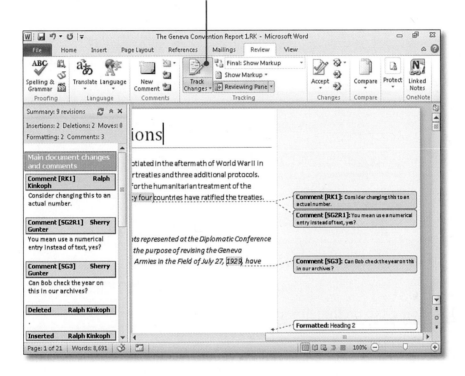

FINDING AND REPLACING TEXT

Sometimes you not only need to find text in a long document, but also replace it with something else. Word's Find and Replace tools take the tedium out of making the same change in several places. Whenever you find yourself about to change something by hand throughout your entire document, stop and see whether Word's Find and Replace feature could do the work for you.

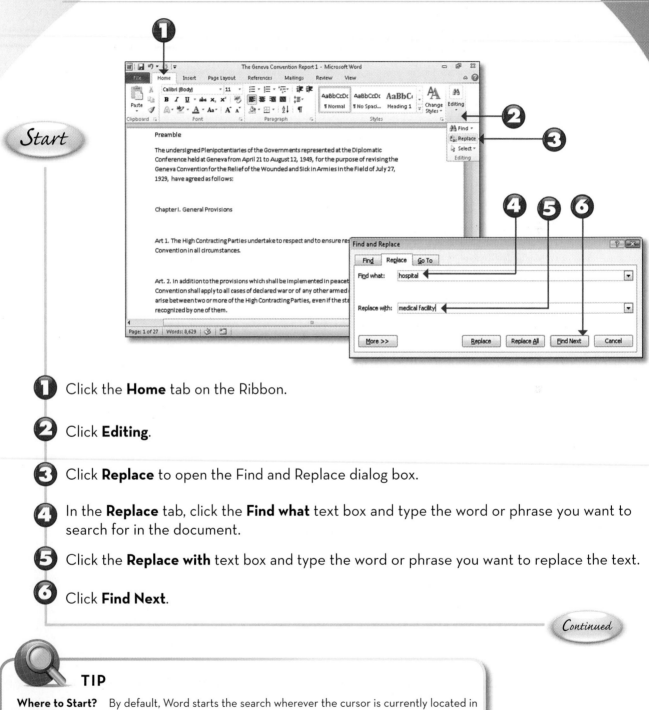

Start

1. Click the **Home** tab on the Ribbon.

2. Click **Editing**.

3. Click **Replace** to open the Find and Replace dialog box.

4. In the **Replace** tab, click the **Find what** text box and type the word or phrase you want to search for in the document.

5. Click the **Replace with** text box and type the word or phrase you want to replace the text.

6. Click **Find Next**.

Continued

TIP

Where to Start? By default, Word starts the search wherever the cursor is currently located in the document. To start the search from the very top, click at the top of the document. ∎

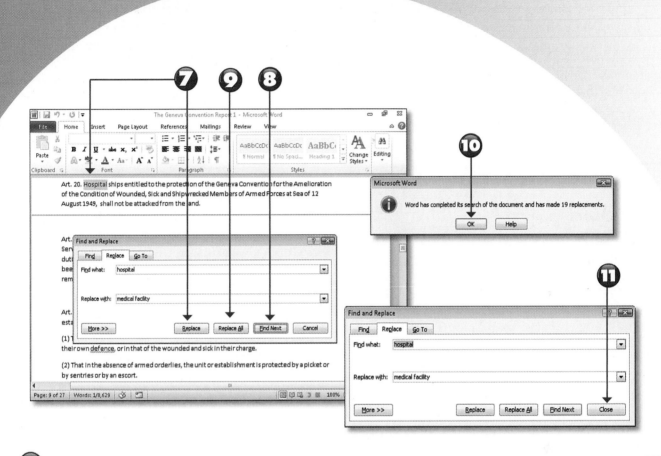

7 Word highlights the first occurrence of the text. To replace it, click the **Replace** button.

8 To look for more instances of the text, click **Find Next** again.

9 To replace all the occurrences with the new text, click **Replace All**.

10 When you finish searching and replacing, a prompt box appears; click **OK**.

11 Click **Close** to close the dialog box.

End

TIP

Find Only   If you just want to find a word without replacing it, click the **Editing** button and click **Find** to open the Navigation Pane to the Search tab. Type in what you want to locate and press **Enter** to search for the text. ■

TIP

More Options   To be more specific about what text you are looking for, click the **More** button at the bottom of the Find and Replace dialog box to reveal a variety of options to narrow the search. ■

CHECKING SPELLING AND GRAMMAR

You can use Word's Spelling and Grammar Checker to help you correct proofreading issues in your document. By default, the Spell Checker is turned on when you start Word, underlining any problems it encounters with a red, wavy line. If the Grammar Checker is on, grammar issues are identified with green, wavy lines. You can also choose to run the Spell Checker anytime you need to review the document. The feature takes you through each problem, one at a time, until the check is complete.

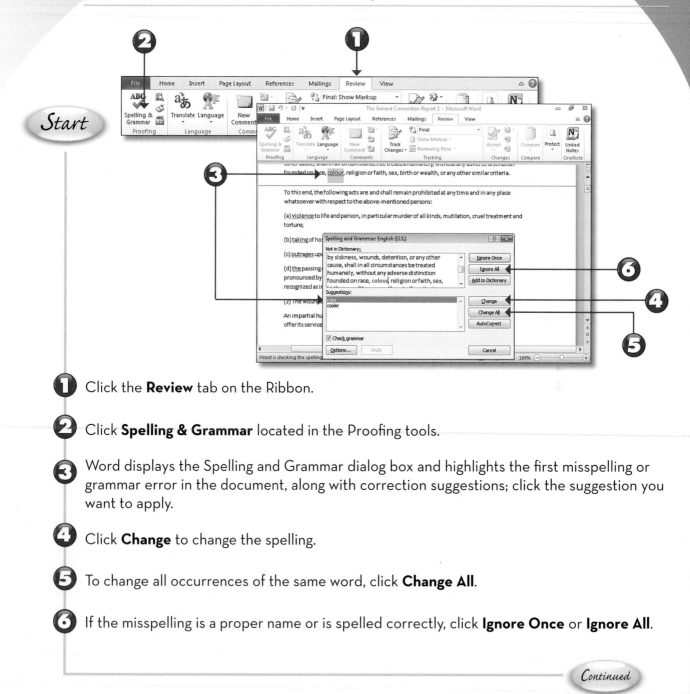

Start

1 Click the **Review** tab on the Ribbon.

2 Click **Spelling & Grammar** located in the Proofing tools.

3 Word displays the Spelling and Grammar dialog box and highlights the first misspelling or grammar error in the document, along with correction suggestions; click the suggestion you want to apply.

4 Click **Change** to change the spelling.

5 To change all occurrences of the same word, click **Change All**.

6 If the misspelling is a proper name or is spelled correctly, click **Ignore Once** or **Ignore All**.

Continued

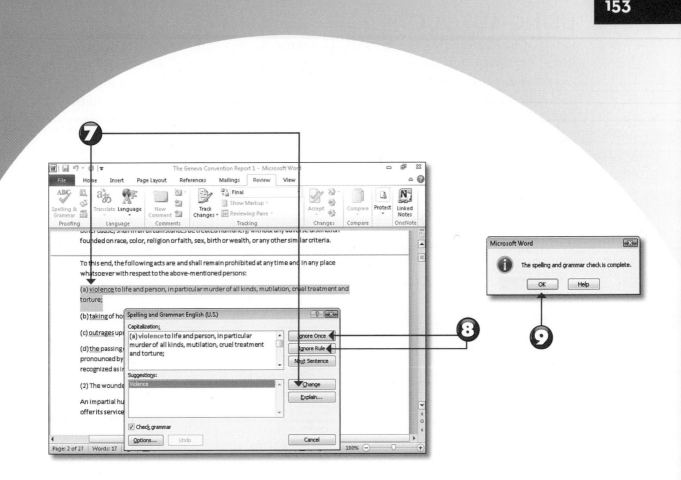

7 If the Check grammar check box is selected, grammar issues are checked along with spelling and any problems are highlighted and marked with green, wavy lines. Click **Change** to change the grammar error.

8 To ignore the grammar rule, click **Ignore Once** or **Ignore Rule**.

9 When the check is complete, click **OK**.

End

TIP

Turning It Off To turn off the Spell Checker, click the **File** tab and click **Options** to open the Word Options dialog box. Click **Proofing**, and then deselect the check box for the **Check spelling as you type** option. To turn off the Grammar Checker, deselect the **Check grammar with spelling** check box. You can also open the Word Options dialog box by clicking the **Options** button at the bottom of the Spelling and Grammar dialog box. ■

USING AUTOCORRECT

Word's AutoCorrect feature fixes spelling errors for you automatically as you type. The feature is turned on by default when you first open Word. AutoCorrect makes corrections based on suggestions from the Spell Checker. It also has its own list of many commonly misspelled words, and you can add your own favorite typos to the list. In addition, you can use AutoCorrect to automatically enter special symbols, long names, or phrases you have to type frequently.

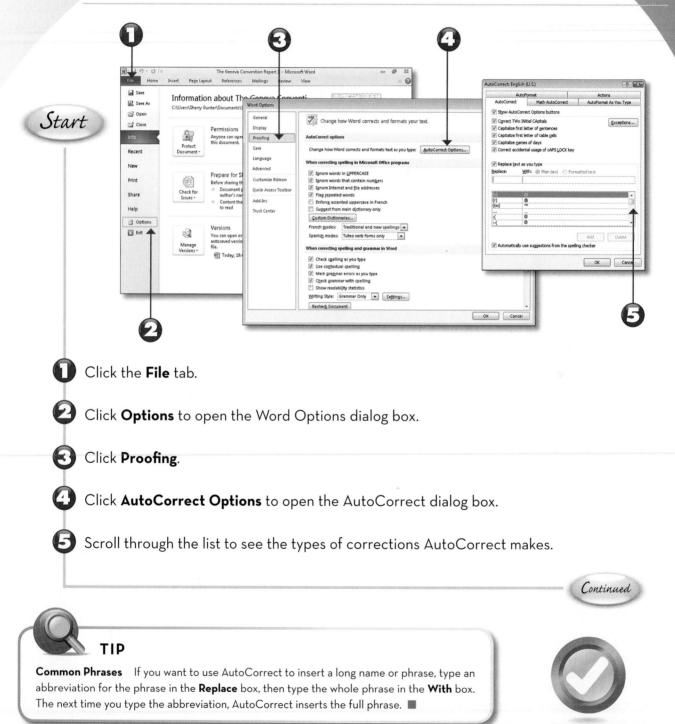

1 Click the **File** tab.

2 Click **Options** to open the Word Options dialog box.

3 Click **Proofing**.

4 Click **AutoCorrect Options** to open the AutoCorrect dialog box.

5 Scroll through the list to see the types of corrections AutoCorrect makes.

Continued

TIP

Common Phrases If you want to use AutoCorrect to insert a long name or phrase, type an abbreviation for the phrase in the **Replace** box, then type the whole phrase in the **With** box. The next time you type the abbreviation, AutoCorrect inserts the full phrase. ■

6 Click in the **Replace** text box and type a word you commonly misspell.

7 Click in the **With** text box and type the correct spelling for the word.

8 Click the **Add** button.

9 AutoCorrect adds the word to the list.

10 Click **OK** to exit the dialog box.

11 Click **OK** to exit the Word Option dialog box.

End

TIP

Remove It To remove a word from the AutoCorrect list, select it in the AutoCorrect dialog box and click the **Delete** button. ■

CHECKING A DOCUMENT FOR HIDDEN DATA

You can use Word's Document Inspector tool to check your document for sensitive information or hidden data. For example, if you plan on sharing the document with other users, you may want to remove any personal information concerning the file. Hidden data, also called metadata, includes elements such as comments, tracked changes, and information about who created the document. With the Document Inspector, you can control what type of content is inspected and if any issues need to be addressed.

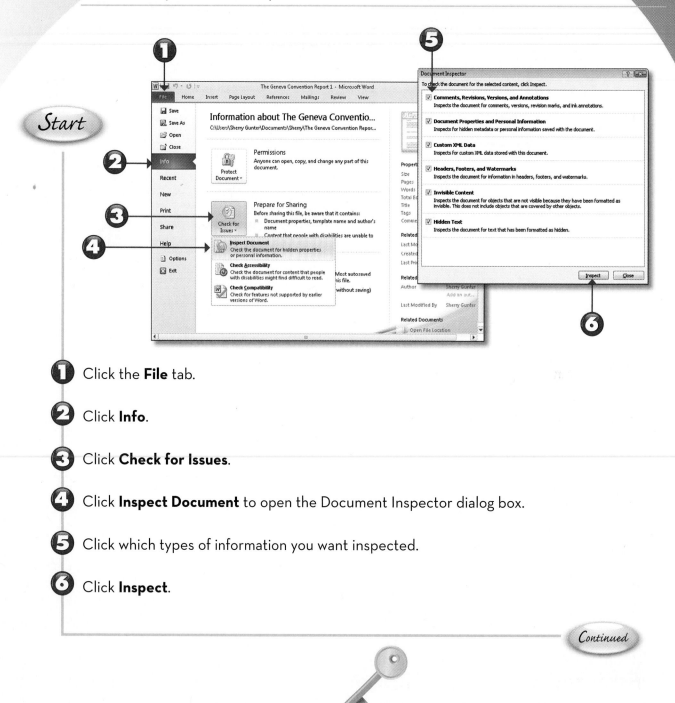

① Click the **File** tab.

② Click **Info**.

③ Click **Check for Issues**.

④ Click **Inspect Document** to open the Document Inspector dialog box.

⑤ Click which types of information you want inspected.

⑥ Click **Inspect**.

Continued

8

Document Inspector
Review the inspection results.

✔ **Comments, Revisions, Versions, and Annotations**
No items were found.

❗ **Document Properties and Personal Information**   Remove All
The following document information was found:
* Document properties
* Author
* Template name

✔ **Custom XML Data**
No custom XML data was found.

✔ **Headers, Footers, and Watermarks**
No headers, footers, or watermarks were found.

✔ **Invisible Content**
No invisible objects found.

✔ **Hidden Text**
No hidden text was found.

⚠ Note: Some changes cannot be undone.

Reinspect   Close

7

Document Inspector
Review the inspection results.

✔ **Comments, Revisions, Versions, and Annotations**
No items were found.

✔ **Document Properties and Personal Information**
Document properties and personal information were successfully removed.

✔ **Custom XML Data**
No custom XML data was found.

✔ **Headers, Footers, and Watermarks**
No headers, footers, or watermarks were found.

✔ **Invisible Content**
No invisible objects found.

✔ **Hidden Text**
No hidden text was found.

⚠ Note: Some changes cannot be undone.

Reinspect   Close

9

7 Word inspects the document and any issues appear listed for you to check.

8 Click **Remove All** to fix an issue.

9 Click **Close**.

End

TIP

Caution   You cannot undo the effects of removing information with Document Inspector. You can, however, restore the removed information by closing the document without saving the changes made by the inspection process. ■

TRACKING AND REVIEWING DOCUMENTS

If you share your documents with other Word users in an editorial environment, you can turn on Word's Track Changes feature and keep track of who makes what changes to the text. For example, if your department is working on a project that involves everyone's input on the team, you can pass the document around and collect everyone's changes, then review the changes, accepting or discarding each one as needed. Track Changes allows you to track comments, insertions, deletions, formatting changes, and more.

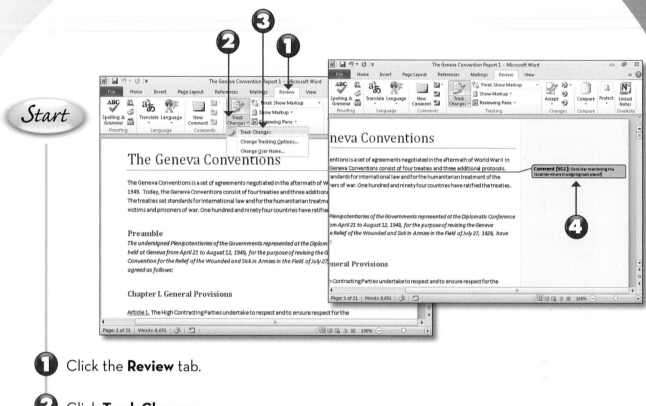

1 Click the **Review** tab.

2 Click **Track Changes**.

3 Click **Track Changes** to turn the tracking feature on. You can now share the document with other users to make edits to the text.

4 Edits you make appear in a comment balloon off to the right of the document page.

Continued

TIP

Comments To add a comment, click where you want it to go or select the text it refers to, then click the **New Comment** button on the Review tab. Type your comment text. To remove a comment, click it and click the **Delete Comment** button. ■

TIP

Reviewing Pane You can click the Reviewing Pane button on the Review tab to open a Reviewing Pane on the left side of the document. This pane lists all the changes, revisions, and comments. You can click an item in the list to quickly move to its location in the document. ■

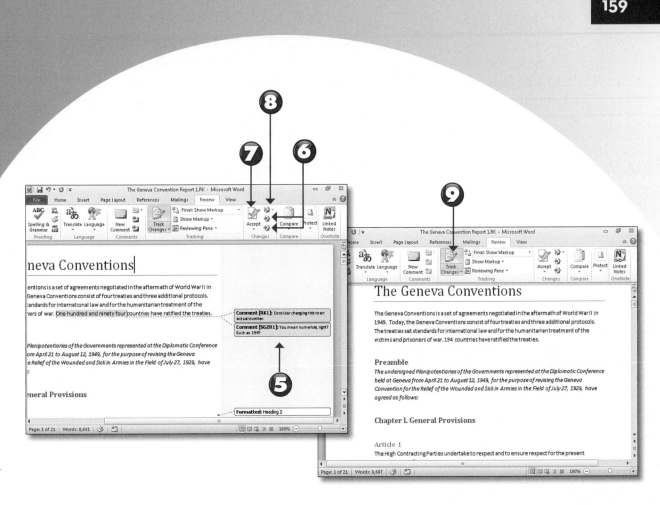

5 Once the document is edited, you can review the changes. Open the document and view the changes. In this example, two users have reviewed the document.

6 Click the **Next Change** and **Previous Change** buttons to navigate between the edits.

7 Click the **Accept** button to okay the change and move to the next change in the document.

8 Click the **Reject** button to forego the change and move to the next edit.

9 When you complete the review, you can turn off the tracking feature; click **Track Changes**.

End

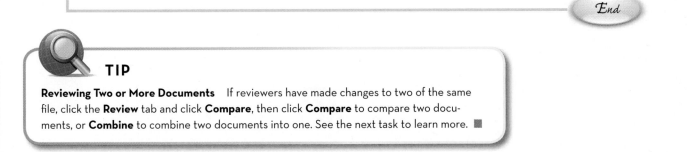

TIP

Reviewing Two or More Documents   If reviewers have made changes to two of the same file, click the **Review** tab and click **Compare**, then click **Compare** to compare two documents, or **Combine** to combine two documents into one. See the next task to learn more. ∎

COMPARING DOCUMENTS

You can compare two documents to see what changes were made in each. You compare an original document with an updated version by creating a third file that has all the differences between the two documents marked. Changes are marked in the same way tracked changes are marked in documents with multiple authors, and you use the same reviewing principles to check each change in the comparison document.

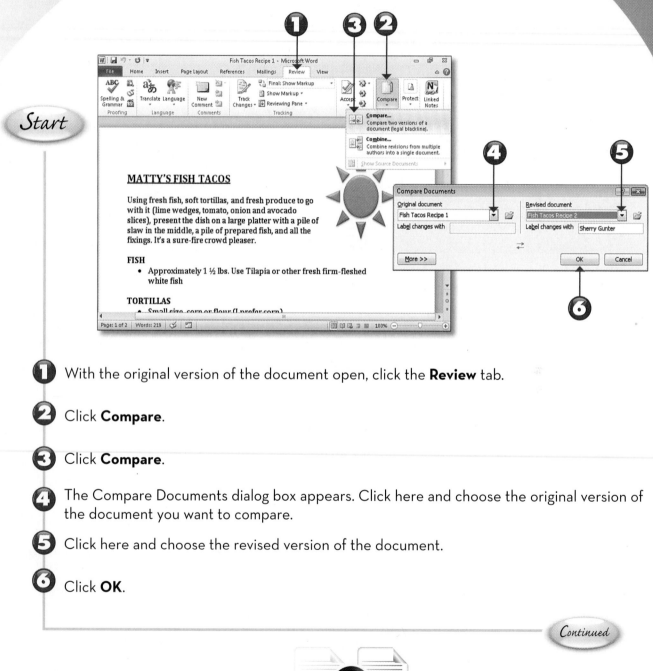

Start

1. With the original version of the document open, click the **Review** tab.

2. Click **Compare**.

3. Click **Compare**.

4. The Compare Documents dialog box appears. Click here and choose the original version of the document you want to compare.

5. Click here and choose the revised version of the document.

6. Click **OK**.

Continued

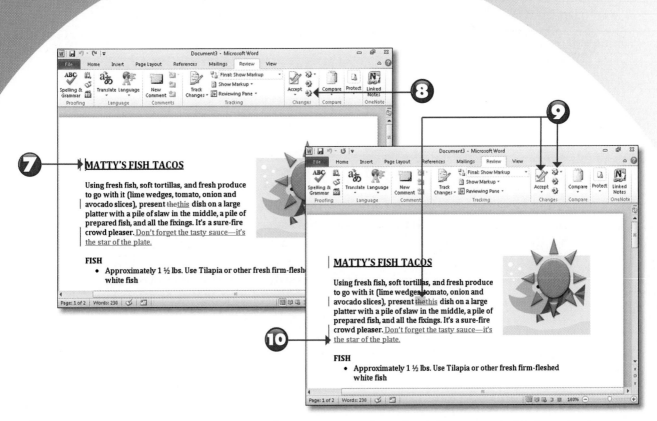

7 Word creates a new document with comparisons from both files noted. Click at the beginning of the document to begin reviewing.

8 Click **Next** on the Review tab.

9 Word highlights the first issue. Click **Accept** to accept the change or click **Reject** to reject the change.

10 You can continue editing the document as needed.

End

TIP

Accepting All Changes   To accept all changes in the document, click the down arrow under **Accept** and click **Accept All Changes in Document**. ◼

TIP

Finding Your Document   If the Compare Documents dialog box does not list the original or revised document you want to use, click the **Browse** button to the right of the Original Document or Revised Document field and choose the desired document from the dialog box that appears. ◼

Chapter 10

PRINTING DOCUMENTS

Creating documents in Word wouldn't be very satisfying without the ability to print out your work. Although the invention of computers was touted as leading to a lessening of our reliance on printed materials and paper consumption, the fact is that we will probably always encounter situations in which we need a tangible copy of a document. With Word 2010, it's easier than ever to print your documents and control the various settings for number of pages printed, collation needs, page orientation, and more. The tasks in this section show you how to view more advanced printing options, print envelopes and labels, and tap into Word's Mail Merge tools to generate mass mailings.

To quickly print the current document using the default print settings, just click this button.

The Print tab in Backstage view displays all the printing options you need to print your Word documents.

VIEWING ADVANCED PRINT OPTIONS

You learned the basics of printing a Word document in Chapter 2, "Working with Word Documents." Now it's time to view some of the more detailed settings available in Word 2010. As you've already learned, the Backstage view (which you access through the File tab on the Ribbon) is the place to go to find all of your document printing options in one convenient spot. You can also use Backstage view to access other printing controls, such as the Printer Properties dialog box and the Page Setup dialog box. The Printer Properties dialog box displays options for the selected printer. The Page Setup dialog box displays options for pages.

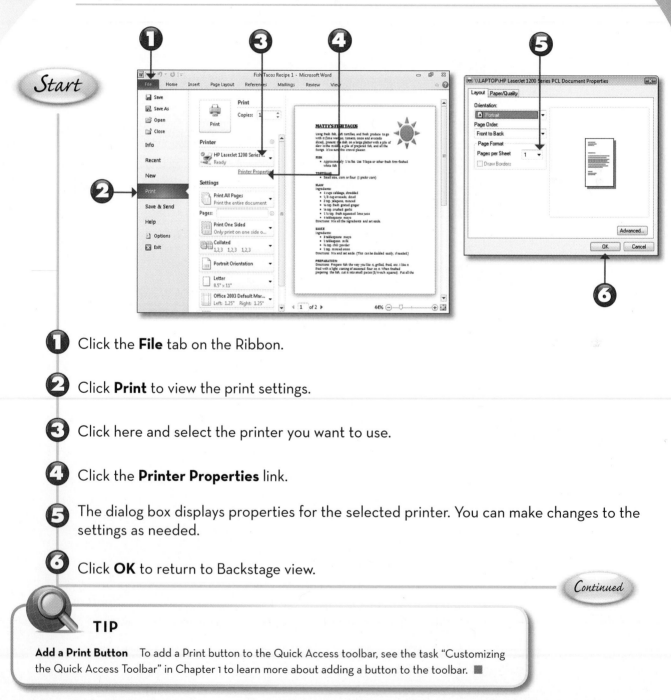

1. Click the **File** tab on the Ribbon.

2. Click **Print** to view the print settings.

3. Click here and select the printer you want to use.

4. Click the **Printer Properties** link.

5. The dialog box displays properties for the selected printer. You can make changes to the settings as needed.

6. Click **OK** to return to Backstage view.

Continued

TIP

Add a Print Button To add a Print button to the Quick Access toolbar, see the task "Customizing the Quick Access Toolbar" in Chapter 1 to learn more about adding a button to the toolbar. ■

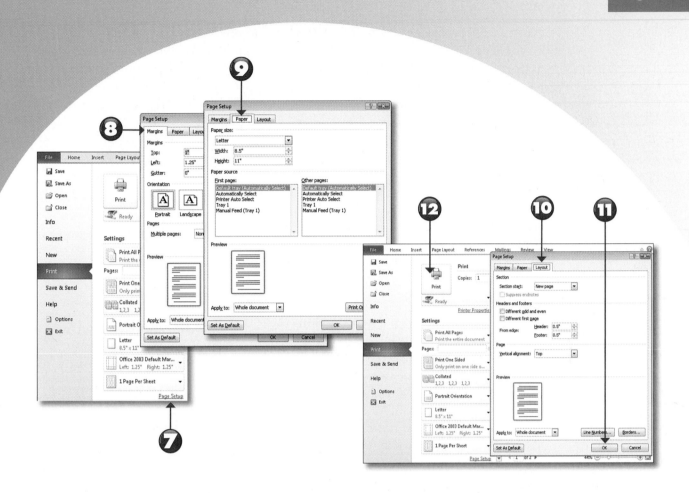

7 Near the bottom of printing options, click the **Page Setup** link to open the Page Setup dialog box.

8 Click the **Margins** tab to make any changes to the page margins.

9 Click the **Paper** tab to control paper size and source.

10 Click the **Layout** tab to make changes to how sections, headers, and footers are printed.

11 Click **OK**.

12 Click the **Print** button to print the document.

End

TIP

More Print Options   The Display tab in the Word Options dialog box offers settings for page display as well as printing options, such as printing hidden text and drawings. Click the **File** tab and click **Options** to open the box. ■

PRINTING AN ENVELOPE

You can turn the address data found in a letter into an envelope that you can print out on your printer. Using Word's Envelopes command, you can quickly whip up an envelope, setting both the sender and delivery addresses, and control how the envelope prints out on your printer. Using the Envelope Options dialog box, you can also change the font, envelope size, and position of the addresses on the envelope, such as moving an address to make way for a pre-printed logo on the envelope.

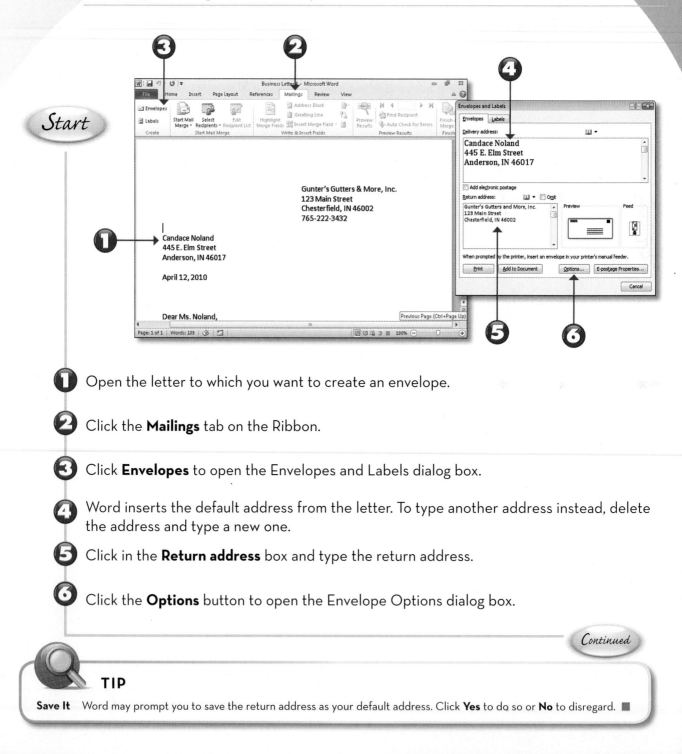

1. Open the letter to which you want to create an envelope.

2. Click the **Mailings** tab on the Ribbon.

3. Click **Envelopes** to open the Envelopes and Labels dialog box.

4. Word inserts the default address from the letter. To type another address instead, delete the address and type a new one.

5. Click in the **Return address** box and type the return address.

6. Click the **Options** button to open the Envelope Options dialog box.

Continued

TIP

Save It Word may prompt you to save the return address as your default address. Click **Yes** to do so or **No** to disregard. ■

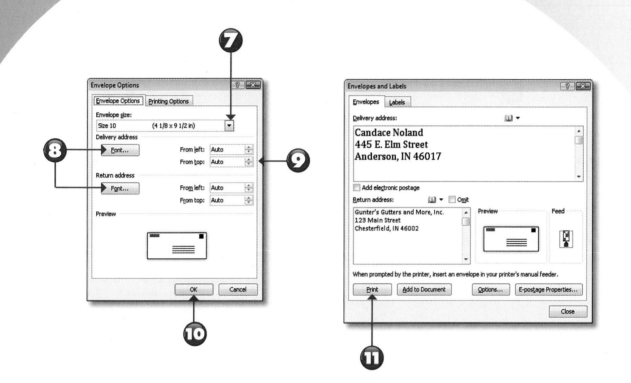

7 To change the envelope size, click here and choose a different size.

8 To change the font for the delivery or return address, click the appropriate **Font** button and choose another.

9 To change the positioning of an address, click here and set new values.

10 Click **OK**.

11 Click **Print** and insert a blank envelope into your printer.

End

TIP

Finding Addresses If you have the recipient's address or your own return address stored in your Outlook Address Book, you can click the **Address Book** icon in the Envelopes and Labels dialog box to access your contacts. Click the button to open the Select Name dialog box, and then click the name you want to use. Click **OK** to add it to the envelope's address field. ■

PRINTING LABELS

Like the previous envelopes task, Word also offers a tool for printing labels.

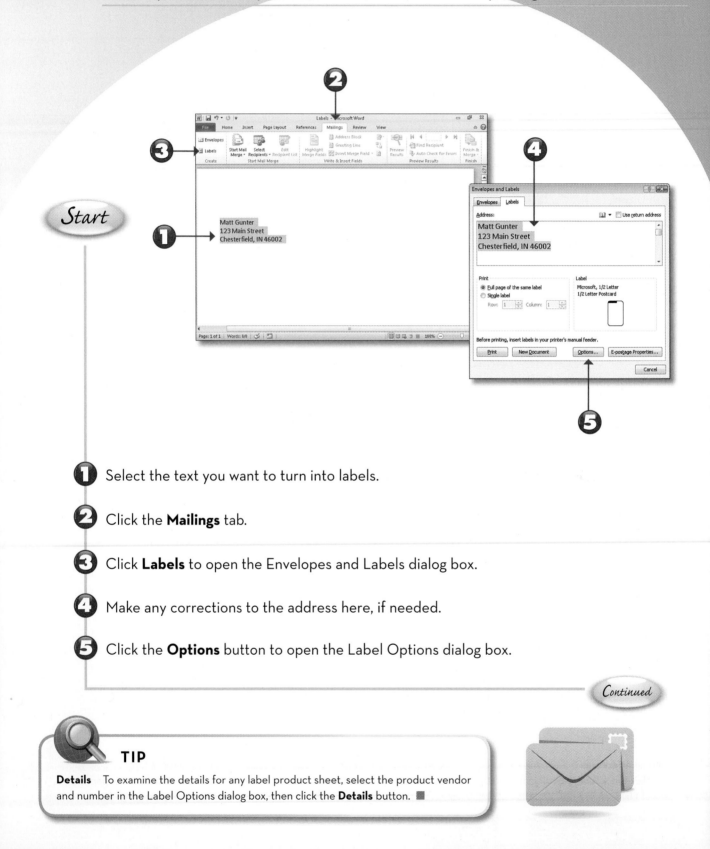

1 Select the text you want to turn into labels.

2 Click the **Mailings** tab.

3 Click **Labels** to open the Envelopes and Labels dialog box.

4 Make any corrections to the address here, if needed.

5 Click the **Options** button to open the Label Options dialog box.

Continued

TIP

Details To examine the details for any label product sheet, select the product vendor and number in the Label Options dialog box, then click the **Details** button. ■

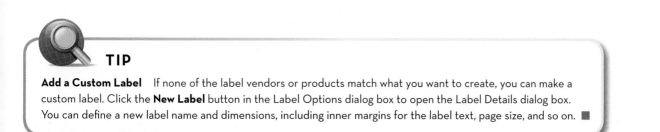

6 Choose a label vendor from the drop-down list.

7 Choose the label sheet's product number from the list.

8 Click **OK**.

9 Insert the label sheets into your printer and click **Print** to print the labels.

End

TIP

Add a Custom Label If none of the label vendors or products match what you want to create, you can make a custom label. Click the **New Label** button in the Label Options dialog box to open the Label Details dialog box. You can define a new label name and dimensions, including inner margins for the label text, page size, and so on. ■

USING WORD'S MAIL MERGE TOOL

You can use Word's Mail Merge tool to create mass mailings, such as form letters or mass e-mails. The easiest way to create mass mailings is to use the Step-by-Step Mail Merge Wizard. It walks you through each phase of the process. You can type up a letter before you get started, or you can stop and do so when prompted by the wizard. You can also choose to insert contacts and addresses from an existing table, from your Outlook contacts, or start a brand new list. For this task, the form letter is already created and contacts are added from the Outlook address book. If you choose different options, your steps may vary slightly.

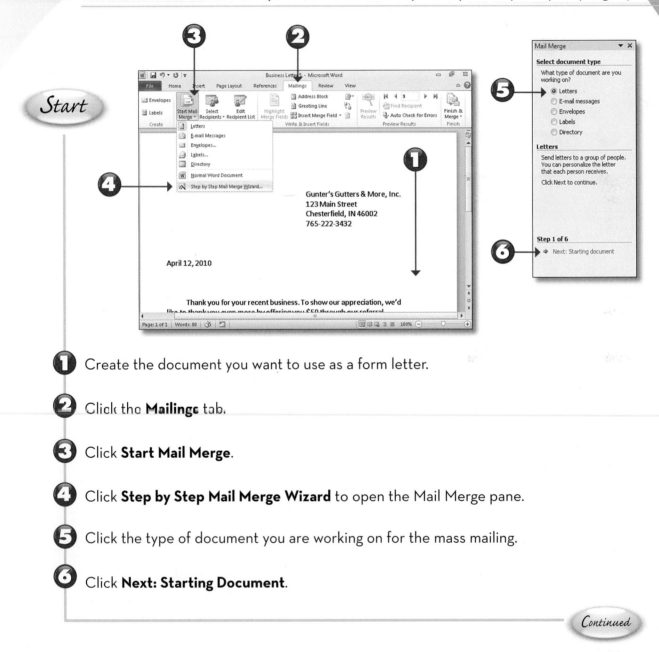

1 Create the document you want to use as a form letter.

2 Click the **Mailings** tab.

3 Click **Start Mail Merge**.

4 Click **Step by Step Mail Merge Wizard** to open the Mail Merge pane.

5 Click the type of document you are working on for the mass mailing.

6 Click **Next: Starting Document**.

Continued

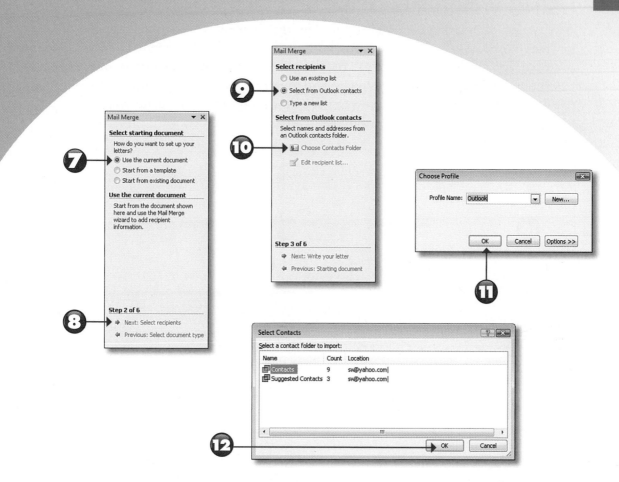

7 Unless you want to use another file as the form letter, leave the **Use the current document** radio button selected.

8 Click **Next: Select Recipients**.

9 Choose which type of recipients you want to use. In this example, **Select from Outlook contacts** is selected.

10 Click **Choose Contacts Folder**.

11 In the Choose Profile dialog box that appears, click **OK**.

12 The Select Contacts dialog box appears; select a contact folder and click **OK**.

Continued

TIP

Use a Template? To use one of Word's form letter templates, click **Start from Template** in Step 2 of the Mail Merge Wizard. ■

USING WORD'S MAIL MERGE TOOL CONTINUED

A large part of creating personalized mail merge documents is designating merge fields in which Word inserts data from your contacts list into the document. In a form letter, for example, you can insert an Address Block field for the contact's address, and a Greeting Line field that takes the person's name and inserts it into the letter's opening salutations. At the end of the Wizard process, you can preview a sample of what the merged document will look like, and then print your finished form letters when ready.

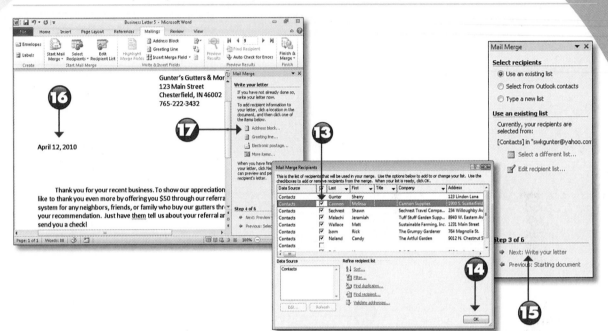

13 Word opens the Mail Merge Recipients dialog box. Check which recipients you want to use for your mass mailing.

14 Click **OK**.

15 Click **Next: Write your letter**.

16 The next part of the process is to identify fields where information from the contacts listed can be inserted into the document. Click where you want to insert a field into the document.

17 Click the type of field you want to insert.

Continued

TIP

What Are Merge Fields? A *merge field* is preset information for automating parts of a document. Merge fields act like placeholders for information that is inserted later. ■

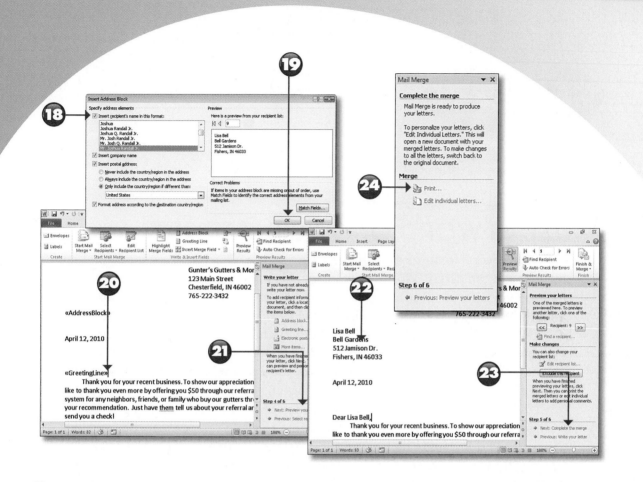

18 A dialog box opens for you to preview what the inserted information from the contacts list will look like and make any changes you deem necessary. In the address block, for example, choose how you want the name and address to be displayed.

19 Click **OK**.

20 Continue adding more fields to the form letter as needed.

21 Click **Next: Preview your letters**.

22 Word generates a preview of the form letter, filling in the fields with information from your contacts list.

23 Click **Next: Complete the merge**.

24 Click **Print** to print out the letters.

End

Chapter 11

USING WORD ON THE INTERNET

There are several features available to help you use Word with the Internet. For starters, you can access Word's online Help files anytime you need help with the program (see Chapter 1, "Getting Started with Word," to learn more about using the Help feature). You can also e-mail a document as a file attachment, a link, a PDF or XPS file, or Internet Fax (with the help of a fax service provider, available for a fee). In this chapter, you learn how to e-mail a document as a file attachment, one of the most common tasks you can perform using an Internet connection and Microsoft Word. In this chapter, you'll also learn how to turn a Word document into a Web page that you can share with anyone using a Web browser, or post onto a Web server for others to view. You can insert hyperlinks in your Word documents that, when clicked, take the reader to a specific Web page. Lastly, you will learn how to upload a Word document to Microsoft's new SkyDrive site. With a Windows Live ID, you can store documents on the site that you can, in turn, access from any computer with an Internet connection.

Backstage view is the place to go to find Internet-related features in Word, such as e-mailing a document.

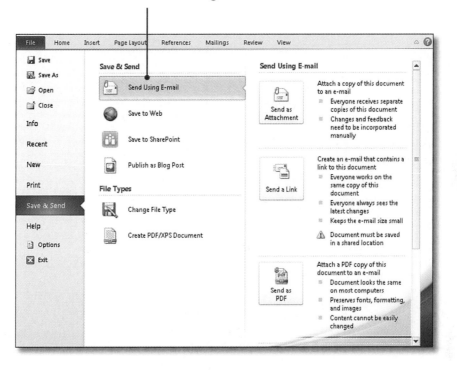

E-MAILING A DOCUMENT

You can e-mail your Word documents to other users. For example, you may want to share a sales report with a colleague. You can send the document as a file attachment and send it using your default e-mail client. The steps in this task show Microsoft Office as the e-mail client. Your own steps may differ if you use a different e-mail program.

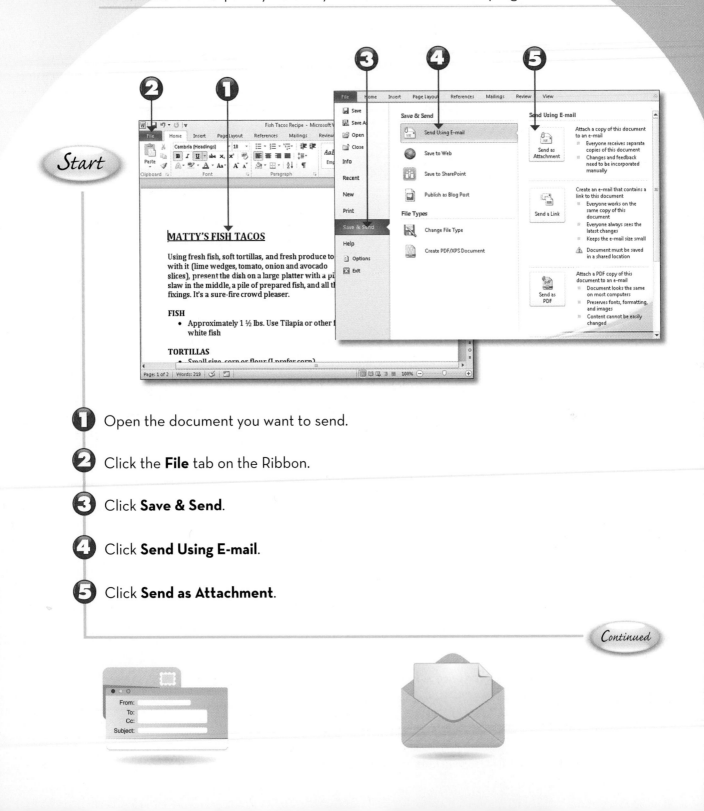

1 Open the document you want to send.

2 Click the **File** tab on the Ribbon.

3 Click **Save & Send**.

4 Click **Send Using E-mail**.

5 Click **Send as Attachment**.

Continued

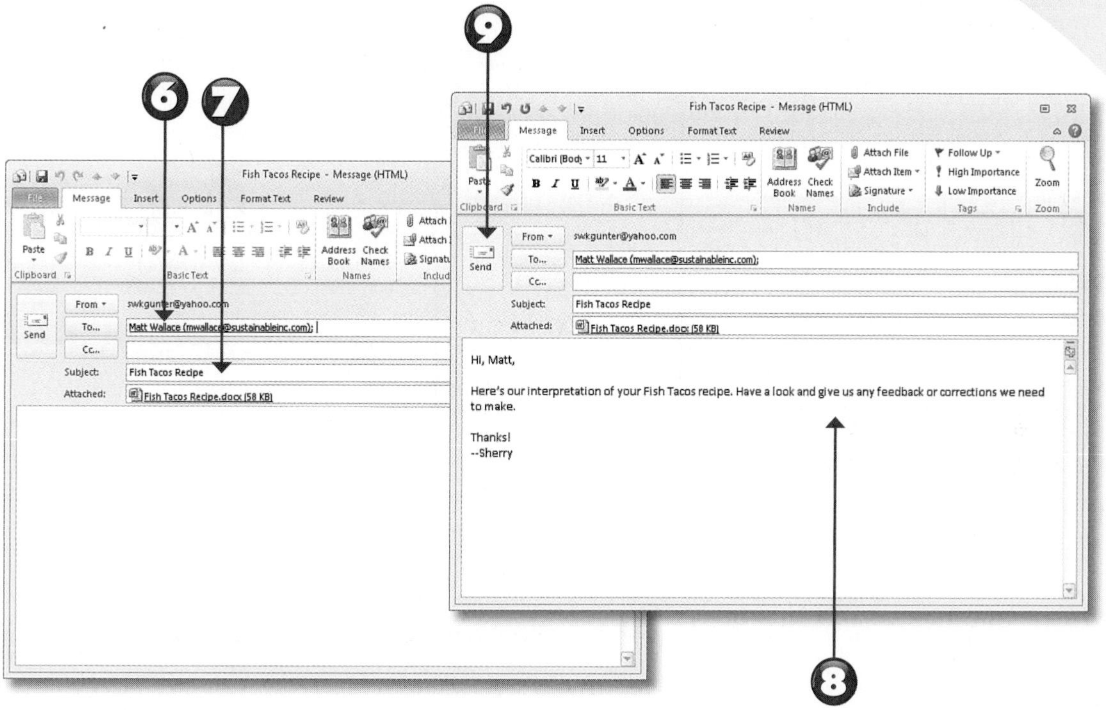

6 Your default e-mail client (in this case, Microsoft Outlook) opens a new message window with the file already attached. Type in the e-mail address (or addresses) you want to send to.

7 Word also inserts the filename as the subject for the message. Type a new subject heading for the message, if needed.

8 Type the message body.

9 Click **Send**.

End

TIP

Change the File Type You can also choose to send the document as a PDF or XPS file, or even as an Internet Fax. Just click one of the other Send Using E-mail options in Backstage view. ■

TURNING A DOCUMENT INTO A WEB PAGE

You can save a Word document as a Web page. Turning your work into HTML format means anyone with a Web browser can view the file. This is a handy technique if the person you're sharing a file with doesn't have Microsoft Word. Just about everybody has a Web browser installed, and with such a program they can view HTML files. You can also upload the Web page to a server to share with Internet users.

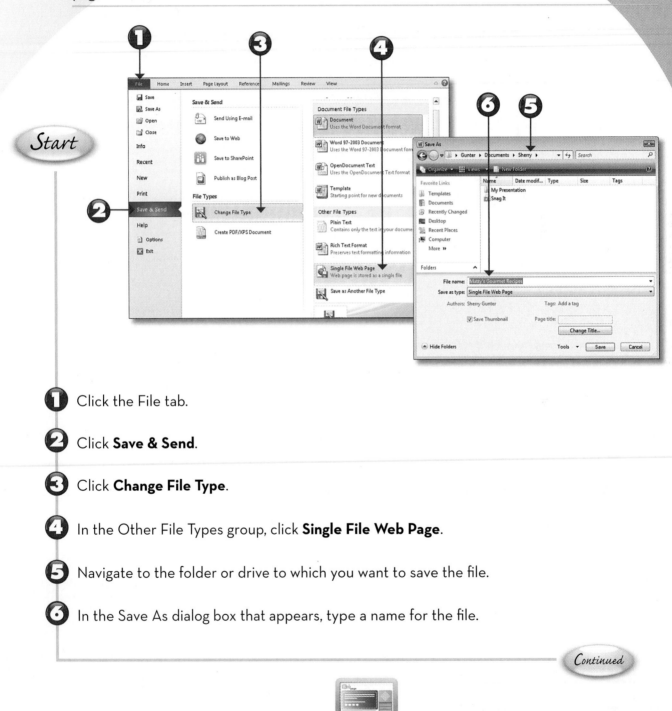

Start

1 Click the File tab.

2 Click **Save & Send**.

3 Click **Change File Type**.

4 In the Other File Types group, click **Single File Web Page**.

5 Navigate to the folder or drive to which you want to save the file.

6 In the Save As dialog box that appears, type a name for the file.

Continued

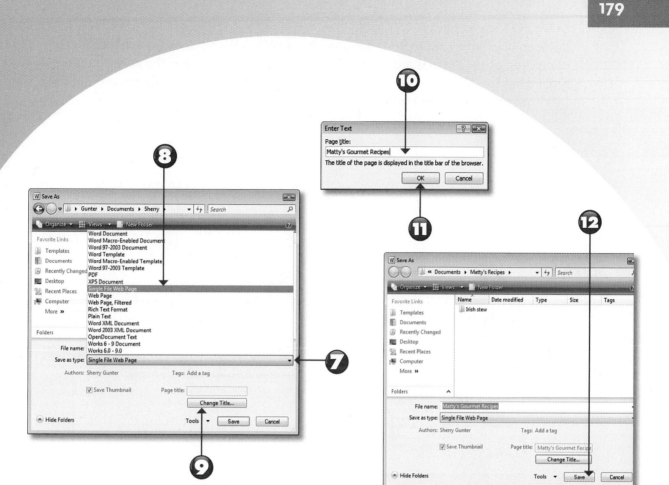

7 Click the **Save as type** drop-down arrow.

8 Click the type of Web page you want to create: **Single File Web Page**, **Web Page**, or **Web Page, Filtered**.

9 Click the **Change Title** button.

10 Type a title to appear in the browser window's title bar.

11 Click **OK**.

12 Click **Save**.

End

ADDING A HYPERLINK

You can use hyperlinks in your documents to link to Web pages, to another location on your computer, other Word documents, or even another spot within the same document. If you are linking to a Web page, you'll need to know the page's URL (address on the Web). This task focuses on linking to a Web page.

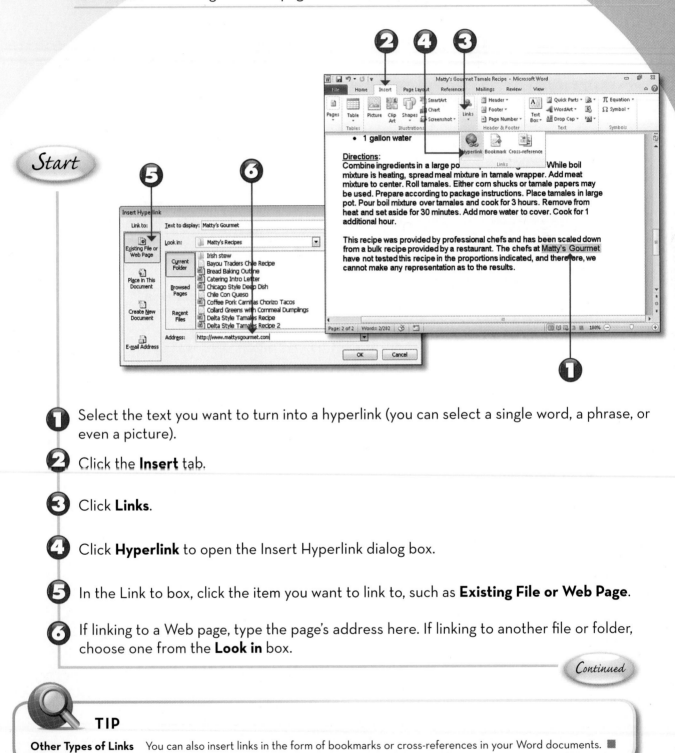

Start

Select the text you want to turn into a hyperlink (you can select a single word, a phrase, or even a picture).

Click the **Insert** tab.

Click **Links**.

Click **Hyperlink** to open the Insert Hyperlink dialog box.

In the Link to box, click the item you want to link to, such as **Existing File or Web Page**.

If linking to a Web page, type the page's address here. If linking to another file or folder, choose one from the **Look in** box.

Continued

TIP

Other Types of Links You can also insert links in the form of bookmarks or cross-references in your Word documents. ■

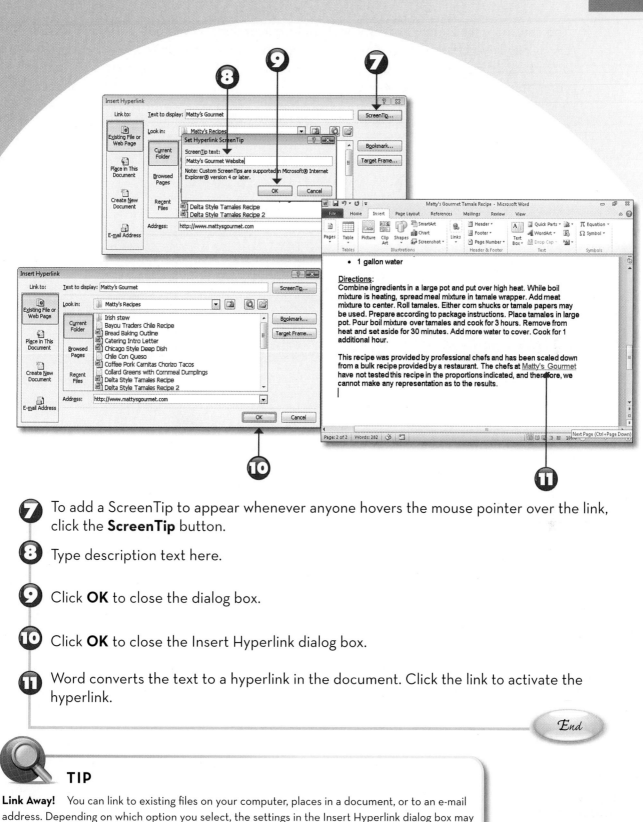

7 To add a ScreenTip to appear whenever anyone hovers the mouse pointer over the link, click the **ScreenTip** button.

8 Type description text here.

9 Click **OK** to close the dialog box.

10 Click **OK** to close the Insert Hyperlink dialog box.

11 Word converts the text to a hyperlink in the document. Click the link to activate the hyperlink.

End

TIP

Link Away! You can link to existing files on your computer, places in a document, or to an e-mail address. Depending on which option you select, the settings in the Insert Hyperlink dialog box may vary. Just fill out the appropriate fields as needed to create the type of link you want. ■

STORING A DOCUMENT ON SKYDRIVE

You can share files online with a Windows Live account and the new Windows Live Sky-Drive. SkyDrive offers you free server storage space you can use to store Word documents, pictures, and more. Once you've placed a document online, you can access it from any computer using an Internet connection. You must sign up for a Windows Live account in order to access the SkyDrive feature from Microsoft. To do so, visit the www.home.live.com website and follow the links for signing up for a Windows Live ID.

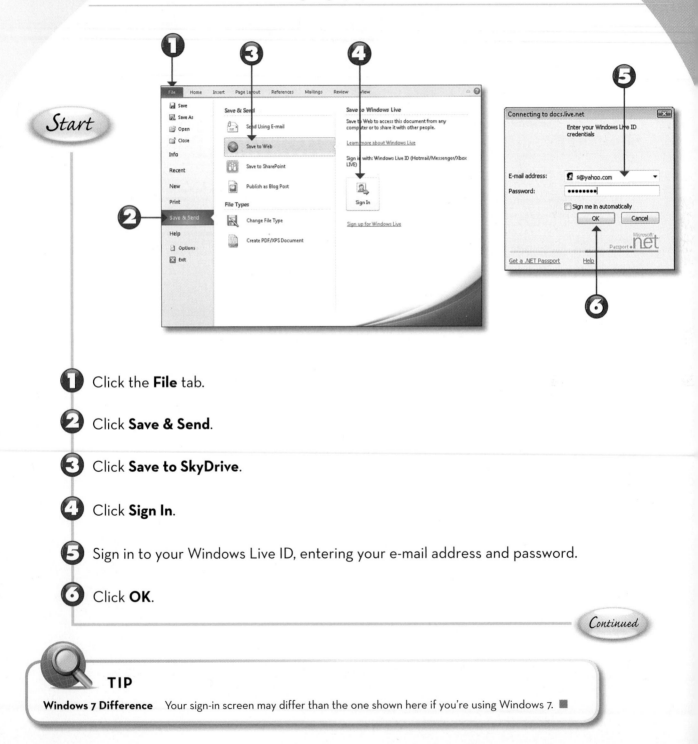

1. Click the **File** tab.

2. Click **Save & Send**.

3. Click **Save to SkyDrive**.

4. Click **Sign In**.

5. Sign in to your Windows Live ID, entering your e-mail address and password.

6. Click **OK**.

Continued

TIP

Windows 7 Difference   Your sign-in screen may differ than the one shown here if you're using Windows 7. ■

7 Click the folder you want to save to, such as the My Documents folder.

8 Click **Save As**.

9 Type a name for the file or use the default filename.

10 Click **Save**.

11 To view your files on SkyDrive, use your Web browser to navigate to **http://skydrive.live. com** and click the **My Documents** folder or the folder in which you stored the file.

End

TIP

Finding SkyDrive   You can type the SkyDrive URL directly into a browser window (http://skydrive.live.com) to navigate to the site, or you can use the link found in the File tab. Click the **File** tab, click **Share**, click **Save to SkyDrive**, then click the **Go to SkyDrive** link and sign in. ■

USING WORD'S GRAPHIC TOOLS

Graphic elements are an important part of creating documents that make an impact and convey your message. Graphic elements are also an important part of giving your documents visual interest and extra polish. Graphic elements can include clip art, digital pictures, drawn shapes and charts, text effects, text boxes, and more. For terminology's sake, we'll just categorize these elements as graphic objects since they can be inserted, moved around, and resized on the document page.

The Insert tab on the Ribbon offers all kinds of graphic objects you can insert into your Word documents.

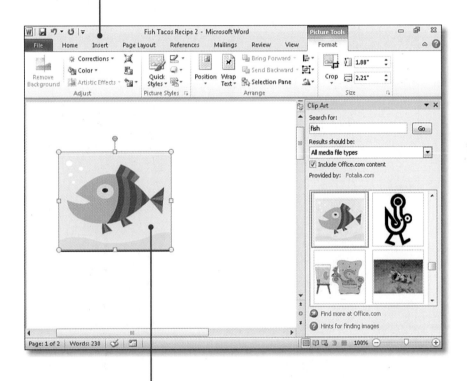

An easy way to illustrate your documents is to use clip art. You can choose from a wide variety of clip art that installs with Word and is also available through the Office.com website.

DRAWING WITH AUTOSHAPES

Word 2010 installs with a large set of pre-drawn shapes, called AutoShapes. For example, you can use AutoShapes to create logos and simple drawings. You can draw basic shapes, such as circles and squares, or more elaborate shapes, such as a starburst or callout balloon. You can also use AutoShapes to draw lines and arrows. Once you draw a shape, you can add a fill color, change the border, and apply special styles, shadow, and 3D effects. The Format tab appears offering all kinds of formatting tools for the shape.

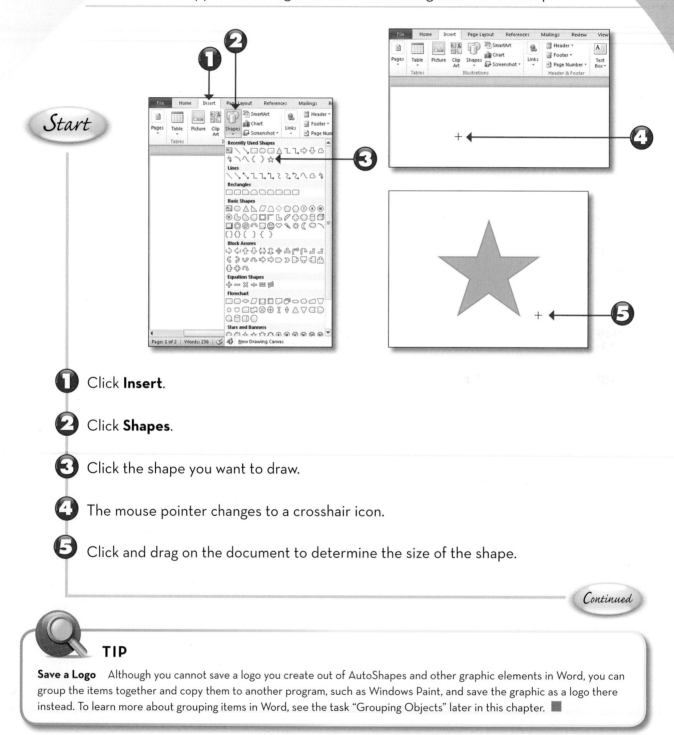

1 Click **Insert**.

2 Click **Shapes**.

3 Click the shape you want to draw.

4 The mouse pointer changes to a crosshair icon.

5 Click and drag on the document to determine the size of the shape.

Continued

TIP

Save a Logo   Although you cannot save a logo you create out of AutoShapes and other graphic elements in Word, you can group the items together and copy them to another program, such as Windows Paint, and save the graphic as a logo there instead. To learn more about grouping items in Word, see the task "Grouping Objects" later in this chapter. ■

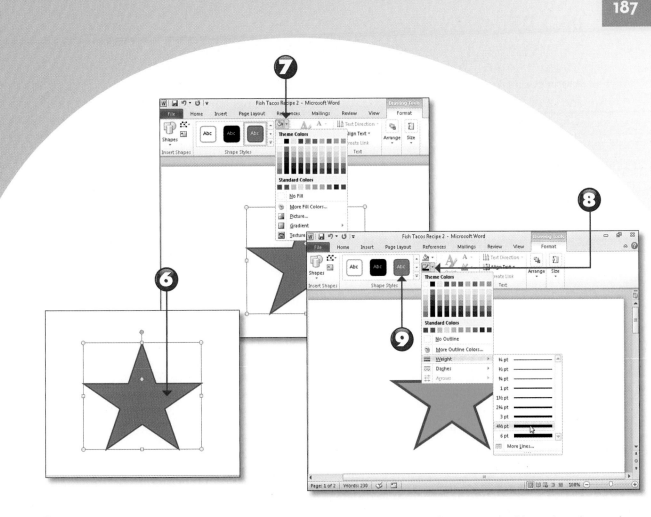

6 Release the mouse button and the shape is completed and surrounded by a border with selection handles.

7 To add a fill color to the shape, click here and choose a color.

8 To change the border, click here and choose a color or line weight.

9 To add an instant style including a fill color and border, click a shape style.

End

TIP

Building Logos   You can build your own logo by layering shapes, WordArt objects, or text boxes. To learn more about WordArt, see the task "Inserting a WordArt Object" later in this chapter. To learn more about text boxes, see "Inserting a Text Box Object." To learn about ordering graphic objects, see the task "Layering Objects." ■

TIP

Formatting Options   You can also find formatting for your shapes in the Format Shape dialog box. Right-click the shape on the document, then click **Format Shape** to open the dialog box. ■

INSERTING CLIP ART

If drawing your own artwork doesn't sound appealing, then add some clip art instead. Clip art is pre-drawn artwork you can insert into your documents and manipulate or format as you like. Clip art comes in a variety of categories and styles, and includes drawings, photos, and even sound or animation clips. You can sort through the available artwork using the Clip Art task pane. You can also include the Office.com website as part of your search for clip art that meets your document needs.

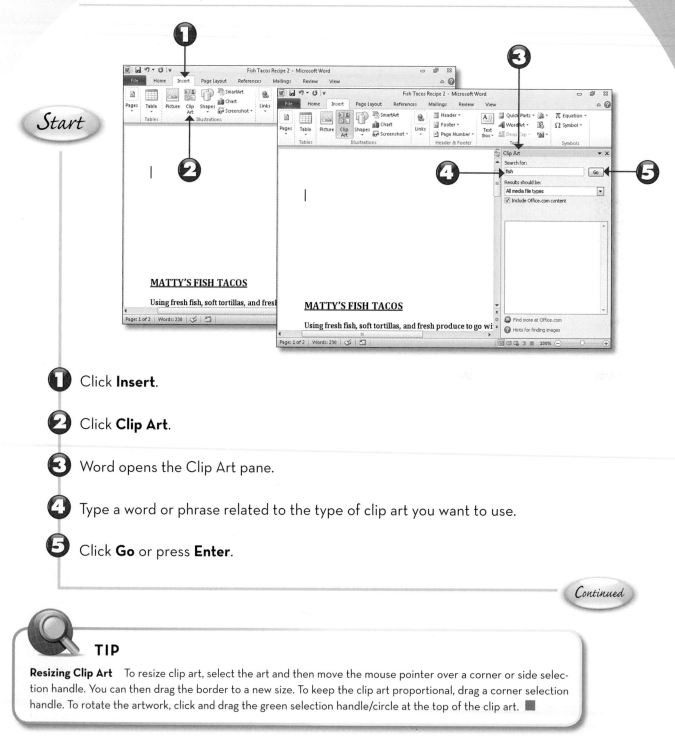

Start

1 Click **Insert**.

2 Click **Clip Art**.

3 Word opens the Clip Art pane.

4 Type a word or phrase related to the type of clip art you want to use.

5 Click **Go** or press **Enter**.

Continued

TIP

Resizing Clip Art   To resize clip art, select the art and then move the mouse pointer over a corner or side selection handle. You can then drag the border to a new size. To keep the clip art proportional, drag a corner selection handle. To rotate the artwork, click and drag the green selection handle/circle at the top of the clip art. ■

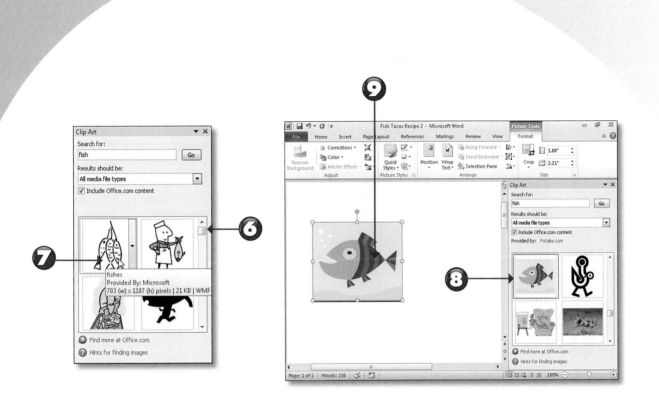

6 The Clip Art pane displays any matching results. You can scroll through the list to view the clip art.

7 To learn more about a particular piece of clip art, simply move the mouse pointer over the artwork to reveal a brief description about the dimensions and file type.

8 When you find clip art you want to use, click it.

9 Word immediately inserts it into the document. You can move or resize the clip art to suit your document needs.

End

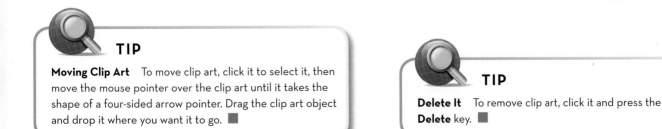

TIP

Moving Clip Art To move clip art, click it to select it, then move the mouse pointer over the clip art until it takes the shape of a four-sided arrow pointer. Drag the clip art object and drop it where you want it to go. ■

TIP

Delete It To remove clip art, click it and press the **Delete** key. ■

ORGANIZING CLIP ART WITH THE CLIP ORGANIZER

You can access clip art libraries stored on your computer in addition to the clip art that comes with Word 2010. The Microsoft Clip Organizer is the place to go to organize and view clip art on your computer. You can use the feature to search for clip art, add and organize clip art, and remove clip art you no longer want.

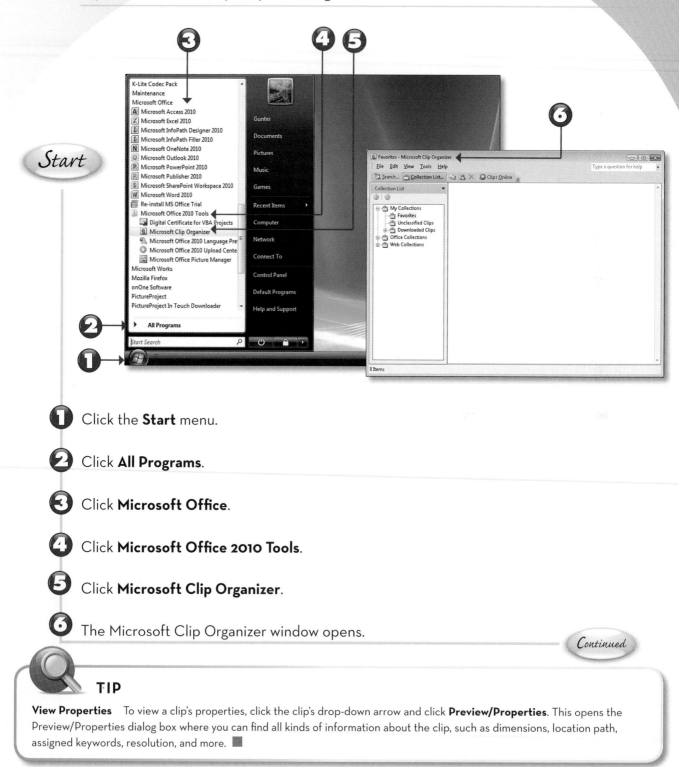

1 Click the **Start** menu.

2 Click **All Programs**.

3 Click **Microsoft Office**.

4 Click **Microsoft Office 2010 Tools**.

5 Click **Microsoft Clip Organizer**.

6 The Microsoft Clip Organizer window opens.

Continued

TIP

View Properties   To view a clip's properties, click the clip's drop-down arrow and click **Preview/Properties**. This opens the Preview/Properties dialog box where you can find all kinds of information about the clip, such as dimensions, location path, assigned keywords, resolution, and more. ■

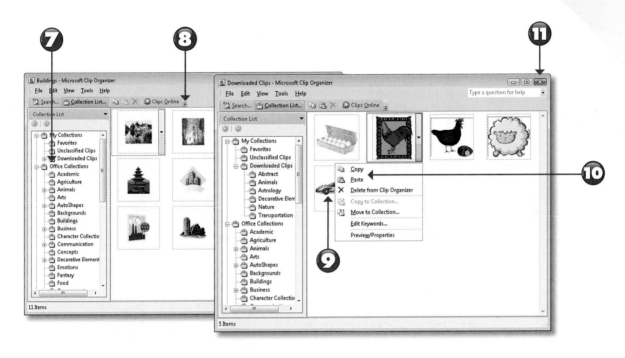

7 The Clip Organizer lists your clip art collections here. You can click a collection folder to expand or collapse the folder view.

8 You can use the toolbar to perform a search; view the collection as a list; copy, paste, and delete clip art; and search for clip art online.

9 To perform an action on a piece of clip art, move the mouse pointer over the artwork and click the drop-down arrow that appears.

10 Choose an action.

11 To close the window, click here.

End

TIP

Searching for Clips To search for a particular piece of artwork, click the **Search** button in the Organizer window's toolbar to open the Search pane. Next, type the keyword you want to search for and press **Enter** or click the **Go** button. Microsoft Clip Organizer lists any matches. ■

FINDING CLIP ART ONLINE

You can also visit the Microsoft Office website and look for more clip art to add to your clip art collections. When you find clip art online, you can download it into the Clip Organizer and use it in your Word documents as well as other Office 2010 programs.

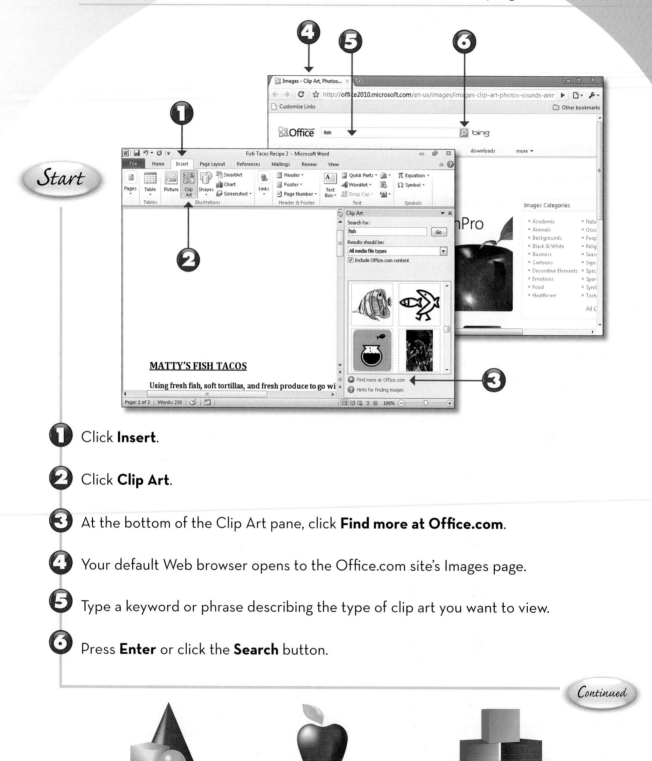

Start

1 Click **Insert**.

2 Click **Clip Art**.

3 At the bottom of the Clip Art pane, click **Find more at Office.com**.

4 Your default Web browser opens to the Office.com site's Images page.

5 Type a keyword or phrase describing the type of clip art you want to view.

6 Press **Enter** or click the **Search** button.

Continued

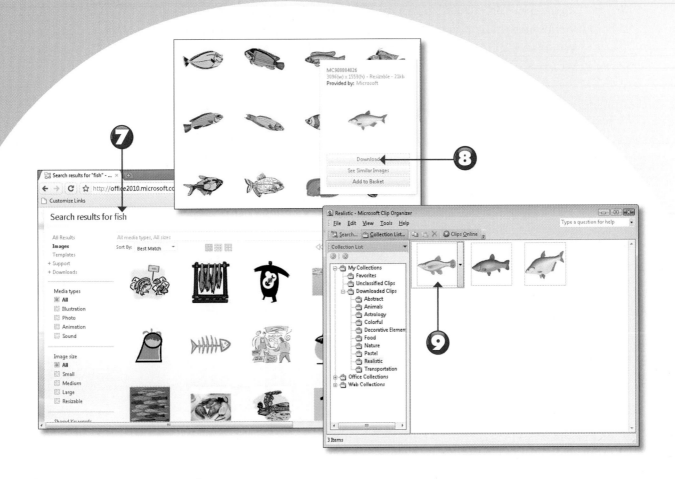

7 The Search Results page displays any matches.

8 Move the mouse pointer over the clip art you want to download and click **Download**.

9 The artwork is downloaded and added to the Microsoft Clip Organizer window's Downloaded Clips folder.

End

TIP

Office.com Anytime you want to visit the Office website and view clip art, simply type in **www.office.com** to open the Microsoft Office Online site and click the **Clip Art** link. ■

TIP

License Agreement If this is your first time downloading clip art, you may need to agree to the Microsoft License Agreement before downloading. Just follow the onscreen prompts as needed. ■

INSERTING A PICTURE

You can insert digital photographs, or pictures, into your document to illustrate and add visual appeal. You can insert JPEG, GIF, PNG, and other popular image file types. Once you insert a picture, you can apply formatting, move or resize the image, or control how text wraps around the picture.

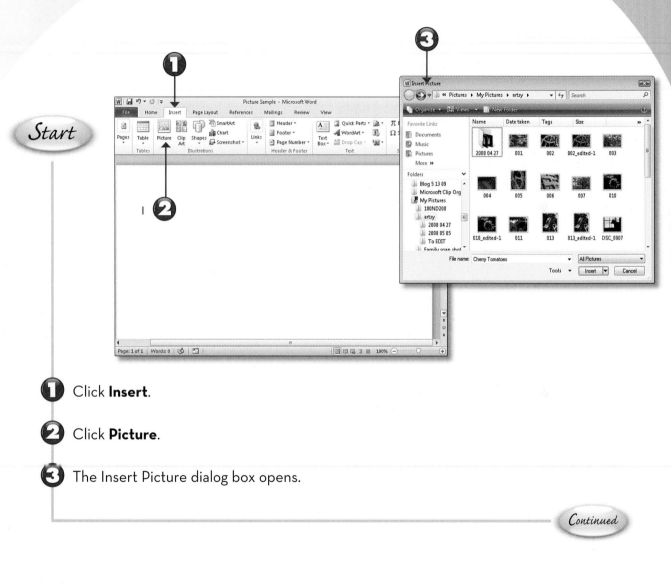

Start

1 Click **Insert**.

2 Click **Picture**.

3 The Insert Picture dialog box opens.

Continued

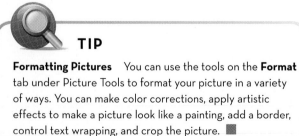

TIP

Formatting Pictures You can use the tools on the **Format** tab under Picture Tools to format your picture in a variety of ways. You can make color corrections, apply artistic effects to make a picture look like a painting, add a border, control text wrapping, and crop the picture. ■

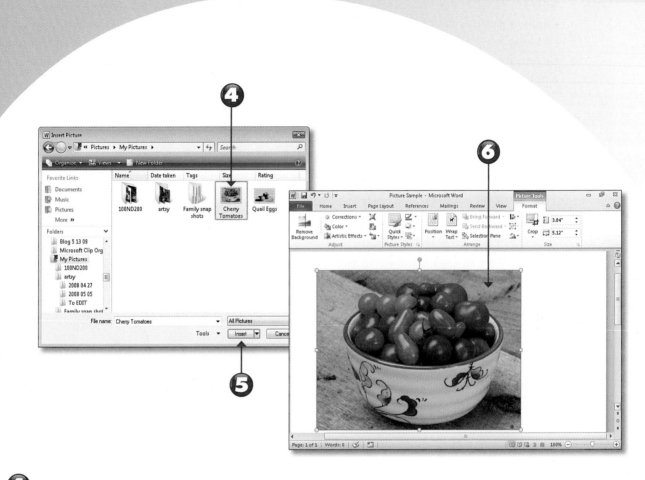

4 Navigate to the file you want to insert and select the file.

5 Click **Insert**.

6 Word inserts the image and displays the Picture Tools on the Ribbon. You can resize or move the image as needed.

End

TIP

Quick Styles You can apply a variety of Quick Styles to your picture to add a border or change the picture shape. Simply click the **Quick Styles** button on the Format tab and choose a style from the gallery that appears. ■

TIP

Delete It To remove a picture from your document, click it and press the **Delete** key. ■

REMOVING AN IMAGE BACKGROUND

New to Word 2010, you can remove the background from a picture using the Background Removal tool. This unique tool acts much like similar tools found in photo-editing programs, allowing you to cut out parts of the background and focus just on the subject of the picture. Depending on the image, you may have to fine-tune the selection process to determine just what parts of the image stay in or are cut out.

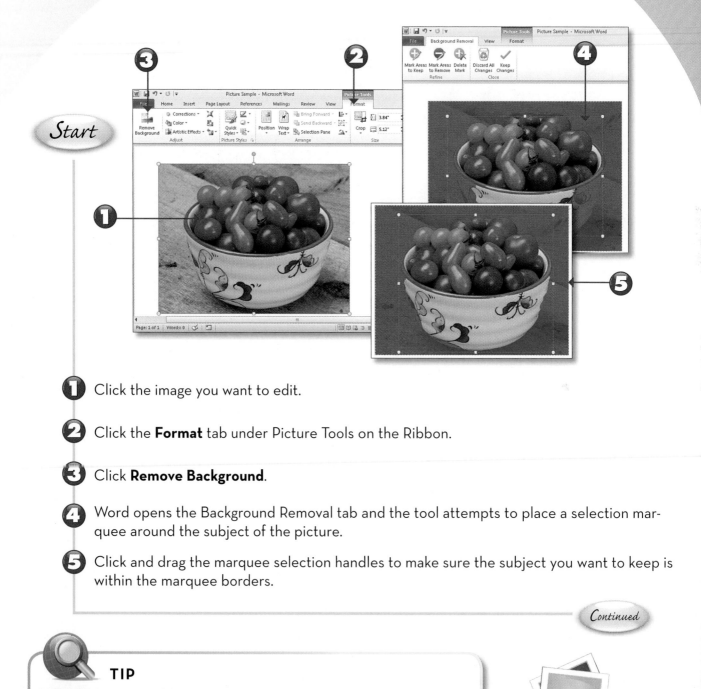

1 Click the image you want to edit.

2 Click the **Format** tab under Picture Tools on the Ribbon.

3 Click **Remove Background**.

4 Word opens the Background Removal tab and the tool attempts to place a selection marquee around the subject of the picture.

5 Click and drag the marquee selection handles to make sure the subject you want to keep is within the marquee borders.

Continued

TIP

More Edits To retouch the image some more, you can revisit the Background Removal tab. Just click the **Remove Background** tool again to view the tab. ■

6 If the Background Removal tool is leaving out an important area, click the **Mark Areas to Keep** button and click the area to keep in the subject.

7 Click additional areas to keep, as needed. To remove an area instead, click the **Mark Areas to Remove** button and click the area.

8 Click the **Keep Changes** button or click anywhere outside the image to view the removal.

9 Word removes the background.

End

TIP

Discard Edits   To return your picture to the way you found it, display the Background Removal tab and click the **Discard All Changes** button. ■

ADDING A PICTURE BORDER

You can add all kinds of borders to pictures you insert into Word. You can choose a border color, line weight, or even use specialty borders with dashes or dots.

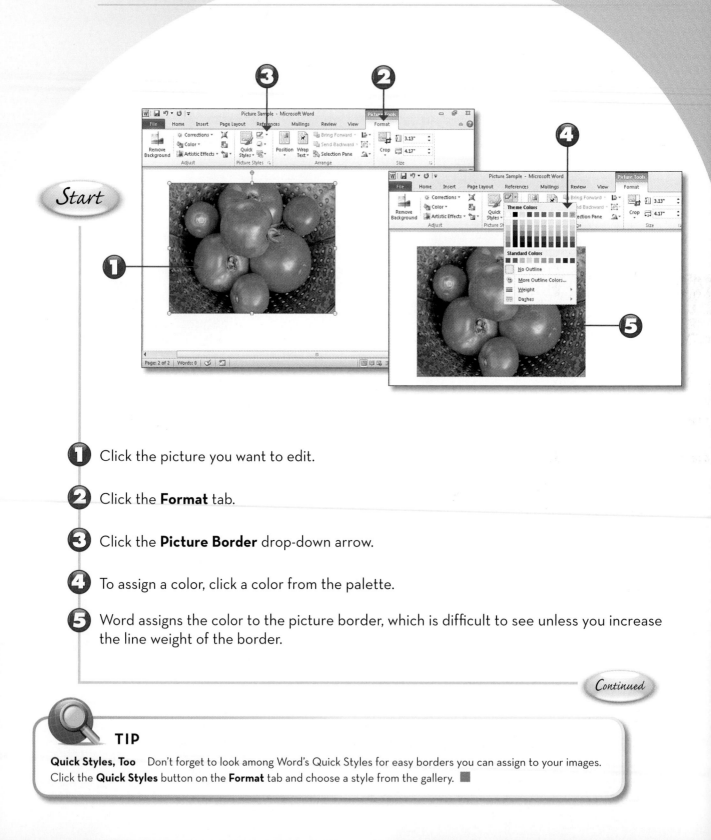

1. Click the picture you want to edit.

2. Click the **Format** tab.

3. Click the **Picture Border** drop-down arrow.

4. To assign a color, click a color from the palette.

5. Word assigns the color to the picture border, which is difficult to see unless you increase the line weight of the border.

Continued

TIP

Quick Styles, Too Don't forget to look among Word's Quick Styles for easy borders you can assign to your images. Click the **Quick Styles** button on the **Format** tab and choose a style from the gallery.

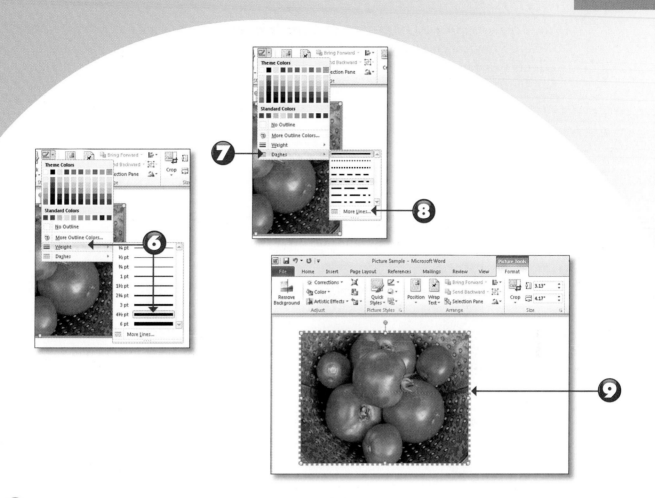

6 To assign a different line thickness, or weight, click **Weight** and click a style.

7 To assign a dash style to the border, click **Dashes** and choose a style.

8 To view additional line options, click the **More Lines** command to open the Format Picture dialog box to the Line Style settings.

9 Word immediately applies any border styles you selected to the picture.

End

TIP

Adding Borders to Other Elements   You can also add borders to other selected graphic objects in Word, including text boxes, WordArt objects, shapes, and clip art. You can find tools for adding borders, or outlines, to graphic elements on the **Format** tab. Click the **Shape Outline** drop-down arrow and choose a border color or line weight. ■

ADDING A PICTURE EFFECT

You can use Word's Picture Effects feature to quickly turn any image into stylized artwork. Picture Effects include shadow effects, 3D effects, bevels, glows, and more. As you view the effects listed in the gallery menu, you can see what each one looks like on your selected image simply by passing the mouse over the listed effect.

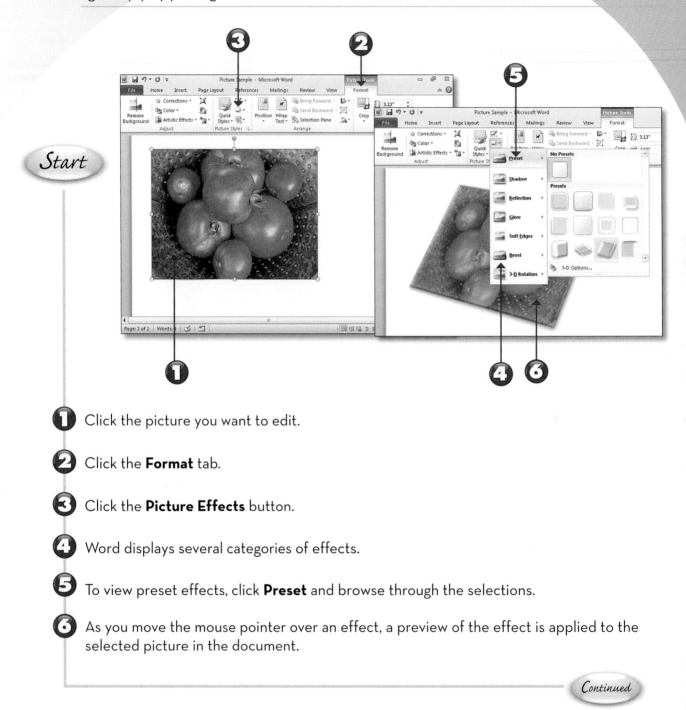

Start

1. Click the picture you want to edit.

2. Click the **Format** tab.

3. Click the **Picture Effects** button.

4. Word displays several categories of effects.

5. To view preset effects, click **Preset** and browse through the selections.

6. As you move the mouse pointer over an effect, a preview of the effect is applied to the selected picture in the document.

Continued

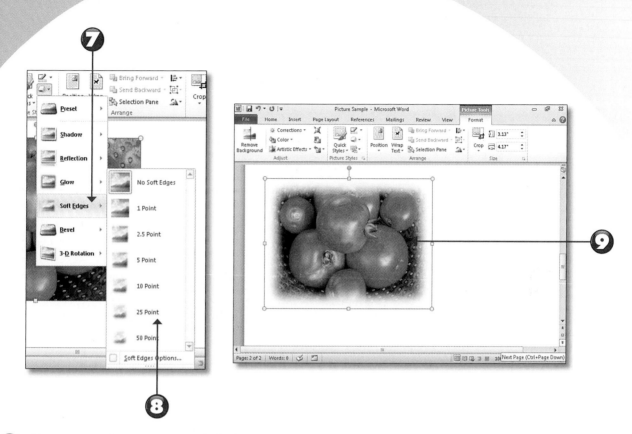

7 To view another category, click the category name to open a submenu of effects. In this example, the Soft Edges effects are listed.

8 To assign an effect, click the picture effect.

9 Word applies the effect to the picture. In this example, a 25 Point Soft Edge effect is applied.

End

TIP

More Options At the bottom of each Picture Effect category, you'll notice an options command, such as **Shadow Options** or **Reflection Options**. You can click this command to open the Format Picture dialog box to the effect's settings. Here you can tweak the effect by making changes to the settings, thus creating new effects tailored to your own making. ■

TIP

No Effect To remove any picture effect you've applied, select the image, click the **Picture Effects** button, click the **Presets** category, then click the **No Presets** effect. ■

CAPTURING A PICTURE OF YOUR SCREEN

Another new feature in Word 2010 is the ability to capture a screenshot, or picture, of your program screen. You can then insert the image into a document, a PowerPoint slide, an Excel spreadsheet, and so on. The screen clipping feature takes a picture of the currently opened program window. If you have several open at the same time, you can choose which one to use. You can also choose to select the portion of the window you want to capture.

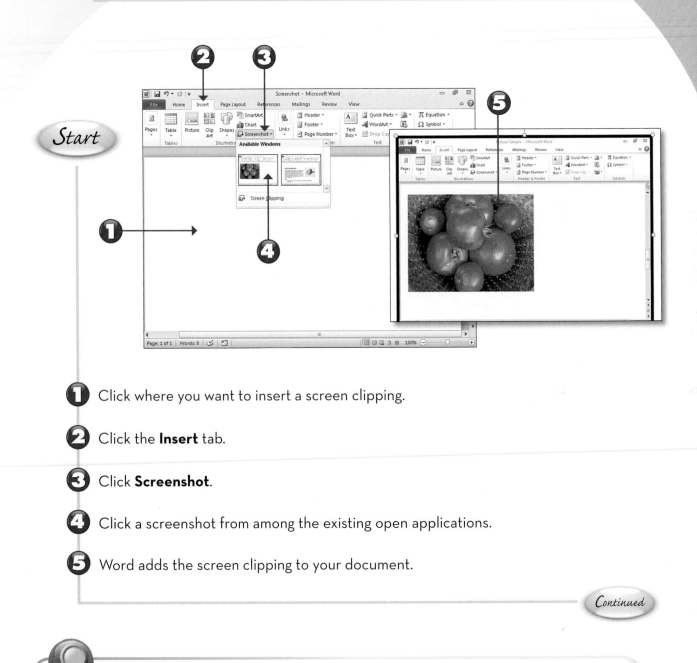

Start

1 Click where you want to insert a screen clipping.

2 Click the **Insert** tab.

3 Click **Screenshot**.

4 Click a screenshot from among the existing open applications.

5 Word adds the screen clipping to your document.

Continued

TIP

Moving and Resizing Once you've added a screen clipping to your document, you can move and resize it just like any other graphic object. The Format tab is available with all the formatting commands you can apply to the image. ■

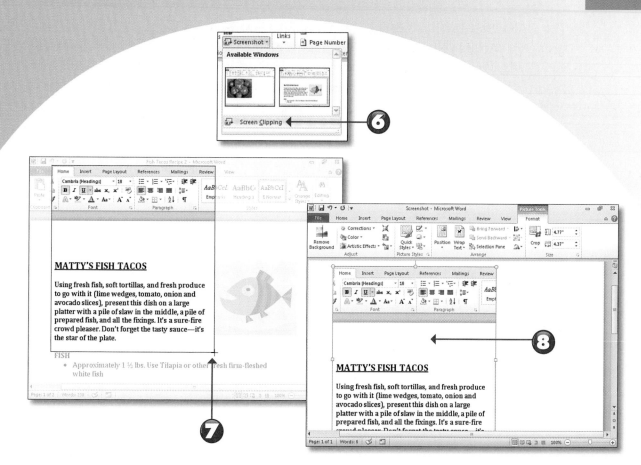

6 To control exactly what part of the screen is captured, click **Screen Clipping** in the **Screenshot** menu.

7 Drag across the portion of the window you want to capture.

8 Release the mouse button and Word adds the clipping to the document.

End

TIP

Clip the Right Window When drawing your own screen clipping, Word automatically displays the program window immediately next to the current program window. For example, if you have three documents open on the Taskbar, named File 1, File 2, and File 3, and File 3 is where you're inserting the clipping, the Screenshot tool assumes you want File 2 as your source. If this is not the case and you want File 1 instead, you'll need to close File 2 so that File 1 is adjacent to File 3 in the Taskbar. ■

INSERTING A WORDART OBJECT

The Office WordArt feature has been around a long time, and in Word 2010, it's better than ever. WordArt lets you turn text into graphic elements in your documents. For example, you can create curved text or shadowed text, or choose from a variety of gradient fill effects.

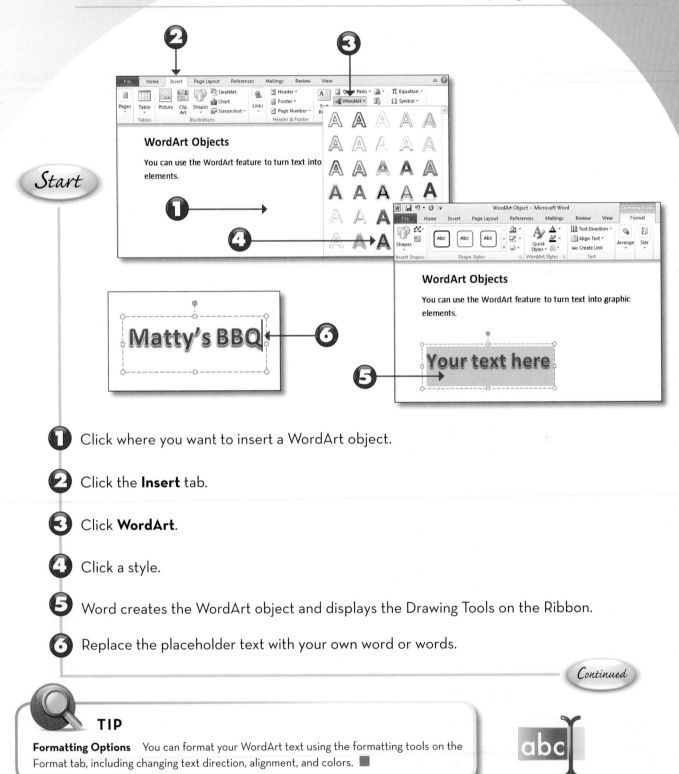

Start

1. Click where you want to insert a WordArt object.

2. Click the **Insert** tab.

3. Click **WordArt**.

4. Click a style.

5. Word creates the WordArt object and displays the Drawing Tools on the Ribbon.

6. Replace the placeholder text with your own word or words.

Continued

TIP

Formatting Options You can format your WordArt text using the formatting tools on the Format tab, including changing text direction, alignment, and colors. ▪

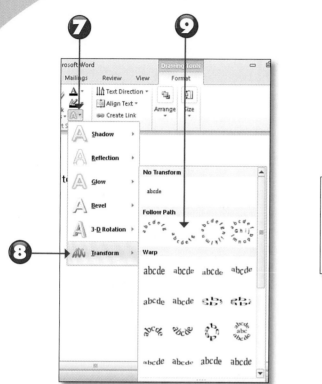

7 To change the WordArt object's effect, click the **Text Effects** button.

8 Click an effect category.

9 Click an effect.

10 Word applies it to the WordArt. In this example, an Arch Up effect is applied to the text.

End

TIP

Format Text Effects Dialog Box   You can change how your WordArt text is aligned in its text box by opening the Format Text Effects dialog box to the Text Box tab. Simply click the **Format Text Effects** icon in the corner of the WordArt Styles group on the Format tab. This opens the dialog box where you can change alignment, text direction, and set internal margins inside the text box. ■

INSERTING A TEXT BOX OBJECT

You can insert text boxes into your documents any time you want to set aside text in its own box, such as a quote or sidebar text. Text boxes act like other graphic objects, and can be moved around the document, resized, and formatted with borders, fill colors, and more. You can choose from a gallery of preset text boxes or you can draw your own.

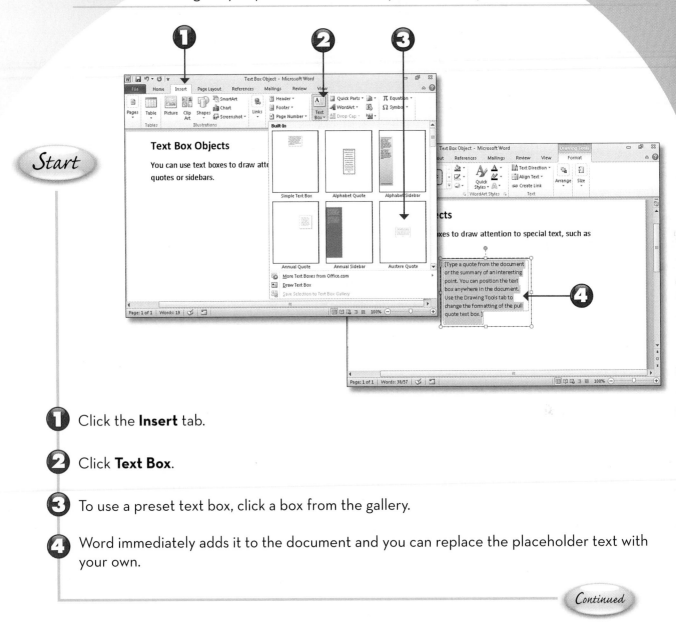

Start

1. Click the **Insert** tab.

2. Click **Text Box**.

3. To use a preset text box, click a box from the gallery.

4. Word immediately adds it to the document and you can replace the placeholder text with your own.

Continued

TIP

Format It   You can format the text inside a text box just like you format document text. Additionally, you can also apply formatting as you would to a graphic object, such as adding a color border, fill color, or applying shape styles. ■

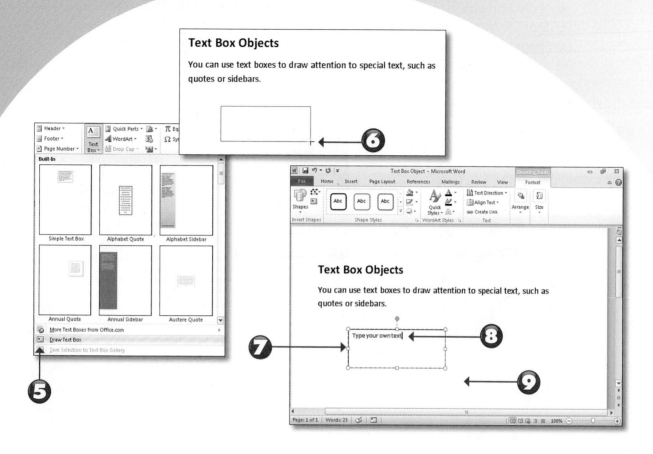

Text Box Objects

You can use text boxes to draw attention to special text, such as quotes or sidebars.

5 To draw your own custom text box, click the **Draw Text Box** command on the Text Box vmenu.

6 Click and drag in the document where you want the text box to go.

7 Release the mouse button and the box is created.

8 Type your text inside the box.

9 Click outside the box to unselect it.

End

TIP

Text Wrap Use Word's text wrapping feature to wrap text around a text box object. Select the text box, then click the Arrange button and click Wrap Text and choose a text wrapping option, such as Tight or Square. ■

MOVING AND RESIZING OBJECTS

You can quickly move and resize graphic objects you place in your Word documents. When you select an object, such as clip art or a picture, it's surrounded by selection handles, tiny squares at each corner and sometimes along the sides of the object. You can use the selection handles to resize an object.

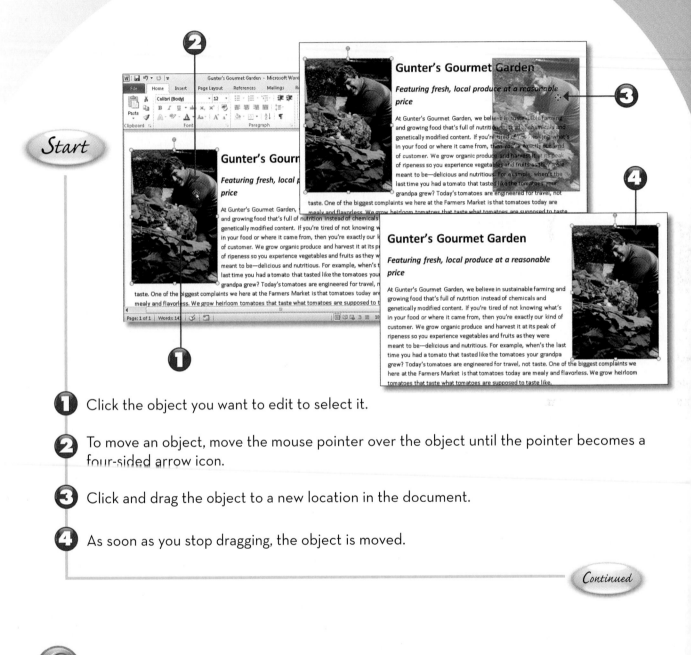

Start

1 Click the object you want to edit to select it.

2 To move an object, move the mouse pointer over the object until the pointer becomes a four-sided arrow icon.

3 Click and drag the object to a new location in the document.

4 As soon as you stop dragging, the object is moved.

Continued

TIP

Keeping Proportions To keep the original proportions, drag a corner selection handle instead of a edge handle. ■

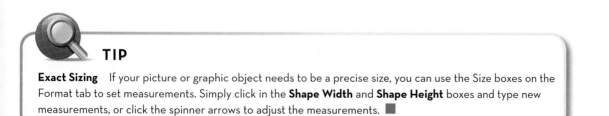

5 To resize an object, move the mouse pointer over a selection handle until the pointer becomes a two-sided arrow icon.

6 Click and drag the handle to resize the object.

7 As soon as you release the mouse button, the object is resized.

End

TIP

Exact Sizing If your picture or graphic object needs to be a precise size, you can use the Size boxes on the Format tab to set measurements. Simply click in the **Shape Width** and **Shape Height** boxes and type new measurements, or click the spinner arrows to adjust the measurements. ◼

ROTATING AND FLIPPING OBJECTS

You can rotate or flip objects to change their appearance or position in the document. You can use the selection handles to flip an object vertically or horizontally, and you can use the rotation handle to rotate an object.

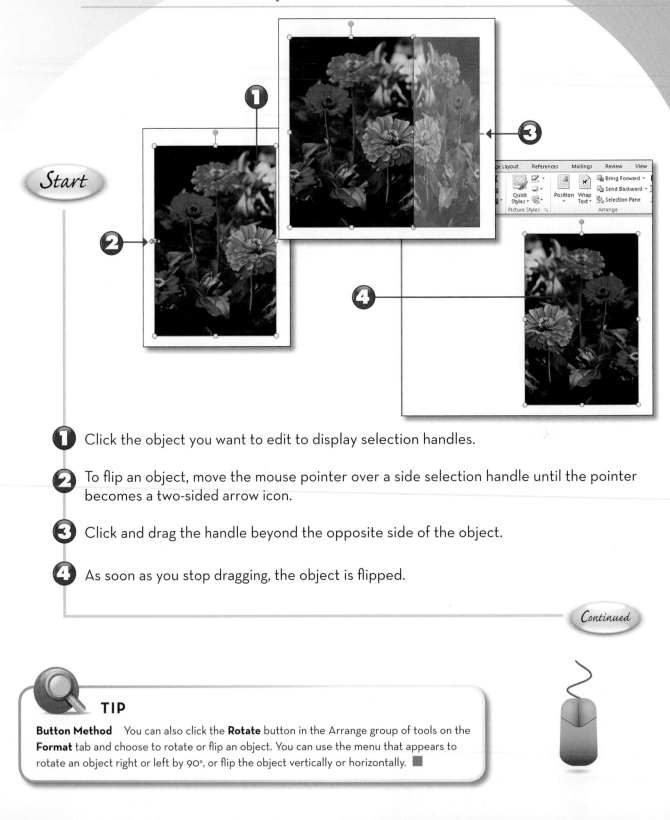

1 Click the object you want to edit to display selection handles.

2 To flip an object, move the mouse pointer over a side selection handle until the pointer becomes a two-sided arrow icon.

3 Click and drag the handle beyond the opposite side of the object.

4 As soon as you stop dragging, the object is flipped.

Continued

TIP

Button Method   You can also click the **Rotate** button in the Arrange group of tools on the **Format** tab and choose to rotate or flip an object. You can use the menu that appears to rotate an object right or left by 90°, or flip the object vertically or horizontally. ■

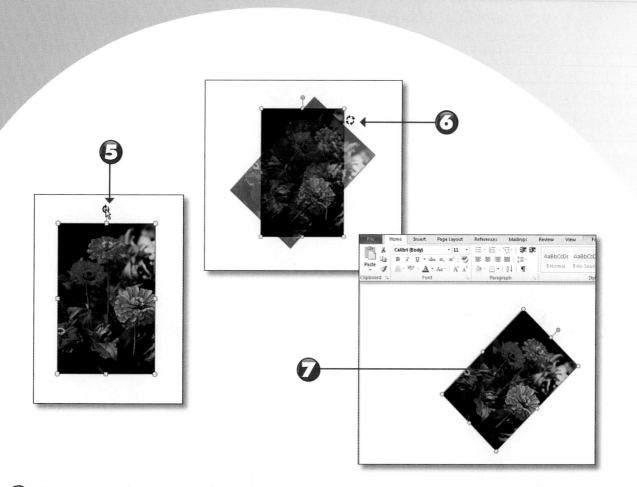

⑤ To rotate an object, move the mouse pointer over the rotation handle until you see a circular arrow icon.

⑥ Click and drag the handle to rotate the object.

⑦ As soon as you release the mouse button, the object is rotated.

End

TIP

More Options For more rotation options, open the Layout dialog box to the Size tab and specify a specific rotation degree. To view the dialog box, click the **Rotate** button on the **Format** tab and click **More Rotation Options**. ■

TIP

Undo Anytime you want to undo your change, whether you flipped or rotated an object, just click the **Undo** button on the Quick Access toolbar. ■

LAYERING OBJECTS

You can layer objects in a document to create logos and complex drawings. When layering objects, you can move a selected object forward or backward in a stack of other objects.

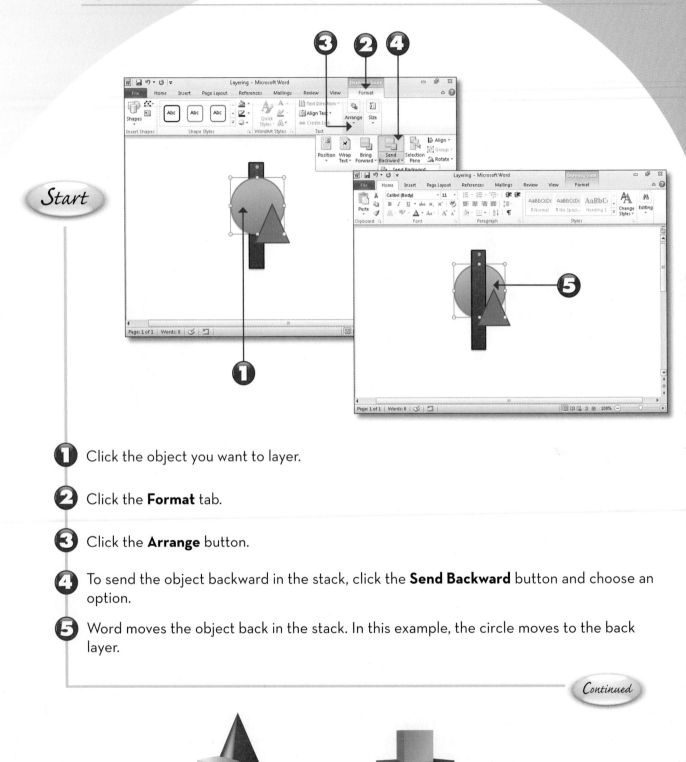

Start

1. Click the object you want to layer.

2. Click the **Format** tab.

3. Click the **Arrange** button.

4. To send the object backward in the stack, click the **Send Backward** button and choose an option.

5. Word moves the object back in the stack. In this example, the circle moves to the back layer.

Continued

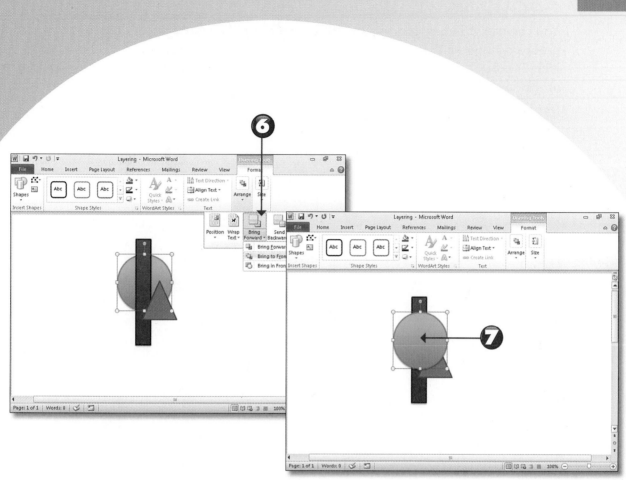

6 To bring the object forward in the stack, click the **Bring Forward** button and choose an option.

7 Word moves the object forward in the stack. In this example, the circle moves to the top layer.

End

TIP

Alignment Options The Drawing Tools or Picture Tools tab has tools for aligning shapes and other graphic objects. Like text alignment controls the positioning of text, graphic alignment tools control the positioning of graphic objects. Using the Align button, you can align selected objects to the left, right, or center, or you can align them vertically to the top, middle, or bottom of the page, or even distribute the objects evenly across or up and down the page. ■

GROUPING OBJECTS

You can use grouping controls to group together objects into one. For example, you might group together all the elements that make up a logo you've created and create a single object, or group several shapes to apply the same formatting all at once or move all the items at the same time. You can leave the group together, or you can ungroup the group and return all the individual elements to their own selectable objects again.

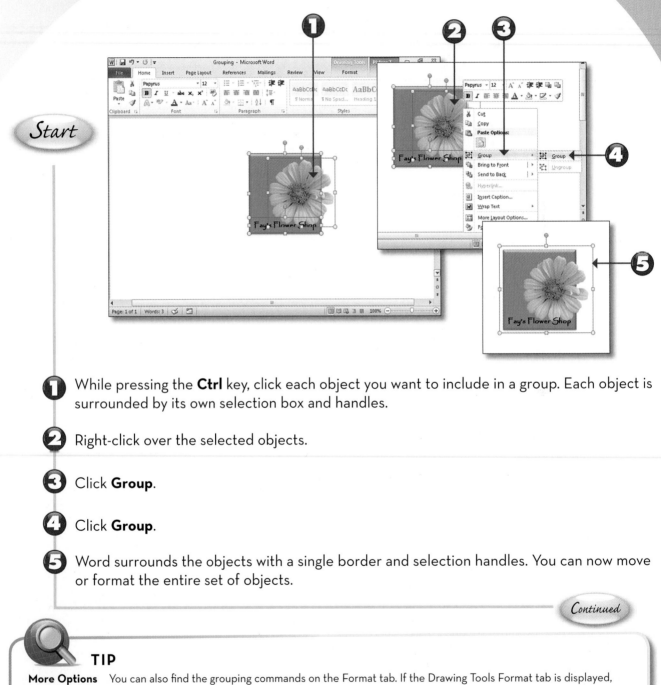

1 While pressing the **Ctrl** key, click each object you want to include in a group. Each object is surrounded by its own selection box and handles.

2 Right-click over the selected objects.

3 Click **Group**.

4 Click **Group**.

5 Word surrounds the objects with a single border and selection handles. You can now move or format the entire set of objects.

Continued

TIP

More Options You can also find the grouping commands on the Format tab. If the Drawing Tools Format tab is displayed, you can click the **Arrange** button, click **Group**, and click **Group** in the menu that appears. If the Picture Tools Format tab is displayed, click the **Group** button and then click **Group**. ■

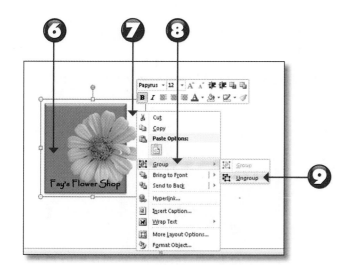

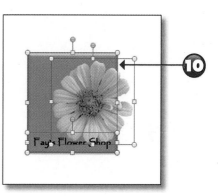

6 To ungroup a set of grouped objects, first select the object.

7 Right-click the selected object.

8 Click **Group**.

9 Click **Ungroup**.

10 The objects revert to their individual parts.

End

TIP

Selection Troubles? If you're having a difficult time selecting individual items to include in a group, try using Word's Selection Pane. If the Drawing Tools Format tab is displayed, you can click the **Arrange** button and then click **Selection Pane**. If the Picture Tools Format tab is displayed, click the **Selection Pane** button. Either route opens the Selection Pane and you can then click items to select for your grouping task.

CROPPING A PICTURE

You can use Word's cropping feature to crop out unwanted parts of your pictures. When activated, you can crop out different sides or corners of an image.

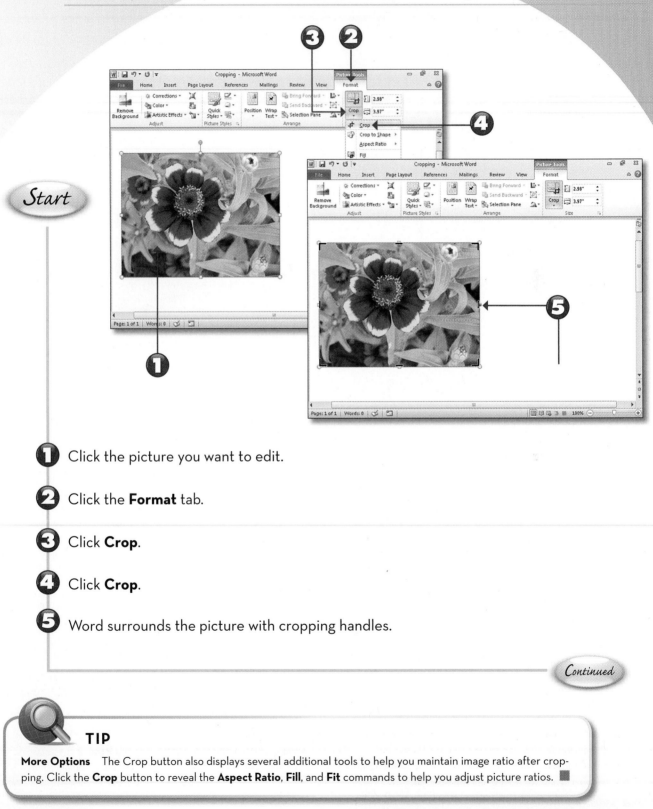

1. Click the picture you want to edit.

2. Click the **Format** tab.

3. Click **Crop**.

4. Click **Crop**.

5. Word surrounds the picture with cropping handles.

Continued

TIP

More Options The Crop button also displays several additional tools to help you maintain image ratio after cropping. Click the **Crop** button to reveal the **Aspect Ratio**, **Fill**, and **Fit** commands to help you adjust picture ratios. ■

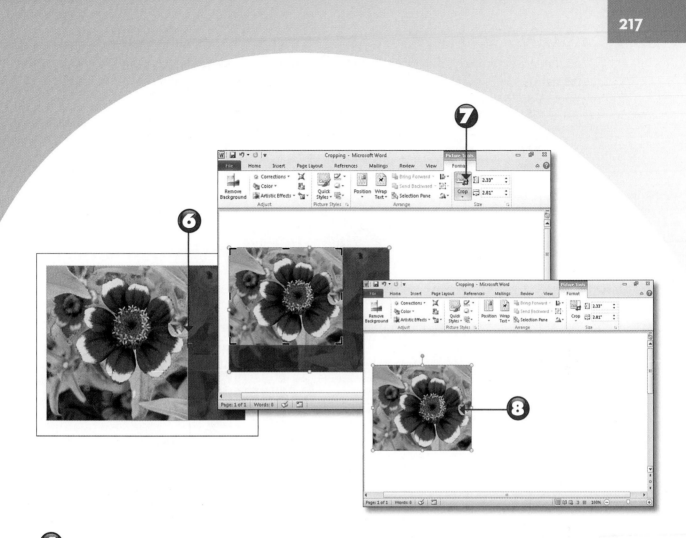

6 Click and drag a cropping handle to crop the picture.

7 When finished cropping, click the **Crop** button on the Format tab again to toggle cropping off.

8 The picture is cropped.

End

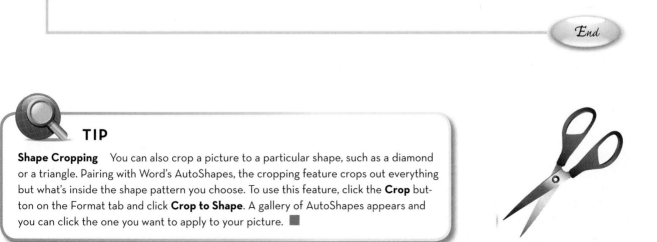

TIP

Shape Cropping You can also crop a picture to a particular shape, such as a diamond or a triangle. Pairing with Word's AutoShapes, the cropping feature crops out everything but what's inside the shape pattern you choose. To use this feature, click the **Crop** button on the Format tab and click **Crop to Shape**. A gallery of AutoShapes appears and you can click the one you want to apply to your picture.

ADDING ARTISTIC EFFECTS

You can add painterly effects and other stylizations to your pictures using Word's Artistic Effects feature. You can choose from a variety of effects ranging from pencil sketch to watercolor sponge.

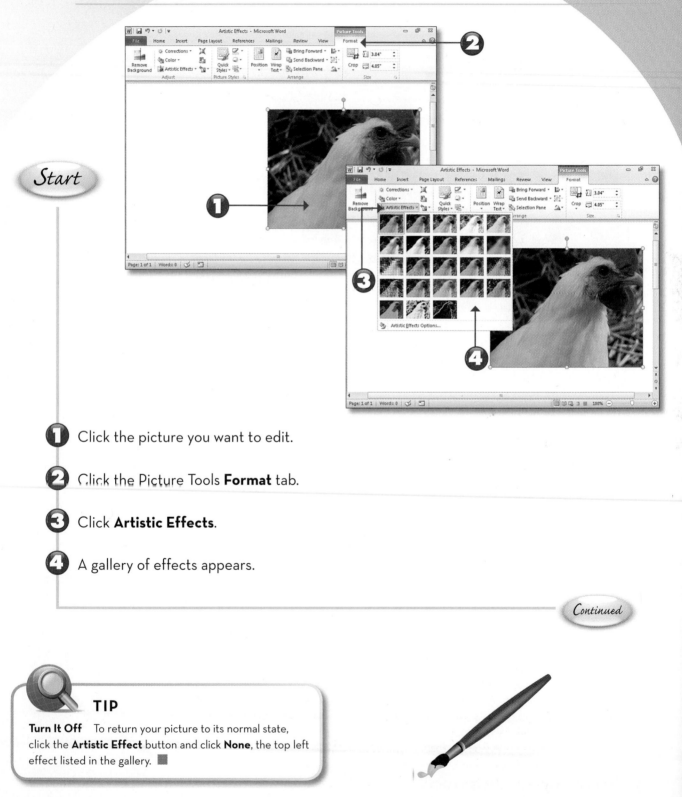

1 Click the picture you want to edit.

2 Click the Picture Tools **Format** tab.

3 Click **Artistic Effects**.

4 A gallery of effects appears.

Continued

TIP

Turn It Off To return your picture to its normal state, click the **Artistic Effect** button and click **None**, the top left effect listed in the gallery. ■

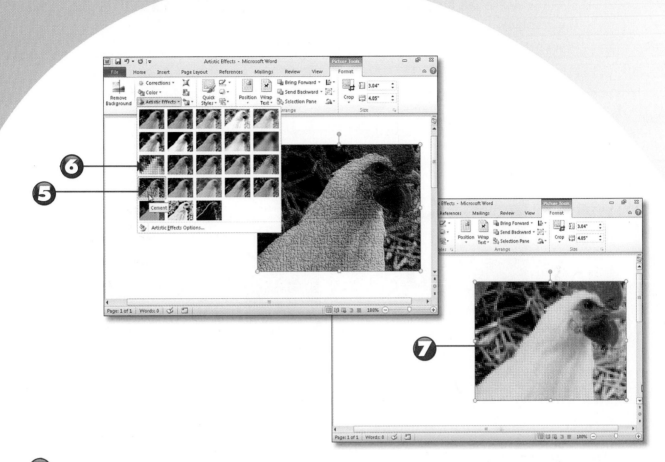

5 To preview an effect, move the mouse pointer over the effect.

6 Click the effect you want to assign.

7 Word applies the effect to the picture. In this example, the Light Screen effect is applied.

End

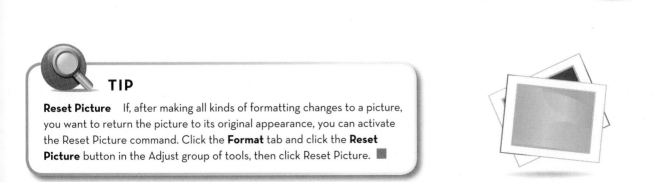

TIP

Reset Picture If, after making all kinds of formatting changes to a picture, you want to return the picture to its original appearance, you can activate the Reset Picture command. Click the **Format** tab and click the **Reset Picture** button in the Adjust group of tools, then click Reset Picture. ■

CONTROLLING TEXT WRAPPING

Text wrapping refers to how document text flows around graphic elements you add, such as pictures or clip art. By default, Word places graphic elements inline with text, which means the graphic object sits on the same baseline as the text. To make the text wrap around the object, assign another wrapping control instead.

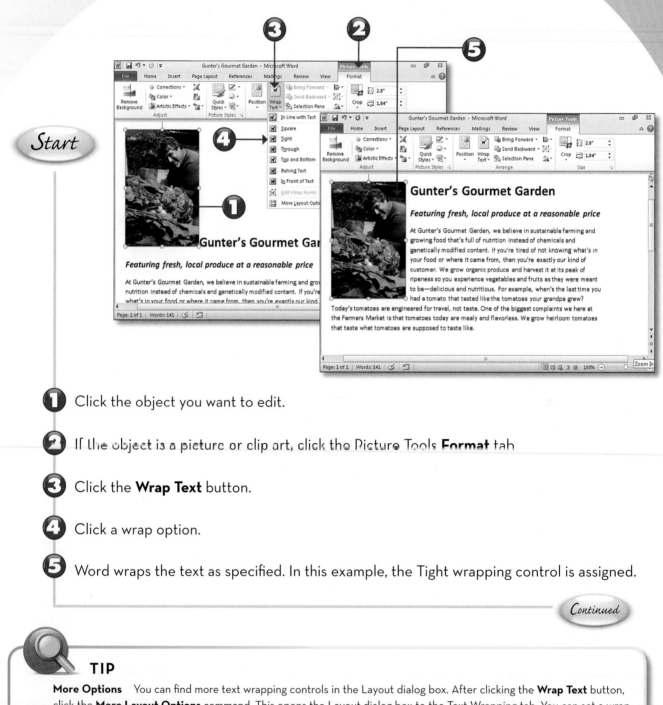

1 Click the object you want to edit.

2 If the object is a picture or clip art, click the Picture Tools **Format** tab.

3 Click the **Wrap Text** button.

4 Click a wrap option.

5 Word wraps the text as specified. In this example, the Tight wrapping control is assigned.

Continued

TIP

More Options You can find more text wrapping controls in the Layout dialog box. After clicking the **Wrap Text** button, click the **More Layout Options** command. This opens the Layout dialog box to the Text Wrapping tab. You can set a wrap option, specify which sides of the object to wrap around, and even control the distance of the object from the text. ▪

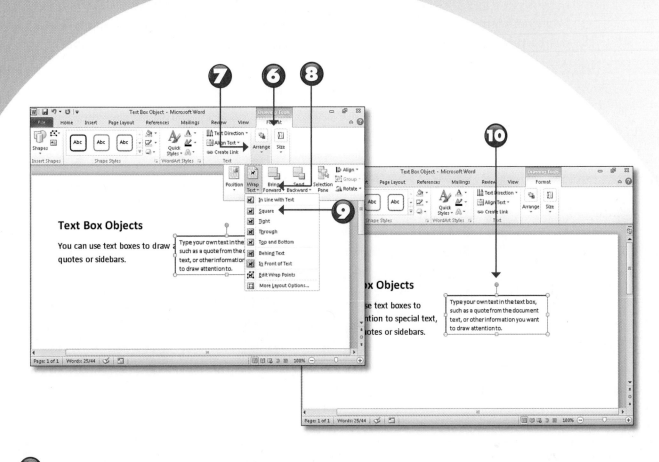

6 If the object is a text box or shape, click the Drawing Tools **Format** tab.

7 Click the **Arrange** button.

8 Click the **Wrap Text** button.

9 Click a wrap option.

10 Word wraps the text as specified. In this example, the Square wrapping control is assigned.

End

TIP

Precise Wrapping   You can apply wrapping points and move them to control the text wrap by clicking the **Edit Wrap Points** command on the **Wrap Text** menu. You can then click to add a wrap point handle to the object and drag it to change the wrapping about the object at that point. You may need to add several wrap points to achieve the desired result. ■

CORRECTING AND COLORING A PICTURE

Word offers two handy photo-editing tools you can use to change a picture's quality: Corrections and Color. You can use the Corrections tool to make improvements to a picture's brightness, contrast, and sharpness. You can use the Color tool to make improvements to the picture's color settings, such as color saturation, tone, and recoloring options.

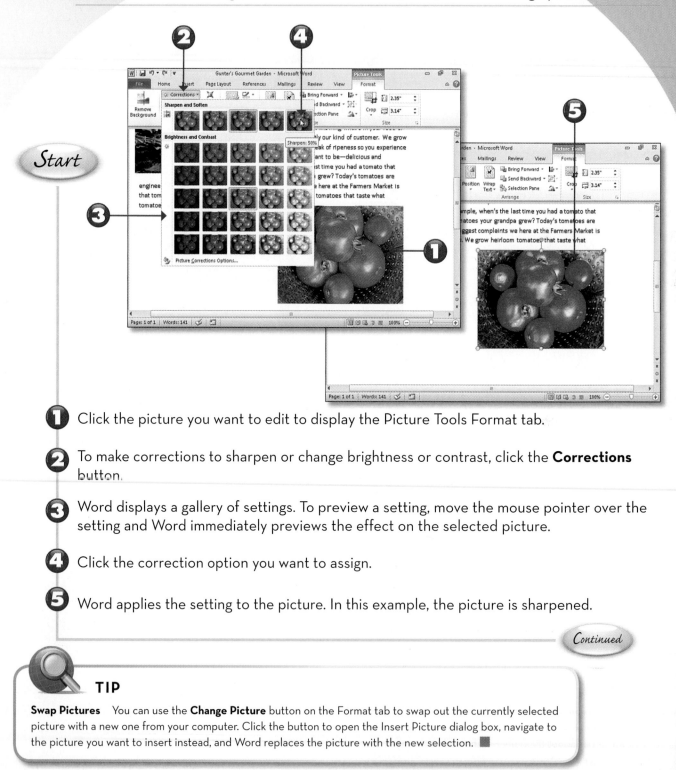

1. Click the picture you want to edit to display the Picture Tools Format tab.

2. To make corrections to sharpen or change brightness or contrast, click the **Corrections** button.

3. Word displays a gallery of settings. To preview a setting, move the mouse pointer over the setting and Word immediately previews the effect on the selected picture.

4. Click the correction option you want to assign.

5. Word applies the setting to the picture. In this example, the picture is sharpened.

Continued

TIP

Swap Pictures   You can use the **Change Picture** button on the Format tab to swap out the currently selected picture with a new one from your computer. Click the button to open the Insert Picture dialog box, navigate to the picture you want to insert instead, and Word replaces the picture with the new selection. ■

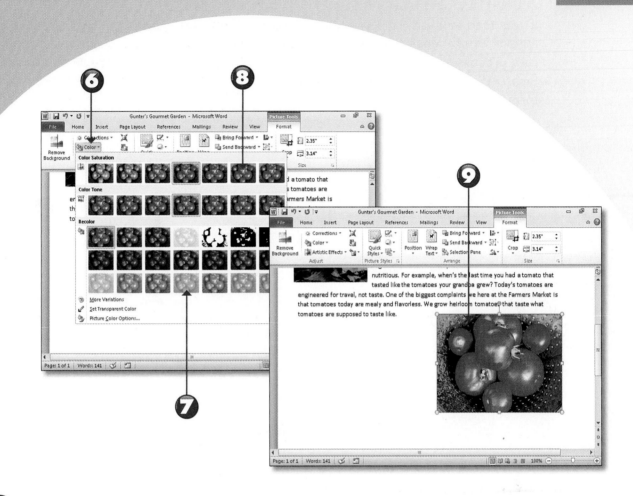

6 To make color changes to a picture, click the **Color** button.

7 Word displays a gallery of color settings. To preview a setting, move the mouse pointer over the setting and Word immediately previews the color on the selected picture.

8 Click the color option you want to assign.

9 Word applies the change to the picture. In this example, the color saturation is adjusted.

End

TIP

Compress Pictures You can compress your pictures to dramatically reduce the overall file size of your document. Pictures are notorious space consumers, so reducing their file size can help speed up downloading or save room on the drive in which you store the document. To compress your pictures, click the **Compress Pictures** button in the Adjust group on the Format tab. This opens the Compress Pictures dialog box where you can adjust the output target and then apply compression. ■

ADDING SMARTART

If you need to insert a diagram of some sort, make things easy for yourself and take advantage of Word's SmartArt graphics. You can use SmartArt to create diagrams for graphical lists, processes, procedures, hierarchies, organization charts, and more. When you add a SmartArt diagram, Word adds two SmartArt Tools tabs to the Ribbon which you can use to format and design the diagram.

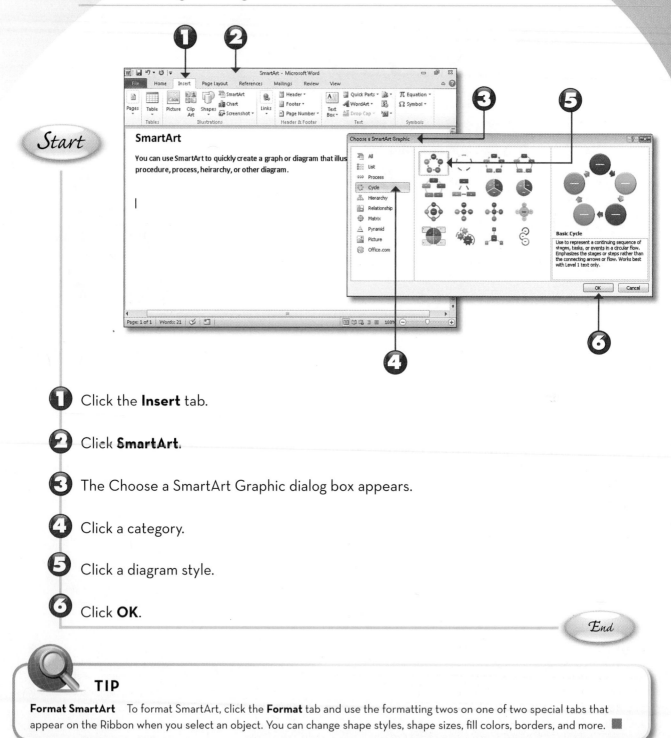

1 Click the **Insert** tab.

2 Click **SmartArt**.

3 The Choose a SmartArt Graphic dialog box appears.

4 Click a category.

5 Click a diagram style.

6 Click **OK**.

End

TIP

Format SmartArt To format SmartArt, click the **Format** tab and use the formatting twos on one of two special tabs that appear on the Ribbon when you select an object. You can change shape styles, shape sizes, fill colors, borders, and more. ■

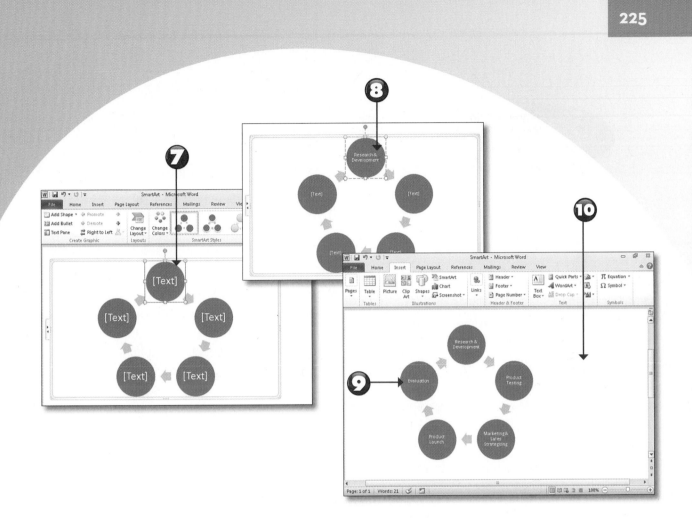

 Word opens a default SmartArt diagram with placeholder text.

8 Click a diagram element and type your own text.

9 Continue adding text to each part of the diagram.

10 When finished, click outside the diagram to unselect the graphic object.

End

TIP

Add a Shape To add a shape to the diagram, click where you want to add a new shape in the chart, then click the **Design** tab and click the **Add Shape** button and choose whether you want to add the shape before or after the current selection. ■

TIP

SmartArt Styles SmartArt installs with a gallery of styles you can apply to change the appearance of your diagrams. Simply click the **Design** tab and choose another style from the SmartArt Styles gallery. ■

Glossary

A

alignment   The way text aligns along the right and left sides of the page. Alignment comes in four distinct settings: left, center, right, or justify.

AutoCorrect   A feature that corrects spelling errors as you type. You can also use AutoCorrect to quickly insert long phrases automatically.

AutoShapes   Pre-drawn shapes and lines you can use to add graphic elements to a document, such as a square or star.

B

bar tab   A custom tab stop that creates a vertical line at the tab stop.

bookmark   A link in a document that allows you to return to a specific location in the document.

border   Lines around one or more sides of a paragraph, page, or object. Word offers a wide variety of line types and colors to choose from.

break   See **page break** or **section break.**

C

cell   A box in a table, formed by the intersection of a row and a column.

center alignment   An alignment option that aligns text between the right margin and left margin in the center of the page.

check box   A small box that you click to enable or disable an option in a dialog box. If the check box has a check mark in it, the option is currently enabled; if the box is empty, the option is disabled. Check boxes are not always mutually exclusive; sometimes you can mark several check boxes in a group.

clip art   A collection of pre-drawn artwork you can use to illustrate your document.

Clipboard   A temporary storage area that holds multiple pieces of cut or copied text or other items. You can paste items from the Clipboard to other documents or files.

context menu   Also called a shortcut menu. A menu that appears when you right-click on something. The commands in a context menu are related to where you click.

copy and paste   To place a duplicate of the selected text or object somewhere else in the document or another document.

cursor   See **insertion point**

custom tab   A tab stop that you insert in a document. When you add a custom tab, all the default tabs to its left disappear.

cut and paste   To move the selected text or object somewhere else in the document or another document.

D

data source   A file that contains the data you will merge into the main document. *See also* **mail merge**.

decimal tab   A custom tab stop that aligns text along the decimal point.

dialog box   A small window that appears when you issue a command or implement a feature that requires more information about how you want to carry out the task.

drag   To press and hold down the mouse button as you move the mouse pointer. You typically drag to move, draw, or select objects with the mouse.

drop caps   A large initial or capital letter that appears at the start of the paragraph and seems to drop below the baseline into the rest of the paragraph.

drop-down menu   A menu that appears when you click a drop-down arrow next to a command or tool button allowing you to select from additional commands or options.

E, F, G

endnote   A reference note that appears at the end of a chapter.

field   A placeholder for information that can be updated. Typical fields in Word include the date field, which displays the current date, or the page number field, which displays the correct page number on each page in a document. *See also* **mail merge**.

first line indent   Only the first line of a paragraph is indented.

font   Refers to a typeface, such as Arial, that defines the shape or character set of text.

font size   Refers to the size of text in a document, measured in points.

footer   Text that repeats at the bottom of every page.

footnote   A reference note that is placed at the bottom of a page.

H

hanging indent   All the lines in a paragraph except the first line are indented.

hard page break   Also called a manual page break, this is a page break inserted by the user to force a page to break at a particular spot; press **Ctrl+Enter** to insert a hard page break.

header   Text that repeats at the top of every page.

hyperlink   A clickable piece of text that links you to a different location within the current document, to another file on your computer or network, or to a page on the Internet.

I

in-line   In-line images are in the same layer of the document as text, so text cannot wrap around them.

indent   To push in the text in a paragraph so that it moves away from the margin. Word offers four indent options: left, right, first line, or hanging.

insertion point   The flashing vertical bar, also called the *cursor*, that marks where text will be inserted or deleted when you type new text or delete existing text.

J, K, L

justify   An alignment that creates both a flush left and flush right edge.

keyboard shortcut   A combination of keystrokes that you can use to issue a command instead of using buttons and menus.

landscape orientation   The document prints so that the long edge of the paper is at the top of the page.

left alignment   An alignment option that aligns text along the left margin of the page.

M, N, O

mail merge   The process of merging a "boilerplate" document, such as a form letter, with a list of data, such as names and addressees, to generate personalized documents.

memory   The temporary storage area in your computer that holds the programs and documents that you currently have open (also called *RAM*). Memory is cleared each time you turn off your computer.

merge field   A field you insert in a main document telling Word where to insert personalized data from a list, such as a person's name or address.

object   A general description for any item or element you add to a document, such as clip art, a picture, or a text box.

option button   See **radio button**.

P

page break   The separation between one page and the next.

paragraph mark   A symbol (¶) that marks the end of a paragraph. Normally hidden, you can turn on paragraph marks using the Show/Hide Paragraphs command.

points   A measurement stemming from the tradition of typography equivalent to 1/72 of an inch. Twelve points make a pica, and 6 picas make an inch. A point is the smallest unit of measure in desktop publishing and commonly describes the height of a font or space between lines of text and other digital elements.

portrait orientation   The document prints so that the short edge of the paper is at the top of the page. Portrait is the default setting for most documents.

Q

Quick Access toolbar   A small toolbar that appears at the top of the Word program window that contains commonly used commands.

quick parts   Pre-made content elements, also called *building blocks*, you can insert into your documents, such as headers.

R

radio button   Also called an *option button*, this button allows the user to choose only one of a predefined set of options.

record   All the information about one person in a data source list, such as a person's name and address. Each record is composed of individual fields for the specific pieces of information, such as first name and last name.

Ribbon   The area at the top of the program window containing tabs of commands and tools.

right alignment   An alignment option that aligns text along the right margin of the page.

S

ScreenTip   A small pop-up box that appears when you rest your mouse pointer over a button or other element that identifies the item. Also called a *ToolTip*.

scroll arrows   The arrows at either end of a scrollbar that you can click to scroll through a document.

scrollbar   A long bar that lets you move through your document with the mouse. The vertical scrollbar lets you move up and down pages, while the horizontal scrollbar lets you move left and right.

section break   Marks the end of a section in your document, storing section formatting information such as margin settings and headers and footers.

select   To mark text for performing an action, such as applying formatting or moving the text.

selection handles   Small squares that surround a selected object, such as clip art. You can drag selection handles to resize the object.

SkyDrive   A free online storage service offered through Microsoft's Windows Live website. You can upload documents to the server and access them from any computer with an Internet connection.

smart tag   When Word recognizes the data you're typing, such as a person's name, and offers a menu of actions you can apply.

SmartArt   A group of pre-formatted, editable diagrams you can use to illustrate a process, procedure, hierarchy, or cycle.

soft page break   A page break inserted by Word when text must flow to the next page.

spinner arrows   Tiny arrow buttons next to an option that let you set a value for the option.

status bar   The horizontal bar at the bottom of the program window that keeps track of pages, line count, column count, and other status information.

style   A set of formatting you can apply to text. You might apply a heading style to all the chapter titles in a document, for example, or a body style for all the chapter text.

T

tab   In a document, a tab refers to the amount of space you indent when you press the Tab key. A tab can also refer to a group of commands organized into a page or section, such as the tabs on Word's Ribbon.

target   The destination to which a hyperlink leads.

task pane   A vertical pane that usually appears on the right side of the program window offering information and options for a particular feature.

template   A rough "blueprint" for a document that controls the layout and contains some combination of formatting and text. You can replace the placeholder text within the template with your own text.

text box   A special box you can insert into a document to hold text, such as a pull quote.

text effects   Special artistic effects you can apply to text to create visual appeal.

theme   Preset formatting that helps you maintain a consistent look and feel throughout a document or documents.

title bar   The horizontal bar that appears at the top of the program window, listing the name of the file and the name of the program.

toggle   A button or keyboard command you click or press once to turn on and once again to turn off.

ToolTip   See ScreenTip.

U, V

upload   To transfer files from your computer to a location on the Internet.

W, X, Y, Z

watermark   A background image that appears behind the document text, usually shaded. Watermarks are commonly used to mark pages with company logos, DRAFT, or CONFIDENTIAL warnings.

wizard   A specialized feature that asks you about what type of document you want to create and walks you through the process, generating a final document based on your choices.

WordArt   A Microsoft Office feature for turning text into a graphic object.

wrapping   Refers to the way text flows around an image or object in a document.

zoom   To change the magnification of a document onscreen. You can zoom in to enlarge a document or zoom out to view more of the contents.

Index

N-O

P

U-V

W-Z

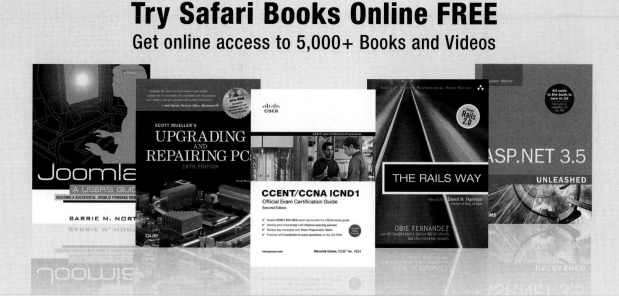

FREE Online Edition

Your purchase of **Easy Microsoft® Word 2010** includes access to a free online edition for 45 days through the Safari Books Online subscription service. Nearly every Que book is available online through Safari Books Online, along with more than 5,000 other technical books and videos from publishers such as Addison-Wesley Professional, Cisco Press, Exam Cram, IBM Press, O'Reilly, Prentice Hall, and Sams.

SAFARI BOOKS ONLINE allows you to search for a specific answer, cut and paste code, download chapters, and stay current with emerging technologies.

Activate your FREE Online Edition at
www.informit.com/safarifree

STEP 1: Enter the coupon code: ZIZJYFA.

STEP 2: New Safari users, complete the brief registration form.
Safari subscribers, just log in.

If you have difficulty registering on Safari or accessing the online edition, please e-mail customer-service@safaribooksonline.com